CONFESSIONS OF AN INTEREST GROUP

CONFESSIONS OF AN INTEREST GROUP

THE CATHOLIC CHURCH
AND POLITICAL PARTIES IN EUROPE

Carolyn M. Warner

PRINCETON UNIVERSITY PRESS   PRINCETON, NEW JERSEY

Library of Congress Cataloging-in-Publication Data
Warner, Carolyn M., 1961–
Confessions of an interest group : the Catholic Church and political parties in Europe /
Carolyn M. Warner.
p. cm.
Includes bibliographical references and index.
ISBN 0-691-01025-0 (cloth : alk. paper). — ISBN 0-691-01026-9 (pbk. : alk. paper)
1. Christianity and politics—Catholic Church—History—20th century. 2. Christian demo-
cratic parties—France—History—20th century. 3. Christian democratic parties—Italy—
History—20th century. 4. Christian democratic parties—Germany—History—20th century. 5. France—Church history—1945. 6. Italy—Church history—20th century.
7. Germany—Church history—1945.
I. Title.
BX1530.2.W37 2000
324'.088'22—dc21
99-41741

This book has been composed in Galliard

The paper used in this publication meets the minimum requirements
of ANSI/NISO Z39.48-1992 (R1997) (*Permanence of Paper*)

www.pup.princeton.edu

1   3   5   7   9   10   8   6   4   2
Printed in the United States of America

TO THE MEMORY OF

Melvin Eugene Norberg

(1898–1983)

Contents

Tables

---------------- *Acknowledgments* ----------------

THIS BOOK began when I gave a hard look at my doctoral dissertation—which dealt with the question of why some Christian Democratic parties succeed in becoming dominant, long-lived organizations, and others fail to do so—and decided that the more interesting question lay in understanding why religious organizations make the choices they do with respect to political parties. The dissertation was set aside for a study of the Catholic Church's strategic behavior.

I have ranged widely in the resources used for data, and in the people I called upon to assist in gathering it. I am grateful to Madame Chantal Bonazzi, Conservateur Général, of the Section Contemporaine at the Archives Nationales in Paris, to Madame Vivienne Miguet of the Archives Départementales du Morbihan, to Monsieur Jean-L. Delmas of the Archives Départementales de l'Aveyron, to Père Ploix and his assistant at the archives of the Archevêché de Paris, for allowing access to parts of the archives under their supervision, and for discussing possible sources. The Chef du Cabinet, Nicolas Desforges, of the Préfecture de Police, Paris, kindly granted access to the Préfecture's documents on the MRP. Monsieur Jean Coville of l'Amicale du M.R.P. allowed me to delve into the Amicale's closet of MRP archives before the archives had been properly catalogued or organized. I thank also the archivist at the Institut Charles de Gaulle, Paris, and Jean-Paul Terrenoire, of the Centre National de la Recherche Scientifique—Centre de Sociologie de l'Ethique, Paris, and Monsieur Noye of the Séminaire St. Suplice for their assistance with archives and data. I am particularly grateful to the late Monsieur Robert and Madame Parker for so generously inviting me into their Paris home to peruse the papers of Madame (Geneviève) Parker's father, the MRP deputy and activist, Ernst Pezet. I am thankful to Madame Georges Bidault for allowing me to examine her late husband's papers.

Madame Semence, of the Fondation Nationale des Sciences Politiques, facilitated access to the Fondation's library collection, which included important archival material on parties of the Fourth Republic. Former MRP deputy Robert Lecourt of Paris kindly consented to an interview, as did the Abbé Rieucau, in Rodez. Professor Jean-Dominique Durand, Université de Lyon, enabled me to get a foothold in Italy, both through his own work on the Italian Catholic Church, and by giving me the names of several Italian scholars to contact. Pierre Milza, of the FNSP Centre d'Histoire de l'Europe du Vingtième Siècle, granted me the dérogation to examine MRP archives, now held at the Archives Nationales. Professor

Jean-Marie Mayeur, La Sorbonne, gave me helpful advice on sources and on European Christian Democracy.

The staff of the Biblioteca di Storia Moderna et Contemporanea in Rome facilitated my research, as did the staff of the Biblioteca Fortunata–Studi Meridionali in Rome. Dario Arrigotti, of the Fondazione Agnelli, Turin, provided numerous helpful letters of introduction. Piergiorgio Corbetta, of the Istituto Carlo Cattaneo, Bologna, as well as the ICC's staff, introduced me to the ICC's remaining holdings on the DC. Professor Daniele Menozzi kindly enabled me to use the library of the Istituto per le scienze religiose, Bologna, and put me in contact with Professor Mario Casella, of Rome. In turn, Casella guided me toward the Archivio Storico dell'Azione Cattolica, where Director Francesco Malgeri and archivist Ubaldo Sulis were most helpful in making important archives available to me. The director of the Archivio Gramsci, Rome, kindly permitted me to use the archives of the Italian Communist Party. The staff at the Istituto Gramsci was most accommodating of my other research needs, as well. Former CISL leader and DC deputy Vito Scalia granted an informative interview; so too the Onorevole Merle, of the DC. Carlo Danè, of the publicity office of the DC, enabled me to consult the original copies of early DC newspapers. I am grateful to the helpful and patient staff of the Archivio Centrale dello Stato in Rome.

Unless otherwise noted, all translations from the Italian, French, and German are my own.

A study of this scope never would have seen the light of day without the financial support of the Krupp Foundation, the National Science Foundation (SES 91-12033), and the Fondazione Giovanni Agnelli. An Arizona State University faculty grant supported additional data collection.

I am grateful to Professor Stanley Hoffmann of Harvard University and Monsignor William Murphy of the Boston Archdiocese for providing letters of introduction to various French and Italian archivists. Ken Shepsle and Jim Snyder's Harvard/MIT seminar on positive political economy provided a stimulating forum in which to introduce and develop many of the ideas in this book. The Minda de Gunzberg Center for European Studies at Harvard provided an unparalleled environment in which to begin, to foster, and to complete this work.

Several friends provided much-appreciated encouragement along the way: Steve Anderson, Annabelle Lever, Jennifer Montana, Susan Scarrow, and Melissa Williams. I deeply regret the untimely death of Brian Baker, who had helped maintain my sense of humor while dealing with the vexations of archival research in France. I thank Malcolm Litchfield of Princeton University Press for his interest in the project and the rapidity with which he moved on it, and Richard Isomaki for his careful scrutiny of the manuscript. Avital Simhony gave a helpful critical reading of the first chapter. David Laitin and Jim Alt compelled me to hone my argument and presentation. Steven White's suggestions for revisions to chapters 6 and 7 were especially helpful, and Maria Mitchell's critique of chapter 9 enabled me to considerably improve my analysis of the Church and Christian Democracy in Germany. David Hollinger kindly proofread a portion of the manuscript to make sure it was comprehensible to general readers. Alex and Thomas Wenner cheerfully delivered eleventh-hour bibliographic assistance. Susan Scarrow, Jorge Domínguez, and Peter McDonough provided extensive and incisive comments on multiple drafts of the manuscript. I particularly thank Jorge for his unflagging confidence in this endeavor and in the author. This work owes an intellectual debt to the many fruitful discussions and written exchanges I have had with Stathis Kalyvas. I am very grateful for the detailed, intellectually challenging and thought-provoking comments of Tony Gill and Peter Hall. I can only hope I have done justice to their efforts. Tony has also been a wonderful sounding board for thinking about religion and politics and Peter a thoughtful, rigorous mentor and critic. The fact that the book exists at all owes much to the ceaseless encouragement of my husband Kurt Wenner and his insistence that I follow out my idea that the Church is an interest group whose actions in politics can be explained by way of a market model. I am deeply grateful to him for his thorough reading, critiquing, and editing of numerous drafts of each chapter, and for his help in so many other ways.

My maternal grandfather had a lively and independent mind. Along with taking me fishing and skiing in his beloved Sierra Nevada mountains, he often told me, "Go out and teach your teachers a thing or two." It is to his memory that I dedicate this work.

Abbreviations

ARCHIVES

AAC	Archivio d'Azione Cattolica, Rome
ACS	Archivio Centrale dello Stato
ADA	Archives Départementales de l'Aveyron
ADM	Archives Départementales du Morbihan
A-MRP	Archives du Mouvement Républicain Populaire
AN	Archives Nationales
APP	Archives de la Préfecture de Police, Paris
APS	Archives de la Préfecture de la Seine
A-RPF	Archives du Rassemblement du Peuple Français
b.	busta
dr.	dossier
f.	fascicolo
MinIntGab	Ministero dell'Interno, Gabinetto
MinIntPS	Ministero dell'Interno, Pubblica Sicurezza
PG	Presidenza Generale (in AAC)

FRENCH ORGANIZATIONS

ACA	Assemblée des Cardinaux et Archevêques
ACO	Action Catholique Ouvrière
CFTC	Confédération Française des Travailleurs Chrétiens
CGA	Confédération Générale de l'Agriculture
FNC	Fédération Nationale Catholique
FNSEA	Fédération Nationale des Syndicats d'Exploitants Agricoles
JAC	Jeunesse Agricole Chrétienne
JOC	Jeunesse Ouvrière Chrétienne
MRP	Mouvement Républicain Populaire
PCF	Parti Communiste Français
PDP	Parti Démocrate Populaire
PRL	Parti Républicain de la Liberté
RPF	Rassemblement du Peuple Français
SFIO	Section Française de l'Internationale Ouvrière
SRP	Semaine Religieuse du Diocèse de Paris
UDSR	Union Démocratique et Socialiste de la Résistance

ITALIAN ORGANIZATIONS

ACI   Azione Cattolica Italiana
ACLI   Associazione Cristiana dei Lavoratori Italiani
CC   Comitati Civici
CGIL   Confederazione Generale Italiana del Lavoro
CISL   Confederazione Italiana dei Sindicati dei Lavoratori
DC   Democrazia Cristiana
MSI   Movimento Sociale Italiano
PCI   Partito Comunista Italiano
PDI   Partito Democratico Italiano
PLI   Partito Liberale Italiano
PNF   Partito Nazionale Fascista
PNM   Partito Nazionale Monarchico
PMP   Partito Monarchico Popolare
PPI   Partito Popolare Italiano
PRI   Partito Repubblicano Italiano
PSC   Partito della Sinistra Cristiana
PSDI   Partito Socialista Democratico Italiano
PSLI   Partito Socialista dei Lavorati Italiani
PSI   Partito Socialista Italiano
PSIUP   Partito Socialista Italiano di Unita Proletaria
UQ   Uomo Qualunque (Fronte dell')

GERMAN ORGANIZATIONS

CDU-CSU   Christlich Demokratische Union Deutschlands–
          Christlich Soziale Union
FDP   Freie Demokratische Partei
KPD   Kommunistische Partei Deutschlands
NSDAP   National-Sozialistische Deutsche Arbeiter Partei
SPD   Sozialdemokratische Partei Deutschlands

MISCELLANEOUS

CCR   *Cahiers du Clergé Rural de France*
SRP   *Semaine Religieuse du Diocèse de Paris*

CONFESSIONS OF AN INTEREST GROUP

CHAPTER 1

Introduction: The Catholic Church and Democracy

IN FEBRUARY 1798, a French general and his troops, aided by the intrigues of Italian republicans and under orders from France's Revolutionary Directorate, besieged Rome. Pope Pius VI fled the Vatican to Florence, where, 13 months later, he was captured by the French army and taken to the south of France. There, on August 29, 1799, the pope, still a prisoner of the French, died. This unseemly introduction to the legacy of the French Revolution and democratic politics ensured that there would be no love lost between the Catholic hierarchy and democratic governments. The Catholic Church had long enjoyed privileged political and social status, and the political struggles in which it engaged were conducted among elites. The rise of democratic politics drastically altered the avenues to power for the Church, the resources available to it, and fundamentally questioned the Church's claims to a privileged position in politics and society. The Church was no longer guaranteed a monopoly on the production of faith, or on the means to secure its own institutional survival.

With the arrival of parliamentary politics the Church had to enter the democratic arena and rely for assistance upon what it regarded as a rather loathsome creature, the party politician. Worse, if the Church were to have any influence, it had to ensure that its members were roused out of Catholic somnolence to vote for the correct politician. The Church had to track legislation and try to influence its formulation and passage. It had to persuade, educate, or compel newly enfranchised Catholics to place their votes with parties and politicians sympathetic to the Church, mobilizing voters to see their interests as coterminous with the Church's. It had to decide whether to contribute resources to party organizations. Even as it tried to restore the status quo ante, the Church began to use lobbying techniques adapted to the democratic context. In short, the Church had become an interest group.[1]

As an interest group, the Church has opted for, or had, different types of political allies over time: sometimes monarchies (or "emperors"), sometimes political parties, sometimes fascist dictatorships. This book focuses mostly on the post–World War II democratic setting and poses the ques-

[1] I use the word *Church* to signify the national Catholic Churches and to describe the Roman Catholic Church, or Vatican. Context will make evident which organization is being discussed.

tion: why did the Church ally with the political parties it did? The French Church, which needed far more help than the Italian to recover lost ground after the war, linked only superficially and briefly with a political party. The Italian Church, emerging relatively unscathed from the war, needed little help, yet forged strong connections with a party. Why did the French Church not expend resources when it needed to, while the Italian Church invested heavily when there was little reason for it to do so? And why did the Churches choose to ally with Christian Democratic parties? The answer is not obvious, because even though those Christian Democratic parties were founded on Catholic principles, there were other parties that were even more strongly pro-clerical. Why did the Vatican, with all its resources, not create its own party but instead ally with one that refused to relinquish itself completely to the Church? Why did the German Catholic Church agree to support a party that had a significant Protestant component? Asking these questions leads to broader questions of why any interest group picks the political party allies it does, and how the interest group manages the relations with them. This book analyzes the Church as a subset of the universe of interest groups. The Church's actions in the context of democratic political systems are poorly understood, as are, surprisingly, those of interest groups. Thus, this study also aims to generate insights about the study of interest groups as well as organized religions in democratic political systems.

This book argues that the Catholic Church is an interest group whose actions can be modeled as if it were a firm in a market seeking a supplier of goods. When an interest group allies with a political party, it usually commits a specific set of assets. Doing so creates a demand for a complex arrangement with a variety of guarantees against being exploited. I present this argument using economic and rational choice terminology and concepts, emphasizing goal-oriented, cost-benefit-calculating behavior.

Previous studies of interest group–party relations have ignored the problems inherent in those relations and thus have been unable to explain puzzling results, such as the ones this book analyzes; namely, why do some interest groups stick with seemingly suboptimal political parties? With few exceptions, previous analyses of the Catholic Church's behavior have stressed its values and cultural presence and thus have been unable to account for the Church's strategic political behavior in a variety of contexts.

Indeed, the standard responses, sociological and functional, to questions about the Catholic Church's, or any interest group's, political party choices are insufficient. The sociological view sees the party as an extension of the interest group in politics; the functional view sees the party as meeting the needs of the interest group. In either case, choice is not involved. If the party were merely an emanation of an interest group in civil society, then one would expect the party to cater to that group and never declare its independence from the group, or vice versa. Yet interest groups and parties seldom are cohesive partners, and they do break alliances.

Both views ignore what a group considers when it chooses a political ally: which party is most likely to enact its policies, which one will have the capacity to do so (e.g., is large enough to influence the government), which one will not sully the group's reputation or drive away members. Supporting a political party, once chosen, is not a costless activity: the interest group must train its members to vote for that party, giving members some skills they may decide to use in a different arena, indeed, which may enable them to leave the interest group. It must invest in organizational resources, not all of which are recoverable should the party fail to do as the group desires (or should the party fail). Such activities divert resources from whatever the group's primary organizational mission was to another—fighting political battles. The interest group must monitor the party to ensure that the party delivers the promised goods. The interest group also risks losing some authority and credibility in society, and among its membership, if politics is regarded by many as a tainted activity.

Using the economic metaphor of a firm in a competitive market searching for suppliers, I unpack the basic factors influencing an interest group's decisions vis-à-vis parties: product quality, reliability, supplier credibility. But the prices attached to the exchange are not determined entirely by the market; depending on exogenous factors, groups attach different values to market trade-offs. Building on work in historical institutionalism, this book proposes a set of factors that affect the prices groups attach to choices: prior and current institutional relationships and structures, and the ideology of the leaders.

INTEREST GROUPS

Interest behavior is central to this study, but what is an interest group? Most definitions include the notion of an organization exerting pressure on government officials and institutions in order to obtain benefits for the group, benefits that are connected to the interests, goals, or desires of the organization. Richardson (1993b, 1) gives a broad definition of an interest group (or, in his terms, pressure group): it is "any group which articulates demands that the political authorities in the political system or sub-system should make an authoritative allocation" of resources to them (cf. Baumgartner and Leech 1998, xxii). Like others, Richardson differentiates the interest group from the political party by stating that the interest group does not itself pose candidates for office. Others define interest groups by what they perceive to be their main function: "using political influence to enhance the well-being of their members" (Becker 1983, 372). Economic theorists, on the other hand, generally define interests groups as organizations seeking rents from the political and economic systems, with rents defined as "differentially advantageous positions and transfers of resources"; benefits, in other words, that are unequally distributed and impose a loss on some (W. Mitchell 1990, 95). Interest groups, by that definition, seek to get more from society than others might think is their "fair share." The ultimate goal is preferential treatment.

Some argue that interest groups should be defined to include government agencies (ministries, departments) and jurisdictions (town, province, municipal district) (Walker 1991, 5; Thomas 1993, 3). Others contend that some interests, while acting as if they were interest groups, should be thought of as "institutions." Their presence has a permanence other associations may not; they are less concerned with satisfying member interests and more concerned about "the needs of the institution as a continuing organization" (Salisbury 1984, 67). While this view certainly applies to religious organizations, it would seem to characterize any interest group. The literature on organizational behavior consistently finds that the leadership of any group with some institutional features (e.g., regularized memberships and officer elections) develops, over time, strong concerns about the organization's survival (Mohr 1982; Panebianco 1982; J. Wilson 1989, 1995).

Interest groups are also institutions: they have identifiable structures, their political activities are exerted in the name of the group, and the rents they gain are distributed in the name of the group. They are not just diffuse social movements; they have leadership succession procedures and an ideology. They provide their members with a mix of selective incentives and collective goods (Moe 1980, 46–57).

THE CATHOLIC CHURCH

The Catholic Church fits the above criteria of what constitutes an interest group. Even prior to the age of democratic politics, it sought preferential treatment from political powers, and it sought rents from economic and political systems (Ertman 1997; Ekelund, Hébert, and Tollison 1989, 309, 329). Pope Pius XII (1939–58) noted that the separation of Church and state left "the Church to provide, with its own methods for sustaining its actions, the fulfillment of its mission, [and] the defense of its rights" (Riccardi 1988, 111). The Church has lobbied democratic governments, via political parties and other means, to retain its monopoly over education and to have the costs of it paid for by governments; it has lobbied them to impose its morals on society through legislation; it has lobbied governments to gain or retain preferential tax status; and it has lobbied to keep some of its employees from being conscripted. The Church seeks to provide its members with collective goods (such as credible answers to philosophical and moral dilemmas), club goods (such as places and means of worship), and selective incentives (e.g., sacraments) (cf. Edinger 1993, 184; Gill 1998; Zwier 1991). To put it bluntly, the Catholic Church is, in addition to being a religion,[2] an interest group.

The Church is, of course, an atypical interest group in several respects. It claims that its principles are universally applicable, including its moral authority, and, in contrast to trade unions and environmental groups, for example, the Church is (usually) regarded by its followers ("members") as being the ultimate moral authority. As Max Weber noted, "a fully developed church—advancing universalist claims—cannot concede freedom of conscience. . . . the formula of the separation of church and state is feasible only if either of the two powers has in fact abandoned its claim to control completely those areas of life that are in principle accessible to it" (1978, 1207). Because the Church has been unwilling to relinquish control over individuals' consciences, and democratic states have been hesitant to allow the Churches to retain that control, the Church's interaction with democratic, secular political systems has been troublesome. Education has been the main battleground. The Church's dealings with political parties can be seen as partly motivated by the effort to exercise control over individuals' minds and beliefs in an era that recognizes "freedom of conscience" and a critical mind as social goods.

Unlike many other interest groups, the Church has been involved in the politics of European countries for centuries and has an even longer institutional presence. These factors may have given many of its leaders a sense of proprietary ownership of "Western Christendom" that other European interest groups lack, and thus intensified the Church's sensitivity to affronts to its perceived prerogatives. The Church also distinguishes itself from other groups by its apparent need to assert its distance from the temporal world while being "operatively present" in it (Poggi 1967, 131). The Church's range of concerns extends further afield than those of other interest groups (Mojzes 1996, 5; cf. Thomas 1993, 3). Unlike labor unions, the Church was not created primarily for the purpose of lobbying governments to get resources for its leadership and members, or for battling an identifiable institutional enemy (e.g. capitalist employers). Whereas the essence of democracy is compromise, many of the Church's demands are not negotiable. Its primary principles cannot be placed on a continuum: it cannot agree that some of its tenets are valid and others not; that some people may divorce while others cannot; or that some reli-

---

[2] Other organized religions can fall into this category. For definitions of religion, see Geertz 1973, 90; Durkheim 1995; Eliade 1987, 282–86.

gions have equal standing with it, but others do not; or that secular education is acceptable for some negotiable segment of the population.

Organizationally, the Church distinguishes itself from many other interest groups, and other world religions, in having an authoritative supranational institution to which all national "branches" are supposed to pay homage: the Vatican. This means that in any interaction between a national Church and a political party, there will be an additional variable: how that interaction affects that Church's relationships with the Vatican, and how the Vatican affects what that Church can or is willing to do in its home country.

The Catholic Church—the "one holy and apostolic Church," is, despite the label, made up of multiple, national Churches, each with its own history, structure, leadership, and political interests. These Churches differ on doctrinal matters, and on pastoral emphases. The national Churches are not franchises of a Vatican corporate headquarters, much as the Vatican has tried to make them so. The national Catholic Churches arose with their own histories, institutional structures, even ideologies, and often have been at odds with the Vatican over maintaining some degree of autonomy. These national differences are not, *pace* Kalyvas (1996, 14), merely quirks that can be dismissed as random variables. The failure to recognize cross-national differences leads to distorted interpretations of Church actions and a failure to recognize the tension between the national Churches and the Vatican. The impact of the resulting tensions, as they are manifested in each country, has been noticeable—on the fortunes of the national Churches, and on decisions pertaining to national issues and politics. Finally, the Church strives to retain control over an aspect of human beings that most interest groups have ceded to the state or to the realm of individual autonomy: values, morals, or conscience.

Indeed, ideologically, the Church claims to be the sole authority for the interpretation of biblical scripture and sees itself as the "teaching authority" on how to live as Jesus demanded, and as the "sacramental agent" that enables Catholics to live the life to which (it says) Jesus called them (Smith 1991, 349). It holds that it "fully embodies and manifests all the institutional elements" necessary for Catholicism (McBrien 1994, 7). Like many other religions, the Church claims to have a monopoly on access to eternal life. Its self-representation, and any legitimacy accorded that, give the Church a substantial claim on the conduct of human activity.

In practice, the Church has occasionally compromised on its principles when it deems doing so necessary to attain some other goal. Catholic doctrine may dictate that the faith and the Church must be preserved and never compromised, but in specific contexts, some Church tenets may be rendered contradictory, and the Church may choose to emphasize one principle over another. Catholic theology is a broad umbrella that sometimes includes contradictions. As such, theology is not always the best predictor of Church political action.

The postwar Italian Church of Pius XII saw no limits on the Church's role in the tutelage of society, culture, or politics. For Pius XII and the Italian hierarchy, Italy, and Rome in particular, was the moral, religious, and civilized center of the world. The Church was far more ready than its French counterpart to see politics as a legitimate arena in which to act; the Vatican's view of itself as being at the center of the Catholic universe made it more willing to invest its resources in political parties, more willing to discount issues of reliability and control.

The point is not to declare that each Church is unique and therefore not tractable for comparisons, but to direct research toward those features of national Churches that, when varying, systematically affect the Churches' political behavior. Ignoring the historical legacy, structure, and leadership of the various Churches prevents us from understanding the different "costs" the Churches assign to courses of action, from understanding why Church priorities and strategies have varied across countries. Those differences in assessments and goals affect what the Churches do in a given situation. Like other world religions, Catholicism's experiences in specific countries gave rise to variations in practices and institutional characteristics. It is important to analyze the recent history of each Church, the battles it has had with secular politicians, parties, and regimes, and the specific popes and their individual policy preferences.

With the spread of democratic government in the late nineteenth and early twentieth centuries, the Church struggled to define its place. For the Church, the problem with democracy is that it recognizes an individual's right to choose, among other things, a government; worse, to choose a sociopolitical ideology and its practices, which in turn have a bearing on religious questions. Since democracy is predicated on the view that power properly resides in individuals, not in a divine being (or an institutional and temporal representation thereof), the Church struggled to either overthrow democracy or find alternative means to convince people that, though some (limited) choices may be decided in the political arena, moral and spiritual matters (and those factors that impinge upon them) are not similarly open to debate and majoritarian decision-making. The cooperation of political parties in the latter endeavor has been a significant but problematic issue for the Church.

POLITICAL PARTIES AND CHRISTIAN DEMOCRACY

The interest group–party link is not unidirectional; because the relationship is interactive, this book pays some attention to the interests of political parties. First, parties seeking elected office want sources of logistical and financial support. Interest groups are one such source. Parties typically seek to gain support at the least cost and, if elected to the governing majority, try to channel government (public) resources, such as subsidies and legislation, to pay for their interest group support. Second, and relevant to the cases here, transitions to democracy pose severe survival problems for new political parties: parties need to establish roots quickly; they need to differentiate themselves from competitors, becoming a known entity distinct from others; and they need to reconcile the ideology of their founders with the perceived demands of the new political context. Interest groups can help, but how do parties establish links with interest groups, old or new?

I focus upon the new parties that were the Churches' most obvious allies—Christian Democratic parties. Christian Democracy is an ideology that, in brief, evaluates social, economic, and political issues and situations using Christian principles. It values democracy for its individual freedoms and as the fairest means to solve economic, political, and social inequalities but, contrary to classical liberalism, sees the individual as an essential member of a family, a spiritual, even supranational, community. It stresses social solidarity, compassion for the poor, and state intervention to ameliorate the ravages of industrialization, seeing class divisions as artificial.[3] Christian Democratic parties need not be exclusively "Catholic": some parties were developed by Protestants (e.g., the Dutch Christian Historical Union); others are "biconfessional" (Germany's Christian Democratic/Social Union, and Christian Democratic Appeal of the Netherlands).

Like parties in other ideological families (e.g., socialism), individual Christian Democratic parties differ in the emphasis they place on points in their programs, on the electorate they target, and on the interest groups they prefer. The parties are, nevertheless, usually classified as center or center-right parties. While their economic program moderates capitalism (and hence differentiates them from liberal parties) and places them in the center of the spectrum, their social program has both conservative (profamily and pro-Church) and nonconservative elements (social welfare programs). Some scholars hold that the parties are "conservatives of the pragmatic and reformist tradition" (Layton-Henry 1982, 17). Yet many of the nineteenth-century Catholic or Christian Democratic parties were anathema to conservatives. While "democracy" is an essential part of the definition, Christian Democratic parties often have within them, or must deal with, the clerical right, whose commitment to democracy has often been questionable, at best. As with other religious ideologies, the notion of Christian Democracy is broad enough to allow for a variety of political

---

[3] These aspects echo Leo XIII's encyclical of 1892, *Rerum Novarum*.

strategies and interpretations (Chassériaud 1965; Einaudi and Goguel 1952; Fogarty 1957, 3–11; Hanley 1994, 4–5; Irving 1979, xvii–xxii; Kalyvas 1996, 1–2; Mayeur 1986; Lynch 1993, 5–20; van Kersbergen 1994, 31–47; von Beyme 1985, 81–96). For instance, the "integralist" strand accepts democracy, but only within the narrow framework of a Christian state. In contrast, the "autonomist" strand accepts a plurality of ideologies and views the separation of Church and state as essential. Other variants of Christian Democracy have a strong leftist streak that challenges class hierarchies.

Precisely at the time when the Churches were grappling with the new sociopolitical environment of postwar Europe, Christian Democratic parties took the reins of the new Italian, French, and German political systems.[4] These parties, Democrazia Cristiana (DC), Mouvement Républicain Populaire (MRP), and Christlich Demokratische Union–Christlich Soziale Union (CDU-CSU), were not creatures of the Catholic Church. They had their own goals and programs that extended beyond, and sometimes did not even include, promoting the dogma and interests of the Church. They had to operate in an environment that was foreign to the Church: democracy involved compromises on goals in the parliamentary and societal arenas. The parties faced a dramatically changed international context yet they had to cope with the Church as an important societal institution that many citizens still regarded as the ultimate moral authority. The parties recognized the potential advantage of cooperating with the Church. However, owing to the different nature of the organizations (party and Church) and their different environments, cooperation was neither automatic nor always desired. It was fraught with pitfalls. Whether and how cooperation was established and maintained is one of the subjects of this book.

In Italy, France, and Germany, the postwar Christian Democratic parties faced significant political challengers from the left and right.[5] There were numerous societal organizations upon which they might have built.

---

[4] The description of the respective political systems is found in chapter 3. Compared to the literature on Socialist and Communist parties, the literature on the postwar Christian Democratic parties is thin, but see Bazin 1981; Pridham 1977; Irving 1973, 1979; Hanley 1994; Cary 1996; Poulat 1986; Verhoeven 1979; Letamendia 1975; M. Mitchell 1995; Sa'adah 1987. The Italian party (Democrazia Cristiana) has received considerable analysis, but usually as an atypical, unique case (Baget-Bozzo 1974), or as an example of a dominant party (Sartori 1967; Tarrow 1990).

[5] From 1945 to 1958, the French Communist Party (PCF) averaged about 25% in national elections; the Italian Communist Party (PCI) ranged from 32% when linked with the Socialists in 1948, to 23% in 1953 and 20% in 1958. The French Socialists (SFIO) averaged about 13% (save 1946, 18%); the Italian Marxist Socialists (PSI), about 13%. In Germany, the Social Democrats (SPD) regularly received at least 30% of the vote, gaining vote share as it shed its classic Marxist heritage.

The internal policy debates that racked the parties were similar; so, too, their structures. The parties had many goals in common: they wanted to create broad-based, cross-class parties, within nominally democratic institutions; however, their strategies, including toward the Catholic Churches, differed. The parties had different ideological conceptions of their roles; they also faced Churches with differing structures and leadership. These three factors affected the parties' willingness, and ability, to take on the Church as an ally, and their relations with their respective national Churches had a significant impact on their early electoral record.

GOALS OF THE BOOK

This book is both theory and subject driven. The cases themselves warrant analysis, while the theoretical model needs to be tested with evidence. The cases are situated in a time when new democratic, political systems were being established, displacing or dismantling (to some degree) the previous authoritarian regime. During such a transition, interest groups have, arguably, a wider range of choices in new party allies and a greater chance of influencing the development of those parties. Transitions may increase the willingness of new parties to find interest group allies, hence to cater to those groups. New parties need roots; old interest groups, such as the Catholic Church, have them. Because transitions are not times of normal politics, leaders and their organizations will be making choices with subpar information. In addition, transitions to democracy pose several problems for those social and political groups that had close ties to the previous regime. A record of collaboration tarnishes the group's reputation; resources that were based on links with the outgoing regime are lost; the public may be vengeful; the group must adjust its ideology to the altered circumstances. How do such interest groups find new allies?

Analytically, an interest group's decision to ally with a political party is more complex than recent works acknowledge (Kalyvas 1996; W. Mitchell 1990). Those works that apply economic models to the behavior of religious institutions have focused on secularization, on the response to religious competition, on the conditions under which Church and state conflict, and on explaining the rationality of religious beliefs and rituals (Iannaccone 1992; Stark and Iannaccone 1994; Keshavarzian and Gill 1997; Gill 1998). They have not explained how religious institutions choose political party allies to deal with some of those same issues. How does the group choose and then control its party ally or allies? What leverage can the party exert on the interest group? Why do parties and interest groups sometimes persist in apparently dysfunctional "relationships"? Any interaction between an interest group and a political party elicits problems of commitment, monitoring, incomplete contracting, fraud, and policy divergence. How did the French, Italian, and German Churches address these problems?

While some of the differences between the Catholic Church and other interest groups affect the Church's assessments of strategy, they do not preclude us from analyzing it as an interest group when it is engaged in politics. The claim that the Church is an interest group has a point: to facilitate a comparative analysis of the Church's actions with other political actors, especially with political parties in democratic political systems. It has the additional point of developing a means of analyzing interest group behavior vis-à-vis parties. I propose an economic model of Church behavior, with the Church as a firm in a competitive market. The model is supplemented by attention to historical legacy, institutional structure, and political entrepreneurship. As with Gill (1998, 4), my focus is on the "*official* political strategy" of the Church, with "official" meaning "that the primary unit of analysis is the national Catholic episcopacy" and the Vatican.[6]

The analysis aims to show why and how the Italian, French, and German[7] Churches sought political allies and provided for their own survival in the years immediately following World War II. At that time, the Catholic Churches had to accept the collapse of regimes they had, in some measure, supported. The Churches also faced a resurgence of Communist and Socialist parties and labor unions, the enfranchisement of women, national governments preoccupied with reconstruction, a decline in the number of practicing Catholics, and serious questions about the Churches' complicity with the Vichy/Fascist/Nazi governments. The end of the war seemed to mark, definitively, the end of the Churches' social dominance. Yet in Italy and Germany, apparently through their links with the Christian Democratic political parties, the Churches successfully competed with other actors for political prominence, for resources, and for maintenance of what they had always assumed were their prerogatives. The French Church did not compete. Explaining the choices of the Churches, and the contrasting outcomes, is the empirical subject of this book. The alliances were problematic: the Italian Church became tightly linked with a corrupt party; the French Church abandoned what was widely regarded as the only honest party in France, and the German Church shared "its" party with a rival denomination.

---

[6] Lower clergy often have divergent political goals that may lead them to prefer different party allies.

[7] I use *Germany* to refer both to pre-1949 Germany, as well as to the Federal Republic of Germany, established 1949 (West Germany), and to Germany after the FRG's unification with the German Democratic Republic (East Germany) in 1990.

PLAN OF THE BOOK

This book ventures into new territory. The Catholic Church in twentieth-century Western Europe has, despite its political and social importance, been a neglected subject.[8] Christian Democratic parties have suffered from a similar lack of scholarly attention. Very little work has explored the conditions under which parties and interest groups support each other, how they exercise leverage over each other, monitor behavior, or decide to withdraw support. While analyzing the behavior of a major world religion in democratic politics, the book also seeks to create a foundation for a theory of interest group–party interaction.

This book focuses on Italy and France, then extends its arguments to Germany. The primary time period is 1944–58, through the establishment of the postwar democracies, but, where relevant, the history of the Church in politics is also addressed. Italy, France, and Germany vary considerably in the extent of Church dominance of the religious, social, and political spheres. The Italian Church was hegemonic, the French Church dominant but, with the French Revolution, was driven into a much more competitive situation with the French state. The German Church competed directly with the Lutheran Church, with which it was compelled to share political, social, and religious power. All three countries have experienced severe Church-state conflicts, the collapse of democracy and its renewal. All three Catholic Churches faced the emergence of Christian Democratic parties in the late nineteenth century and the question of what to do about them; all three worked with nondemocratic regimes in the twentieth century that granted them special prerogatives; all three then faced the collapse of those regimes and the task of integrating themselves into the postwar democracies, which were characterized by the presence of well-organized, adamantly secular parties.

Yet the Churches vary significantly in their histories, structures, and leadership and the political parties and systems with which they worked. For the Churches, these countries are crucial cases: Italy is home to the Vatican, France is home to the Catholic Church's "eldest" or first and traditionally most important "daughter," and Germany is where Catholicism was most directly challenged by an alternative to it—the Lutherans. Were Catholicism to, in some sense, fail in any one of these countries, its power and authority worldwide would be severely diminished. Understanding how the dominant religious organizations in Western Europe coped with democracy and struggled to guarantee their organizational

---

[8] Studies of the Vatican itself are similarly scarce, but see Hanson 1987; Vaillancourt 1980; and Reese 1996.

survival should provide clues as to how other religious organizations in Western Europe and elsewhere might go about doing the same, and what factors might influence their strategies.

The book proceeds as follows: chapter 2 expands on the argument, surveying the field on interest groups, and religion in politics, and suggests that the Church's actions, as an interest group, can be modeled as a firm in a market seeking a supplier for a product. That said, the chapter shows that it is necessary to move beyond the model in order to understand the "prices" the Church assigns to particular strategies. Prices are affected by historical legacy, institutional structures, and by the group's political entrepreneurs—its leadership. Chapter 3 traces the historical trajectories of the Italian and French Churches leading up to the end of World War II. It shows that the divergence in the structure of the Churches, in the constellation of allies, and in the bargains struck with the fascist/authoritarian rulers in the twentieth century gave the Churches (and parties) different starting points after World War II. Further, variations in alliance patterns were affected by the timing of papal intervention (including who was pope and when). Chapter 4 shows the divergent interests and ideologies of the Italian and French hierarchies, discussing their sources and consequences.

I analyze the decisions of the two Churches to support Christian Democratic parties, and at what level, in chapter 5. The Italian-French comparison shows that the Churches made their decisions based on factors highlighted by the economic model and, significantly, that historical legacy, structure, and the Church leadership weigh heavily in strategic calculations of "costs" and "benefits." I find that the Church discriminates on the basis of party policy, capability, and reliability. The next chapter follows the interest group–party dynamic by examining the case of "exit" from the party link (by the French Church) and "voice" (by the Italian Church). Sunk costs and potential benefits are weighed on different scales, leading to different choices by the two Churches. Chapter 7 asks how, once an interest group has decided on a strategy vis-à-vis parties, the group mobilizes its members to cooperate and to assist in implementing the strategy. Chapter 8 asks three questions about parties: first, why does a party link with any interest group? Second, how does it choose among interest groups? Third, how does it control the group it has linked with? A preliminary answer comes from the market model, in which the party is the buyer (of political support) and the interest group is the seller. As with interest groups, parties weigh costs and benefits on scales molded by historical legacy, structure, and their leaderships' perspectives. Chapter 9 extends the reach of the argument by applying it to a third case, that of Germany. The German case, involving a Christian Democratic party supported by both the Protestant and Catholic Churches, provides further evidence of the value of treating religious institutions as interest groups, modeling them as firms in a competitive market. Chapter 10 discusses the implications of the argument for analyses of contemporary Catholicism, other religious organizations in politics, and interest groups.

This book creates an economic model of Church behavior and sees how far it fits the facts of the three cases, on the premise that if there is a good fit, the parsimony of the model argues strongly for it. Further, it goes to great lengths to trace the thinking of the historical actors, to show that the author's concept of how they were formulating and choosing strategies is not simply an abstract model but a good reflection of how they were talking and of the kinds of considerations they had in the decision-making context. The book is an "analytic narrative": it is narrative in the attention it accords "stories, accounts, and context. It is analytic in that it extracts explicit and formal lines of reasoning, which facilitate both exposition and explanation" (Bates et al. 1998, 10).

My work attempts to marry two approaches that often talk past each other. Those who use economic theories to model political behavior may acknowledge leadership, entrepreneurship, and ideology (though they usually dismiss their importance) but seldom import those factors into their analyses (Gill 1998, 8, 195–96; Kalyvas 1996, 19). Those who focus only on "soft" variables such as historical legacy and leadership ideology (Mainwaring 1986, 5; Pattnayak 1995, 7) lose the explanatory rigor of instrumental, cost-benefit models. My claim is that while we can model the Church, and any interest group, as if it were a firm in a competitive market, we must also attend to how its historical trajectory, institutional relationships, and the actions and ideology of its leadership affect its calculations and behavior in that metaphorical market. It is this argument that I elaborate upon in the next chapter.

Interest Groups, Political Parties, and Religion

> The problem of religion, intended in its lay
> rather than its confessional sense, is that of
> the unity, sanctified by faith, between a world
> view and a conforming norm of behavior;
> but why call this "religion" and not call it
> "ideology" or simply "politics"?
> *(Gramsci)*

GRAMSCI notes the similarity between religion, which provides an interpretive map for the world, a system for evaluating the justice of distributive schemes, as well as ethical and behavioral codes to follow, and ideology, which, by most definitions, does the same. Once one agrees that a religion is an ideology, then it is indeed a short step to participating in politics, much of which is about whose worldview, including distributive criteria and behavioral norms, is going to prevail. I join a growing number of writers who argue that the Catholic Church (and any organized religion) is a strategic, calculating, and influence-maximizing organization. Specifically, I analyze the Church's behavior vis-à-vis political parties as if it were an interest group. Given that perspective, I then use an analogy: the microeconomic analysis of a firm in a competitive market. The analogy highlights the risks, costs, and benefits the Church/interest group faces when dealing with a political party. This is an unorthodox position. I also take seriously the fact that the Church (in each country) is a religious organization with a long history, a particular structure, and varied leadership. To be able to assess the impact of these three factors on the Church's political strategies, it is essential first to have a general model of interest group–party behavior that addresses the questions of why an interest group supports (or invests in) a party, how the interest group and party monitor and sanction each other, and under what conditions one of the two organizations might resort to exit. The analogy of the firm serves that purpose. It is also necessary to understand how my argument builds upon or departs from other arguments about interest groups, and about the Catholic Church and Christian Democratic parties. The review of those arguments shows that common conceptions of interest groups inadequately address the strategic, calculating nature of interest groups vis-à-vis parties. Studies of the Catholic Church and Christian Democracy either conflate the two or stress their differences at the cost of ignoring the strong incentives the Church has to cooperate with the dominant political actors (be they parties in a parliamentary system or authoritarian regimes).

INTEREST GROUPS AND THE LINKAGE FUNCTION OF PARTIES

Interest groups have been studied as the representatives of particular subgroups in society that then link with political parties to be represented in the policy process. Groups place their demands, and a political party transmits them, as if it were just a "transmission belt," to the political system (Eldersveld 1964; Lawson 1980; Becker 1983, 372; Zeigler 1993, 30–48). The interest group approaches a party, or forms one itself, when it wants something that can be provided best or only through the political system. At most, the party is a broker between interests, automatically aggregating group demands and transmitting their preferences. Alternatively, the interest group creates its own party: As Angelo Panebianco says of the Italian Christian Democratic party, "it is a party born from the direct will of a religious institution" (1982, 229). In a similar vein, Lipset and Rokkan (1967) argue that when there are conflicts between major sociological and economic blocs at the extension of mass suffrage (voting rights), parties form to represent those blocs. The party is the extension of the group, or bloc, in politics (Galli and Prandi 1970). There is little attention given to the party as an organization with its own interests seeking to make other actors the agents that serve its own ends.[1] There also is a presumption that the party–interest group link, once formed, is on autopilot.[2] Scholars have not tackled the question of why interest groups choose one party over another as their political ally or representative, nor how the groups might handle the interaction.

Panebianco (1982) diverges from the transmission belt view in noting that some parties will be more independent than others of external sup-

---

[1] Lipset and Rokkan (1967) speculated on the influence the organizational efforts of parties, once created, could have on why cleavages endure in political systems, but not on how the socioeconomic group might manipulate the party, or vice versa.

[2] An exception is some of the literature on labor unions and Social Democratic parties, which focused attention on the quandary of a labor union when "its" party is in power (Gourevitch et al. 1984). Kalyvas (1996) recognizes the initial tensions between the Church and Christian Democratic parties but implies that once the Christian Democratic party is formed, the Church has no influence over it, and that the Church's attitude toward it is of no consequence to the party's future electoral or organizational success or behavior.

porting organizations. That difference can be explained by the conditions in which the party is "born" and institutionalizes itself (1982, 104). Generally, new parties that became governing parties immediately, such as the CDU-CSU and DC, are weakly institutionalized, dependent on external organizations and political patronage. Duverger observes that Christian Democratic parties are more likely to have strong horizontal linkages that the parties use "to control organizations ancillary to the party" (1954, 51). But he does not explain why or when the ancillary organization (or interest group) might substantially control the party. More concerned with analyzing internal party organization, Panebianco and Duverger also do not explain why sometimes an interest group or, in Duverger's terms, an ancillary organization, later abandons the party, or vice versa.[3]

Recent work theorizes that parties in established democracies no longer depend upon their base or affiliated interest groups; instead they form a "cartel" in which they set prices and the distribution schedule for state resources to be administered under the auspices of the governing parties (Katz and Mair 1995). If so, that leads to the question of how parties are able to use interest group links to become independent of them, while rendering groups dependent upon the parties.

INTEREST GROUPS, PUBLIC POLICY, AND THE STATE

Others note that interest groups themselves "provide an important link between the governed and the government," and that that link is "in some cases more significant than that of political parties" (Thomas 1993, 1). But if part of the government includes elected officials who represent particular parties, then the analyst trying to understand how interest groups influence "government" cannot ignore the interest group–party link. While recent studies agree that interest groups are only one facet in a complex geometry (Walker 1983, 403; Richardson 1993a, 5–10; Thomas 1993), they have not looked systematically at the groups' interactions with political parties (Baumgartner and Leech 1998; Petracca 1992). Ehrmann (1957) and LaPalombara (1964) provide a wealth of information but few hypotheses.

Interest groups have, on the other hand, often been studied from the perspective of their relationship to "the state" or "government," and,

---

[3] In examining internal party factional battles, scholars note the role that party factions, representing different interest groups, have on the ability of one faction to prevail, or for the conflict to be resolved with a particular outcome (Kitschelt 1994; Koelble 1992a; Panebianco 1982). They do not address the question of why the group supports the faction, what tactics the group might employ to gain more leverage, or when the group is likely to desert it in search of a better deal.

since parties in democracies occupy some state offices, we might look to this literature for insights on interest group–party dynamics. This body of scholarship has three subsets. The first emphasizes that the state has interests and goals of its own, and institutional structures that make the state a proactive organization (North 1981; Levi 1988; Evans, Rueschmeyer, and Skocpol 1985; Nettl 1968). Interest groups, from this perspective, lobby the appropriate branch of the state, perhaps developing a regularized relationship with it. The interest group's influence is, however, held at bay by the relative autonomy of the state (with the degree of autonomy varying by state structure). The literature is silent on the question of where parties fit in the state structure—are they internal or external to it? That silence is rather curious: though political parties are frequently major actors *within* the state and governing institutions, scholars of the state have ignored them, and, thus, have ignored the dynamics of interest group–party relations. If the state is relatively autonomous, one might ask why interest groups nevertheless form and lobby for particular policies. The autonomous state literature only raises more questions about the observable efforts of interest groups to support specific parties.

The second literature subset is that of corporatism, meaning state recognition or sponsorship of organized societal groups and their negotiations. This body of scholarship also accords some degree of autonomy to the state, taking "as its starting point the role of the state in shaping interest representation" (Collier and Collier 1979, 967). Interest groups are "formally incorporated into the public policy-making process and provided by the state with certain benefits in exchange for their cooperation and their restraint" in their demands (Keeler 1987, 9).[4] However, the parties that often foster the corporatist arrangements have not been central to the analyses (Keeler 1987; F. Wilson 1987; S. Berger 1972; Schmitter and Lembruch 1979). The focus of the literature is on whether corporatism exists (e.g. Keeler 1987; F. Wilson 1987) and, if so, what its impact is on a country's political economy (Goldthorpe 1984; C. Maier 1987).

Both literatures (state autonomy and corporatism) contribute some important insights—that the structure of the state and the actions of its agents shape policy, and that the state can, and often does, privilege one set of organized interests over another. Yet political parties are, in varying degrees, critical to state policies, to the formulation of the state's goals, and are often the actors that establish and sanction "corporatist" style arrangements. As Keeler's study notes (1987), corporatist arrangements

---

[4] The corporatist literature grew out of the observation that interest group–state interaction did not conform to the classic pluralist model in which an "unspecified number of multiple" interest groups lobby the state in whatever fashion and have no representational monopoly within their sector, nor state-granted privileges (Schmitter 1974, 96).

are not static, and it is usually a political party or interest group that disrupts them (cf. Sabel 1981). Interest groups are said to be unlikely to disrupt such arrangements because they would have to sacrifice "a host of organizational benefits" (Keeler 1987, 214), yet it is not evident that groups necessarily gain more by being in such arrangements than by leaving them and then requiring the state to pay a higher "price" to lure them back.[5] The influence interest groups have over parties, the extent of the parties' dependence upon them for electoral survival, and the interest group's dependency on one or several parties, are all factors that affect the extent of a state's autonomy and the goals it seeks, as well as the state's choice of which group or groups to privilege in its own efforts to retain its monopoly on power.

The third set of scholars studying interest groups and their relationship to the state are those who apply economic theories to the study of political behavior. Due to their rent-seeking activities (efforts to acquire special economic or political treatment), interest groups have been a subject of significant work by economists and some political scientists. Here again, the interest group–party link is absent. Catalyzed by Stigler and Friedland's (1962) and Olson's work (1965), scholars have examined the role of interest groups in economic growth and government regulations. Interest groups pressure the "government," the latter made up of "elected officials" and "bureaucrats" (W. Mitchell 1990) for favorable rules. The government is the broker of a cartel of industries acting as "pressure groups" (Becker 1983; Posner 1974; Peltzman 1976).[6] Interest groups' ability to attain rents depends partly on what voters will tolerate. The government is expected to respond to voters and not to interest groups when consumers "become discontented and angry enough to vote against incumbents held responsible for their higher prices" (W. Mitchell 1990, 91). Politicians only enter the picture either as unitary actors or individual free agents. They seek to deliver favorable rents to the interest group coalition that helps them stay in power, setting rent amounts at the level just below the taxpayers' threshold of revolt (supporting rival politicians) and setting rent prices (North and Thomas 1973; Levi 1988; Tullock 1967; Krueger 1972).

This is an imaginary world. In assuming away institutions, it argues that groups and politicians and the government respond instantaneously to

---

[5] Schmitter notes that corporatist systems should have a "resilience unmatched by more pluralist arrangements" (in Keeler 1987, 330 n. 4) because of the "sunken institutional costs." Whether and why that is the case remains to be analyzed.

[6] This literature is primarily focused on the United States' political system. It uses the word *government* to mean what other scholars refer to as the *state,* and it also uses *government* to refer to the current administration. When discussing this literature, I will use *government* in their understanding. However, elsewhere, it means the current administration of the state.

"price" signals. They don't. Because governments and their states have specific structures that distort, block, or amplify signals, it is essential to incorporate institutions into the analysis of interest group–government interaction. Politicians are virtually always embedded in a party. Parties, among other things, are institutions. That fact makes a difference to their incentives, and abilities, to provide rents to rent seekers. Party structures (and ideologies) make a party more receptive to, and more capable of responding to, some groups' demands than others. If parties are significant actors in the government, the government's response will vary partly with the extent of penetration of the parties by interest groups, by the groups' hold over the voters, including the group's ability to keep the voters from reacting as "free agents." Since states "perform functions and have capacities unavailable to interest groups" (Howell 1997, 4), the latter will, under some circumstances, turn to the state. The structure of the state affects the relative power of parties and permanent government bureaucracies, and thus an interest group's incentives for lobbying the one or the other. Interest groups have institutional structures that affect the leverage they are able to exert over parties and governments; these structures facilitate some actions and hinder others.

The market analogy and the imputation of strategic behavior to groups raise a key question: why does an interest group opt for a "contract" with just one party? In a competitive market, a group would seem to be better off if no one party has a monopoly on the representation of its interests in government. If the interest group is a sizable one, whose votes (and members) can make a difference to a party's electoral fortunes, then the question is heightened. Shouldn't the group prefer competition for its support? The answer lies partly in the fact that, to the extent that political parties do not manufacture the same "product" (policies varying by party), the number of "suppliers" to any interest group's specific interests is limited. Further, there may be barriers to new entrants: new parties that might be willing to supply an interest group with the desired policies find the cost of entering the market prohibitively high (electoral laws are one obvious barrier).

Most studies of interest groups are studies of economic groups (unions, employers' federations, industry organizations, etc.). Yet, as Olson (1965) indicated in his writing on collective action, there is little reason to expect the dynamics of interest group action to be significantly different for non-economic groups (ethnic separatists, religious groups, environmentalists, etc.). While the specific content of what each group wants may be different, groups of all types lobby and invest support in parties to obtain their desired benefits. Groups will be concerned about providing specific benefits to their members, as well as reaching policy goals. Granted, some groups, because of their structure and ideology, are more inclined (all other things being equal) to seek partisan assistance than others. The power of interest groups to affect areas of politics about which politicians are concerned (vote-winning issues) varies, as do the costs and benefits to the groups of allying with one or more parties. That these factors are at work in a wide variety of interest groups is important to understanding the decisions of religious organizations to invest support in political parties, and their struggles to supervise the investment afterwards.

RELIGIOUS INTEREST GROUPS AND PARTIES

Recently there has been an upsurge in the activism of religious groups in politics. The scholarship on these groups, primarily religious nationalist movements, has focused on what motivates them to form where and when they do, and on who supports the parties presumed to be attached to them. It has produced few insights about why and when a group is likely to support one or many parties, when it is more likely to form its own political party, or what the tensions are between the party(ies) and the group. Considering that their political goals are, in a generic sense, quite similar to those of other interest groups (influence the political system to sustain their organization, give them a monopoly on representation of their sector, and infuse the legal code with their prescriptions), we can expect religious groups to take into account a similar set of factors in response to the questions of whether and how to influence politics.

The more established literature on the Catholic Church and the so-called Catholic parties—Christian Democratic parties of Western Europe—has tended to distort key aspects of empirical phenomena by taking as given that Christian Democratic parties are a natural outgrowth of Catholicism. In this view, various popes thought that the Church needed political representation and defense, and so created and maintained Christian Democratic parties (Miccoli 1973, 189). As an Italian Communist Party activist said, "Because it is one and the same with the Church, Christian Democracy is a party that has twenty centuries of life."[7] Christian Democratic parties are simply Catholicism in another guise (McMillan 1996, 34–68), established and directed by the Church (Boutry and Michel 1992, 101, 673; Hughes 1965, 111; Lynch 1993, 1214).

This view is problematic for multiple reasons. First, it cannot explain the initial and recurring hostility of the Church to Christian Democratic parties, nor why Christian Democratic parties fail in areas with a high percentage of practicing Catholics (e.g., France), nor the timing of a

---

[7] Archivio Gramsci, Archivio Partito Comunista Italiano, MF 4185, Cosenza, 51948, Comitato Esecutivo, Signore Cannataro, Aug. 7, 1948, p. 07185-0653.

Christian Democratic party's emergence. It also cannot explain why the Church sometimes stopped supporting such a party. Second, it is flawed for assuming that the formation of a party is not problematic and has no collective action costs and no costs for the Catholic Church (cf. Kalyvas 1996). Religious orientations do not automatically become encapsulated by political organizations, nor do religious institutions automatically want to be affiliated with a political party. If anything, some Christian Democratic parties formed partly out of some Catholics' dissatisfaction with the Church's policies and responses to political situations. Third (*pace* Kalyvas 1996, 5, and Mayeur 1980), the postwar Christian Democratic parties were *not* merely lifted from storage as a continuation of the prewar Catholic or Christian Democratic parties. Maintaining that they were, while a convenient shorthand, seriously distorts the process of postwar party formation. Fourth, Christian Democratic parties are *not* the direct political emissaries of Catholic theology and social policy. To put it in economic terms, the Christian Democratic parties are not vertically integrated into the corporate structures of the Church.

Those scholars who recognize that Christian Democratic parties and the Church are two distinct organizations have focused on classifying party differences and describing their evolution (Duverger 1954, xxxii–iii; Mayeur 1980; Hanley 1994, 3; von Beyme 1985, 85–89).[8] Other studies of Catholicism and Christian Democracy emphasize the historical uniqueness of each case. Various historical peculiarities preclude causal comparison. While history is significant, the task is to identify, through the use of cross-national comparisons, those elements of the historical trajectories that vary somewhat systematically with outcomes. "History" establishes structures, organizational ideologies, and reputational legacies, all factors that affect an organization's contemporary existence.

In his notable study *The Rise of Christian Democracy in Europe*, Stathis Kalyvas (1996) attempts to provide a theory of the formation of confessional parties that accounts for the micromotives of individuals and counters the assumption that the party is an automatic extension of the Church in politics. It is his attention to the Church and the party as separate actors that is germane to the study here. The key variables are whether the Church mobilizes Catholics through ancillary organizations, and whether the Church thinks the republican regime afflicting it is going to collapse soon. Kalyvas takes as his cases the fate of Christian Democratic movements and parties of the late twentieth century in six European countries[9]

---

[8] Von Beyme draws attention to the tensions between the Church and "the Christian social movement" in stating that relations between the two "were too fraught to further the formation of a 'Catholic International' " akin to the Socialist International (1985, 81).

[9] France, Belgium, the Netherlands, Austria, Germany, Italy.

and argues that, given the organizational costs of mobilization, the Catholic Church had no need or desire to mobilize Catholics and Catholic ancillary organizations unless there were real threats to the Church.[10] Similarly, politicians had no need to ally with the Church unless there were no alternative means of electoral success and survival. If the Church were to risk entering the political arena, it needed a guarantee of electoral success, and success depended upon having organized groups of Catholics available to campaign and vote for a political party.

In Kalyvas's five cases where confessional parties formed, the Church, with its prerogatives concerning family and education policy under severe threat from the (secular) liberals who controlled the government, decided to create ancillary organizations, thinking this was just a temporary measure (the organizations could later be demobilized). Merely doing so, however, did not reduce the liberal threat, so the Church mobilized these organizations to support conservative political candidates who were, in turn, willing to support its agenda on education and family policy. When, to the surprise of the Church and conservatives, the candidates supported by Catholic Action (the preeminent example of a Catholic ancillary organization; see chap. 3) did very well, the Church had little choice but to recognize the confessional party. The Catholic political party had been created—unwanted by its very creators.[11]

The confessional parties, to reduce dependence upon the Church, declericalized themselves by redefining Catholicism. Thus, the process of party formation provided entrepreneurs and other lay Catholics with new opportunities and new identities. Where such parties formed, the Church was worse off than it had been in its prewar alliances (with conservatives): it "lost its monopoly over the definition of Catholicism and the representation of Catholics" (255).

There are three theoretical problems with this study.[12] The first concerns the "costs" of mobilization. It is commonplace in analyses of strate-

[10] Forming ancillary organizations meant losing some control over Catholics. The latter would find new opportunities for status and leadership and have alternative bases of legitimation. Forming a party would be even worse—the party would begin to define what it was to be Catholic, and provide more outlets for participation, affirmation, and solidarity to Catholics.

[11] In the nonformation case, France, the Church apparently did not think the Third Republic would survive. It banked on the Republic's early demise and the return of a clerical-monarchist regime. Thus, it did not think it necessary to pursue the costly route of organizing Catholic ancillary organizations. Ultimately, the Church decided that the Third Republic would not go away, so it acted to mobilize Catholics. Yet it was "too little, too late" (Kalyvas 1996, 165). The organizational space was already filled by Socialist and radical grassroots organizations. The conservative candidates did not succeed electorally. Thus, to both the Church and conservatives, Catholicism looked like a losing political issue.

[12] Empirical problems are noted in chapter 3.

gic interaction to invoke the costs of action relative to the benefits when trying to explain choices made "under constraints" (Kalyvas 1996, 18). The problem is to estimate or measure those costs and benefits. In doing so, it is important to consider the lens through which the organizational leadership evaluated "prices."

Mobilization may not have been as costly as a focus on identity formation might suggest. For individuals to vote for a particular party, they need not be possessed of a particular identity. Coercion (denial of sacraments, of livelihood) were common techniques of "persuading" Italian Catholics to vote for the postwar Christian Democratic party. Those Catholics did not have to be incorporated into Catholic Action movements; the Church could get what it wanted—support for its political programs—through the less costly route of coercion. Moreover, the Church in some cases could derive clear political and financial benefits from its association with a governing confessional party (e.g., the church tax in Germany, lucrative development schemes in Italy).[13] I suggest that, contrary to Kalyvas's argument, costs, or the "prices" assigned to various strategies, are dependent heavily on specific national and historical contexts and on leadership.[14]

The second theoretical issue is that of the leverage each organization can exert over the other even after the Christian Democratic party formed. Kalyvas's work points toward the need for a better understanding of interest group–party interaction. He rightfully notes that the Church and the Christian Democratic parties competed and disagreed over political goals, but he rules out any influence by the Church. In fact, Church-papal political preferences influenced the governing coalitions the Christian Demo-

---

[13] The empirical record contradicts Kalyvas's contention that electoral success of the nascent Christian Democratic party was the final necessary step in having the Church accept its existence: the Italian Church abandoned the Italian Popular Party (PPI) in favor of the Fascists, and the French Church did not stick with the initially electorally successful Mouvement Républicain Populaire (MRP) after World War II. The argument leads to ambiguous assessments: on the one hand, the formation of Catholic parties was costly to the Church's ability to control the definition of Catholicism, and to represent Catholics; on the other hand, *non*formation was costly to the French Church (Kalyvas 1996, 18–19, 165–66).

[14] Vaillancourt goes so far as to argue that "Catholic parties are even more effective than Catholic Action as instruments of control. Using the votes of the laity as a political power base, Church officials try to build up their various bases of control. Ecological power, remunerative power, social power, legal power, traditional power are all reinforced when a Catholic party is strong in a country" (Vaillancourt 1980, 176). This challenges the idea that Catholic parties exact severe costs on the Church. Lay Catholics may become politically aware and look to the party for guidance, but the Church can always curb that through its various powers. Webster notes that "in sponsoring or at least permitting lay Catholic parties with some degree of political autonomy, the Papacy has renounced no part of its claim to a rightful empire over the minds of men, but has rather chosen a new method in harmony with the mass organization of the modern world" (1960, 185).

cratic parties formed.[15] Interest groups possess resources, such as their authority over their members, which they can deploy *after* party formation in order to restrict the party's options.

The third concerns the level of abstraction. Recent studies of the Church in politics tend to assume one model of the Church and the Christian Democratic party, each having fixed preferences (Kalyvas 1996; Gill 1998; Irving 1979). Church and party behavior varies across countries as a function of the external sociopolitical context. This approach exaggerates the similarities between organizations at the expense of significant variation in key features of the individual national Churches that affect Church-party relations, and it has no means of discussing the differences in national Church policies, or of explaining the dominant position of some Christian Democratic parties in postwar Western Europe and their virtual disappearance in other countries.

Kalyvas's key contributions are in highlighting (though to the neglect of other factors) the role of strategic calculations in the process of party formation and the potential for disagreement between the Christian Democratic parties and the Church. This book builds on Kalyvas's insights that the Church acts strategically and that Christian Democratic parties are organizations with interests often distinct from the Church. The book also builds, more generally, on concepts from economic theories of organizational behavior. It takes seriously the view that political entrepreneurship and organizational culture also affect an interest group's, and a political party's, decisions.

THE CHURCH AND THE POLITICAL MARKET FOR RELIGION

Going one step further than Kalyvas, several scholars have analyzed organized religion as if it were a firm competing in a market (Ekelund, Hébert, and Tollison 1996; Gill 1998; Stark and Iannaccone 1994; Stark 1993). The benefits of such an analysis come from the way the analogy captures the conflictual, competitive nature of religions. Since organized religions each claim universality, they each strive to drive the others from the market, or at least gain the biggest market share.[16] New religions typically have low start-up costs and low overhead and hence can compete effectively with established, high-overhead religions such as Catholicism (Gill 1998,

---

[15] For example, it took Pius XII's death in 1958 and the election of John XXIII to enable the DC to undertake its "opening to the left" *(Pacem in Terris)*. This enabled the DC to split the "Marxist" left and reduce the PSI to a dependent governing ally (Pollard 1996, 91–92).

[16] Religions, however, have varied over time in their efforts and desire to recruit new members.

177–82; Iannaccone 1994, 71, 159). Many organized religions seek to maximize their market share, measured by influence, number of believers, and amount of revenue, and turn to political parties and governments in order to obtain restrictions on market entry (i.e., have that religion declared the state religion) and subsidies for their activities. Religions compete not just with other religions, but with other organizations, especially the state and parties, for membership, revenue, and authority (Keshavarzian and Gill 1997; Gill 1998; Kalyvas 1996). This is behavior typical of interest groups. Studying the Church as an interest group enables us to generalize about interest group–party behavior, and to understand how a major world religion copes with secular politics. Indeed, I suggest that the economic analysis can be fruitfully extended to the study of interest groups in general, and it is here that I begin the explication of my argument.

ASSET SPECIFICITY

How would an economic approach explain an interest group's decision to create a party or, instead, to support one that already exists or is forming? In economic terms, the decision is about whether to vertically integrate in order to produce the desired product or to purchase it on the market. Firms vertically integrate when the following conditions obtain: frequent transactions, a high level of market uncertainty, and asset-specific investments (Williamson 1979; Chisholm 1993, 144).[17] In short, services produced at lower cost internally will be undertaken by the firm itself; those available more cheaply in the market will be contracted for (McChesney 1991, 81, 83). I deal first with asset specificity. Such investments are "specific" to a particular transaction, or set of transactions, and are "appropriable" by either party to the transaction (Klein, Crawford, and Alchian 1978). The value of the commodity is unique to that exchange relationship. Asset specificity motivates vertical integration in the following manner: "If both a buyer and a seller contemplate a transaction which requires investments that are unique to that particular exchange relationship, then the two parties are locked into a bilateral monopoly structure. Once this investment is made by both parties, either or both parties might engage in opportunistic behavior" (Chisholm 1993, 144). Each party, knowing the other has invested heavily in the exchange, has an opportunity to en-

---

[17] There is a debate in the economic literature over whether vertical integration is related more to transaction costs (Williamson 1979) or to sunk costs (G. Whyte 1994). As both factors seem to be at work in interest group–party relations, this dispute will not be resolved here.

gage in "opportunistic behavior," that is, failing to deliver the desired product when or as wanted, or even expropriating the invested assets (cf. Frieden 1994).[18] If the assets being exchanged have little use or value outside that exchange relationship, then the parties to the exchange are stuck maintaining the relationship or investing new resources in seeking a different (new) partner (G. Whyte 1994, 188).[19] In such cases, it is expected that the buyer of the product (or the investor) will try to vertically integrate by incorporating the manufacturer (or host site) into its corporate structure, or, if that is not possible, create the equivalent.

Interest groups and parties are involved in a similar relationship. Applying the concept of asset specificity to the question of when an interest group will create its own political party yields the result that it should not happen often. To understand the level of contracting or vertical integration likely, one must ask, what is the relative degree of specificity of assets being exchanged by a group and party? In setting up the relationship, a group might provide the party: (1) access to its organizational facilities; (2) the reputation of being its party; (3) training of its staff for campaigns; (4) voter education; (5) votes; and (6) financing. Regarding the first asset, an interest group could fairly easily prevent the party from using its facilities, provided the group did not build facilities for the party and then sign over the deed. Second, reputation has a lag time but is not insuperable. Third, the basic skills to train campaign staff have value when transferred to other parties. There may be skills specific to one party (how to write propaganda for it, personal connections established that later have to be reoriented or have no value outside that party). The labor of interest group activists may become a specific asset if the party lures the activist away by offering a new venue for personal and financial rewards (Kalyvas 1996). Fourth, voter education is specific to the extent that voters are easily habituated to vote for one party but hard to deprogram.[20] Fifth, votes allegedly have the same face value no matter which party receives them, but in real

---

[18] Another way of looking at interest group support of a party is to construe it as an investment, subject to the same hazards that foreign investors face. If so, then the questions are directed at determining whether the assets invested are discrete and specific to a particular location, hence easily expropriated ("nationalized") by the host society (or political party), or whether the assets invested depend for their value on being linked to the network run by the investor.

[19] There is some debate about whether the issue is one of "sunk costs" or just the effect those costs have on the resources of an actor to exit the exchange relationship. In theory, it should not matter to an economic actor how much has already been expended in an exchange, but rather the use value that can be gained from the exchange compared to the cost of starting a new relationship and breaking the existing contract. However, it has been found that individuals and groups do weigh resources expended in and of themselves, regardless of "future costs and benefits" (G. Whyte 1994, 299).

[20] This is an area still much debated in political science.

terms, the value depends on whether other parties need or want them.[21] If there is greater competition for the votes of some types of voters, then the group that represents them may be able to redeploy those assets (the votes it represents) in another party. Sixth, financial support, once given and consumed by the party, cannot be redeployed, so to the extent that a group must commit finances to a party for it to succeed, that group has specific assets invested in the relationship.

The issue is not just whether an asset can be redeployed easily by the group or seized by the party, or whether the value is only in that relationship, but whether there are obstacles to the group's supplying itself with alternatives. The costs of forsaking an established relationship, usually termed "sunk costs," but perhaps more appropriately called opportunity costs, act as strong disincentives to exit (G. Whyte 1994; cf. Pierson 1997). Thus, to avoid the greater costs of exiting, the buyer may have to endure opportunistic behavior on the part of the seller. To the extent that most assets exchanged by an interest group and party are specific to their particular relationship, one might expect to find a group creating its own party or taking over an existing one.

But asset specificity is only one factor weighed by an interest group; the second consideration is the *transaction costs* of frequent interaction. Rather than having to lobby politicians each time a relevant policy issue is broached, an interest group would find it less costly to supply its own preprogrammed politicians. This would obviate the group's need to expend organizational resources finding suppliers and negotiating a price for services to be rendered by the external party's politicians.

The third factor is the level of uncertainty in the "market." The questions here ask, Are political conditions stable enough? And are the incentives structured so that the group can expect the party to deliver what it promises? Conditions of high uncertainty give a group a strong incentive to build its own party rather than face the costs associated with volatile or nebulous conditions.

Finally, the *core competencies* of the organization must be evaluated. What is the organization good at doing, what is it structured to do, and, given those features, how difficult would it be to take on the new tasks? Organization theorists remind us that the leadership of a firm (or interest group) is concerned not only with identifiable costs, but also with how taking on a new production function will alter the firm's or group's "organizational mission" or raison d'être (J. Wilson 1989, 1995).

Both the Italian and French Churches had concerns about the risks of committing their own assets to external political parties, even as they also

---

[21] The discussion of the specificity of assets a party might exchange will be found in chapter 8.

had incentives to reduce the costs of negotiating with politicians, and to have some certainty in the uncertain, new postwar political environment. The degree to which the Churches' core competencies lent themselves to constructing their own political parties is difficult to determine. On the one hand, the Church's hierarchical structure, its disdain for democracy, its reluctance to compromise its principles (except when organizational survival is at stake), and its belief in its monopoly on truth, do not seem appropriate for the compromising, pluralist, less hierarchical, and overtly nondogmatic features of democratic party competition. On the other hand, the function of priests giving sermons is not far from that of politicians giving speeches: both seek to persuade or compel adherence; priests are well positioned for door-to-door campaigning, for political education, and for turning religious festivals into campaign rallies. The Church had already paid the start-up costs of constructing an organization; mobilizing that organization for other activities would be relatively easy. Finally, the Church's attitude toward democracy need not be an insuperable barrier: not all parties are convinced of the value of the democratic system in which they operate.

Specific assets are not the sole determinant of whether a group creates its own political party or instead engages in various types of contracts with parties. The point is that when the profitable opportunities that a group wants to exploit require the deployment of specific assets, the group will weigh the potential profits against the risks of committing assets that later cannot be recouped or redeployed. Additional factors weigh on the decision. An interest group will also consider the social legitimacy of building its own party, the presence or absence of a likely party ally previously constructed by politicians, whether it sees democratic political competition as an area in which it can operate without severely undermining its original mission, and whether it can, in organizational terms, afford to commit to that activity. Political actions that in Italy were seen as acceptable for the Catholic Church by most of the population were inconceivable in much of France, thus limiting the French Church's ability to construct a party, even if it had wanted to do so. Both Churches had concerns about the negative effects on them as religious institutions resulting from engaging directly in political competition. In both countries, these issues were made less pressing by the emergence of Christian Democratic parties that seemed willing to work for many of the Churches' goals.[22]

---

[22] Granted, the rise of the nascent parties was facilitated, especially in Italy, by Church assistance. The Churches found it organizationally less costly to negotiate with and invest in emerging external parties (suppliers) rather than integrate all political party functions into the organization of the Church. This is discussed at length in chapter 5.

POLITICAL CONSEQUENCES OF COMPETITION
FOR MARKET SHARE

The Church, like other interest groups, tends to be a proactive organization, that is, it may decide to support a political party to improve its position even in the absence of a threat from the government to its position. The Church, as Gill (1998) amply demonstrates, is concerned about the ever-present threat of competition from other religions and other ideologies. While the state may threaten to revoke the Church's "license" to practice, or impose severe restrictions on how, when, and where it may conduct its operations, other religions and ideologies may *reduce* the Church's market share. In a democracy, the Church may seek to pressure the state, via political parties, to grant it a monopoly on the religious "market," or at least to subsidize its operations, giving it a competitive advantage over other groups. The Church would be engaged in political exploitation, defined as using government action to force consumers to buy at the price the interest group demands (Mitchell and Munger 1993, 324–27). The Church, like other interest groups, may try to use the state to increase its control over its own staff (closed-shop practices, appointment procedures, "suppression of substitute goods," monopolies on training and educational facilities). In turn, political parties in the government may be able to act as a cartel manager, offering regulatory services for a price (votes, logistical support) to an interest group (W. Mitchell 1990, 90).

Some of the Church's struggles for presence involve maintaining its trademarks and sole distribution rights to the "product": ritual and salvation. Rather like a multinational pharmaceutical company, the Church exhorts Catholics to use the name brand instead of a generic alternative and not accept apparent substitutes. Having Catholicism declared the religion of the state was and is a (shortsighted) preferred solution (cf. Stark and Iannaccone, 1994), so too that of having rival cults banned. This is one reason Fascism was so attractive to the Church—with competitors outlawed, all rents accrued to the Church. This desire for monopoly prompted the French Church to see the MRP as somewhat wanting as a political ally: the MRP showed itself all too willing to accept non-Catholics (as did the DC, though not officially).

ADVERSE SELECTION AND MALFEASANCE IN CONTRACTING

A critical reading of Kalyvas's work and research on corporatism leads us to ask more about the costs to each organization in interest group–party linkages. Kalyvas suggests that the Church hesitates to support a party because it would lose control over its constituency (one of its assets would be expropriated). The corporatist literature assumes that any group wants state benefits and therefore is willing to enter into state-sponsored or state-sanctioned corporatist arrangements. But how does a group know whether a political party or the state intends to, or can, deliver the promised benefits? As a contracting agent, the group faces risks that in the economic literature are termed *adverse selection* and *malfeasance*. An interest group encounters adverse selection because it does not know the talents, capacities, and intentions of the party as well as the party does. It must make its best guess that the party has not misrepresented its abilities and intentions to the group. Further, the interest group might be exploited by the party it supports, expending resources for which it is not compensated. The problem is the common one of "malfeasance," in which one agent to a contract pays for goods or services that are to be delivered sometime in the future by another. That situation gives the receiving agent an opportunity to leave the contract unfulfilled. Applying this to interest group–party relations, if a group expends organizational resources on a party in an electoral campaign and the party wins office but fails to deliver the stipulated policy, the group's resources have been wasted. This is in addition to the problem that future circumstances may prevent the receiving party from being able to fulfill its promises.[23] The problem is one of committing assets without the guarantees that hierarchical control provides over the agents with whom the group is contracting.

Nevertheless, under certain conditions, interest groups do support political parties. The next section summarizes what will be dealt with at greater length in chapter 6.

SELECTING A PARTY ALLY

It is perhaps obvious to say an interest group will support a political party when that party has some good (product) the interest group wants. In light of the malfeasance problem, the interest group (and party) looks for mechanisms and circumstances that reduce the probability that it will be cheated by the other organization (cf. Mitchell and Munger 1991, 12). Each organization will assess the other's capacity to credibly commit itself: what authority does the leadership have? What capacity to sanction member deviance or police itself? What control over other factors influencing

---

[23] Hinich and Munger (1994) pose a similar problem for voters choosing candidates for legislative office. They argue that ideology provides the substance that overcomes the "contracting" dilemma. Certainly ideology is a potential signal of policy inclinations but, by itself, may not be sufficient to overcome adverse selection or moral hazard.

the delivery of the "purchased" product? What is its time horizon (will it need to engage in another exchange in the future)? Economic reasoning suggests that an interest group will support a party when the interest group is familiar with its candidates; when political conditions are relatively predictable, transparent, and structured so that it can be confident the party will be able to deliver policy as promised; and when the party is not in a position to expropriate the group's assets.

These elements are optimal market conditions that seldom obtain in real political (or economic) circumstances. Yet contracting and exchanges occur. In adverse conditions, groups try to minimize risk, with their propensity to make party alliances depending heavily on the opportunity costs of *not* doing so.

This economic approach leads to a set of questions seldom recognized by traditional approaches to interest group–party relations: how to manage the ongoing relationship and whether to use voice or exit when problems arise.

MONITORING EXIT AND VOICE

Since the constituencies, environments, and goals of a party and interest group are not coterminous, interest groups and the parties they support have disputes about their respective policies, actions, and expectations. How does an interest group control a party after it has contracted with it for services? The two main enforcement mechanisms are voice (complaining), and exit (withdrawal of support). Complaints, as Albert Hirschman rightly noted (1970), have more impact when linked to a credible threat of exit. The question then is: when does an interest group decide to exit? When does it decide not to "renew" the contract or to break it? There are multiple reasons one can adduce to explain why a group would want to withdraw support from a party, the primary one being that the party cannot or will not deliver the "product" that the group "purchased." Interest groups and political parties part company on occasion; the Catholic Church sometimes withdraws its support of governments and parties. When is this most likely to happen? The obvious answers would seem to be when the party no longer delivers what the group wants, or when the group finds a better deal elsewhere, that is, a new affiliation that it believes will promote its goals more effectively.[24] Yet, as Hirschman pointed out with reference to consumers and defective products, "exit" is observed

---

[24] Another factor concerns internal group politics: when some group members, dissatisfied with the party, threaten exit from the group, the interest group leadership may abandon the current party to save the organization.

less frequently than one might expect. He notes that sunk costs, and the unavailability of suitable substitutes, strongly affect the decision to exit.

Exit is most likely to occur when the barriers or disadvantages to doing so are low: those cases in which the group has invested relatively few specific assets or other resources in its links with the party and/or in which there is a suitable substitute—another party able to serve the group's interests. In such instances, the group thinks the value of making marginal adjustments to the previous party is less likely to produce the desired long-term effects than the act of switching to the new partner (party). In the terminology of Hirschman (1970): the cost of voice (complaining, negotiating, and waiting for a satisfactory response) is greater than the cost of exit (severing the old affiliation).

To this point it would seem that understanding interest group–party interactions is simply a matter of specifying the costs and then seeing whether there were factors that offset them. Different circumstances make some choices costly in one country and cheap in another. However, while that analysis is crucial, it is also essential to recognize that the same types of interest groups and parties may, because of differences in key aspects of their history, structure, and leadership, assess costs differently, and hence make different choices about broadly similar issues. Different national Churches have different organizational histories, as do different Christian Democratic parties. The variance in the attributes of actual organizations (history, structure, leadership) matters, not just the variance in context. Ignoring the variations limits the understanding of different "costs" the Churches assign to courses of action, of different priorities. Those differences in assessments and goals affect what the Churches do.

HISTORY

Interest groups are put on different trajectories, depending on the context in which they operate and the choices their leaders made at times of flux. A group's resources are not entirely, if at all, comprised of liquid assets; should the group be faced with a situation that demands a different response (and that favors a different organizational configuration), resources the group expended in one area may not easily be transferred to another. The accretion of previous experiences predisposes the organization toward some types of behavior because the group has adapted to a particular context and developed tools appropriate to it.

When Marx wrote that "men make their own history, but not as they please," it is not likely that he had the Catholic hierarchy in mind, though the statement applies to its members. The interaction between the national Catholic Churches and the nascent republican regimes of the late 19th century, the conflicts between the national Churches and the Vatican, and the activities of Catholic activists bequeathed the post–World War II Churches and Christian Democratic parties a set of orientations and institutional structures that constrained some, and facilitated other, actions. The actions and opportunities of the Catholic Churches in France, Italy, and West Germany after World War II were strongly affected by the Churches' actions and political status during the interwar years and the war itself, specifically the institutional and ideological distance they did or did not establish from the Fascist regimes.

STRUCTURE

The structure of the organization affects how it processes information and its ability to react in particular ways at key moments to threats and opportunities. Opportunity costs give actors incentives to stick with an existing arrangement and thus limit considerations of viable alternatives (Pierson 1997). Structure also affects the institution's capacity to follow through on commitments.

Structure refers as well to the broader context in which an organization operates: the electoral system, the formal arrangement of the state, and the organization's competitors. Existing institutions affect the incentives and constraints and the way in which individuals (and organizations) perceive those and can pursue their goals. Institutions privilege some actors and strategies and discourage others. Institutions, then, can be seen as independent variables. The differing powers of state institutions (parliaments, bureaucracies, judiciaries) to effect policy outcomes will influence interest groups' decisions on where to concentrate their efforts (Thomas 1993; Hall 1993). If, as was the case in postwar Italy and France, the parliament is relatively influential, interest groups will focus their efforts on political parties. Institutions are, however, somewhat resistant to change (Hall 1993; Pierson 1996) and can be expected to have a long-term impact on behavior patterns. The French Church's seemingly incoherent response to the attacks of the secular state was partly due to its decentralized structure. Structure, however, does not explain *why* the Italian Church chose to support just one party (the DC), or, in economic terms, to make an extensive organizational investment in the DC.[25] The question is all the more acute for the fact that the Church did not use its already existing ancillary organizations (Catholic Action) but created new ones: the Civic Committees. Nor does it adequately explain why the

[25] Within "structure" I am subsuming the Catholic laity and its role in setting limits on the Church's options (and do likewise with interest group membership).

French hierarchy largely abandoned the MRP and could not or did not wish to make an organizational investment in an alternative.

The analysis of the Catholic Church highlights a serious problem of the existing literature on institutions and the individuals who run them, and that is the tendency to see the institution in service to, as the agent of, its members or constituency—the "principals" who have merely delegated authority to the institution for some specified purpose(s). Yet some interest groups, by virtue of their institutional structures and the interest they claim to represent, possess considerable means to turn the tables on their "principals": Catholics are not the principals of the Church. The premise of (most) religions is that the individual is the agent (in some fashion) of a Supreme Being, and of that Being's earthly organizational forms. If the Catholic Church ever were the agent of Catholic principals, it long ago appropriated the religion and reversed the principal-agent roles.

POLITICAL ENTREPRENEURS

Political scientists who point to organization leaders and their ideology as significant for understanding organizational strategies do so at some risk to their acceptance in the discipline. The dominant view is that individual leaders who do not behave as structural or game theoretic assumptions would lead one to expect (rationally, according to the incentives of their situation) are weeded out by various selection mechanisms (Aldrich 1995; Mayhew 1974). Thus, the value of focusing on leaders in explaining differences in outcomes across large cases is held to be trivial. Moreover, it is hard to know their ideology independently from observing the behavior that the ideology allegedly explains. Yet, much of politics is about selecting leaders. Indeed, leaders are significant for two reasons. First, they are usually best positioned to have anything like a comprehensive view of their organization's situation; they provide direction and control the agenda (which has a powerful effect on decisions). Second, leaders are political entrepreneurs. They solve collective action problems for a group in exchange for a cut of what the group is able to produce and achieve. They take risks with the organization.

The minimalist view of a leader is nevertheless powerful: a leader has an impact if only by virtue of control of the agenda, establishing what others in and external to the organization must react to, and priorities for the use of the organizations resources. While real changes in orientation may not take hold unless they are accepted by the organization's followers, leaders can initiate change, stall it, or influence its direction. Timing can also have significant consequences for outcomes (Pierson 1997). Because of that, leaders' decisions can have definitive effects on their organizations.

Conclusions drawn from experience affect how the leadership reacts to new situations. The accretion of experience develops a worldview and the meaning one attributes to issues and events; that view may resist easy change, exerting an independent effect on elements said to affect it. Ideas outlive the experiences that gave rise to them. Leaders may well use an organization to impose their view on the world, as well as to further their own interests; to do so, and to maintain their hold on power, they engage in organization-building activities. Leaders, working with the "historical structures" at hand and in turn attempting to shape those structures, try to form the alliances that they anticipate will operate to their benefit and be in keeping with their vision of the group and its roles, and reduce the likelihood that disgruntled members and activists exit or join a minority faction. When faced by a "cost," some leaders more readily discount it than others. Pius XII was a decisive simplifier, clearly dividing Italy into two camps: Communist and anti-Communist. In France, Archbishop Cardinal Suhard was rather vague about the attitude to be adopted by the Church and Catholics toward Communism. The responses of the two Churches to the "Communist threat" was in fact noticeably conditioned by their leaders.

Even in rigid, tradition-bound organizations, leadership makes a difference. The Catholic Church's hierarchical structure would seem to be devoid of room for innovation or discretion; the Church is an institution characterized by innumerable formal rules, procedures, and objectives. It would seem that who leads the organization could scarcely make a difference to the Church's orientation and behavior. Popes, bishops, and clergy, have, however, changed the Church's orientation, its relations with political parties and regimes, its definition of its core organizational tasks, and its dogma. Some doctrines are sufficiently vague, and contradictory enough, to allow for different (and new) interpretations.

IDEOLOGY

Economic theory suggests that the priority of any organization is the maximization of its utility; organization theory suggests that the priority of any organization is survival (Panebianco 1988; J. Wilson 1995). Yet "utility" and "survival" mean different things to different organizations and the political entrepreneurs within them. Organizations differ in their purposes, in the policies they thus prefer, and in their ideologies. In crude economic terms, these differences affect the organization's preference functions, and the choice of which "utility" is to be maximized. Put differently, the role the organization assigns to itself in the political system (and the role others assign to it) and the meanings it attributes to events, situations, and other organizations affect the actions it takes. The ideas that founders and activists bring to the organization, the significance of the organization to other interest groups and parties, the meaning it has for the public, all affect the organization's strategies. The actions an organization recognizes as facilitating survival will depend upon the leaders' and activists' definition of organizational survival. The pursuit of utility maximization and survival is not just different in each country because of different contexts, but also because of the organization's institutional relationship to prior regimes, its leadership, and its structure.

SUMMARY

The real market for political parties is defined by
major investors, who generally have good and
clear reasons for investing to control the state.
(*Ferguson 1995, 379*)

Although Ferguson was referring to business and financial institutions, this chapter has argued that the Catholic Church, as embodied by the Vatican and the national Churches, can be analyzed as a firm making investments in the political system. It seeks particular outcomes and, taking into account factors impinging on contracting decisions, invests its resources in activities designed to bring about those desired political and social policy outcomes. Catholic Churches in democracies have, at times, thrown their weight behind political parties. To understand their choices, it is necessary to analyze the Churches with some of the tools economists use to analyze the contracting behavior of firms. However, the evaluations made by the Catholic Churches are conditioned by a set of factors not typically given weight in economic models: the effects of historical legacy, of structure, and of leadership.[26]

Those factors are essential to the explanation of why the Catholic Church allied and remained allied with the Christian Democratic party in Italy and Germany, but not in France; to explaining why the latter party failed to become a dominant party; and to understanding the techniques each Church adopted in order to influence the Christian Democratic parties and to control the political preferences and behavior of their members. Chapter 3 takes up the contribution of the Churches' historical legacies to explaining the Italian and French Churches' behavior.

---

[26] My arguments, derived from thinking about interest groups, logically apply to the wider universe of interest groups, though I cannot, in this monograph, make an empirical test of that claim.

The Constraints and Opportunities of History

AT THE liberation of Paris in August 1944, the cardinal archbishop of Paris, Emmanuel Suhard, was refused entrance to his own cathedral at the celebratory service. At the liberation of Rome in 1943, Pope Pius XII was feted by tens of thousands at St. Peter's Square. During the Constituent Assembly sessions in France, the French Church asked only that modest state subsidies to private schools be restored. During the same deliberations in Italy, the Vatican demanded that Catholicism retain its status as the official religion of Italy. In France, the Church did not, as a unit, support the new Christian Democratic party, nor uniformly withdraw support from it later. In Italy, the Church led the electoral battle on behalf of the new Christian Democratic party. Why such differences between the Churches in the face of similar occasions?

What this chapter shows is that, through their own prior actions and through differences in structures the Churches had put themselves, or been placed, on different trajectories. Their history had left a legacy that in this case had traceable effects on its beneficiaries (or victims). One of the most important effects of historical legacy on an interest group in a new political system is a group's relations with the previous regime. Another is the structures and resources the organization has; a third is the orientation of its leadership. As this chapter will show, before we can understand the differences in organizational development and strategies, we must take account of the outcome of the prior interorganizational struggles, institutional structures, and the political entrepreneurship of organizational leaders.

UNDERSTANDING THE ROLE OF HISTORICAL TRAJECTORIES

To argue thus is to make a path dependent argument. Path dependency relies on the contention that, as Margaret Levi writes, "once a country or region [or organization] has started down a track, the costs of reversal are very high. There will be other choice points, but the entrenchments of certain institutional arrangements obstruct an easy reversal of the initial choice" (1997, 28). That "track" is marked by institutional structures that constrain some, and facilitate other, actions. It is also marked by ideological orientations that often outlive the circumstances that gave rise to them. Events and relationships create memories that actors carry and respond to (Rousso 1991). Even when utilizing the market analogy, it is clear that interest groups enter a new competitive market encumbered and with a restricted set of options.[1]

A group's connections (or lack thereof) with the previous regime affect its reputation, its ideological compatibility with actors in the new political system, its policy goals, the encumbrances to be overcome, and what demands can be made. The prior regime becomes a foil for the reactions of societal and political actors. The previous regime is influential because it created or sanctioned institutional arrangements that may be repudiated in the new regime, leaving those involved tainted by association. They become less than desirable allies for the political and societal actors wanting to build a new society. The old regime conferred power on some, denied it to others. The new regime may require a balancing of accounts, altering how actors can pursue their interests. It alters how actors see their interests and brings forth orientations that did not previously exist. The old regime gives a platform to new societal actors and interests, including, of course, its own opponents. It may leave institutions and orientations that are hard to dismantle because of vested interests; actors find that the opportunity cost of continuing along the same path is significantly less than the cost of switching.

The second major aspect of a historical legacy is the structure of the interest group and the structure of the state. Variations in the structure and extent of institutional resources help account for variations in organizations' behavior. Institutions also facilitate or hinder various actions, making some more costly than others. New political systems are not blank slates; they are marked by distinct institutional features carried over from earlier ones. A better understanding of interest group–party interaction comes from not merely taking those features as given, but in examining where they come from. Past interactions close off some options and, given new conditions, leave some actors in more advantaged positions than others.

In many ways it is tempting to attribute differing interest group strategies to differences in interest group, party, and state structures alone. Yet there is another aspect of the historical legacy that conditions in important ways the behavior of groups and parties: how prior struggles and experi-

---

[1] Path dependence is sometimes misunderstood to be fully deterministic: once a choice is made, it is irreversible. Instead, path dependent arguments emphasize that, in the presence of certain institutional arrangements, the costs of reversing the initial decision are high, making change less likely than if the costs were low. Research then focuses on how and why some structures impose high costs to reversals (Steinmo, Thelen, and Longstreth 1992).

ences have shaped the group's (and, particularly, the leadership's) outlook. This latter factor goes under different names, sometimes called *interpretive frames* or *worldview* (Hattam 1992), sometimes *repertoires* (Clemens 1997), sometimes *organizational culture* (Ouchi and Wilkins 1985; J. Wilson 1989, 1995). I focus on the interpretive frame of the group's leadership and, like the authors cited, contend that how the leadership sees the world and the tools at hand has an impact on its evaluation of strategies. Earlier struggles in building and preserving the organization establish flash points, issue areas that are more sensitive to one organization than to another. The French Church of the postwar years and its dealings with political parties make little sense unless one knows about its Gallican past, the French Revolution, the Dreyfus affair, the Separation Law, the absence of a large prewar Christian Democratic party, and, finally, Vichy. The Italian Church is comprehensible only if one knows its origins as the seat of Roman Catholicism, its early struggles with unified Italy, its interactions with the prewar Christian Democratic party, and Fascism.

The Italian Church's historically derived, and politically reinforced, position at the center of Catholicism gives the Church a more extensive realm with which it is concerned and a greater sense of responsibility for institutional survival, magnifying its sensitivity to events at the "core"—Italy. This sense of responsibility gave the Church an exaggerated fear of the threat from Communism. The French Church, as the first to be chased out of power by a secular, liberal European government (such as it was in 1789), was quickly rendered more dependent upon the papacy (a dependency the French Church fought) and more sensitive to charges of clericalism. The struggle within the French Church over whether, and how, to reduce its dependency interfered with its efforts to repel liberal advances through partisan allies. Anticlerical hostilities seemed to chasten the Church and render it more cautious after the war, limiting its political demands to state subsidies for private schools.

The advent of liberal democratic governments in the late 1800s in Western Europe (and Latin America) was marked by sharp conflicts between the Catholic Church and the secular state. The state challenged the Church for access to revenue (mainly by expropriating and/or taxing Church properties); for control over education and Church employees (e.g., military conscription), and for determining the marital status of its citizens (e.g., by mandating civil marriage ceremonies). Perhaps most galling to the Church was the liberal state's assertion that human reason was the ultimate arbiter of truth and could provide "for the welfare of men and institutions" (Pius IX 1864, 8). These challenges sent the Church searching for allies to fend off the attacks. As in the postwar years, the Church sought to create or to find allies that would effect change in the direction it wanted. The choices were consequential for the fate of the early-twentieth-century democracies and, to some extent, for the types of alliances possible after the war.

This era was also marked (as were earlier eras) by conflicts between the Vatican and the national Churches. The French Church's long-standing perception of itself as a national Church independent of Rome, the "Gallican Church," made for conflict within France and between the French Church and the Vatican. Its decentralized structure was in part a result of this battle. Fearing that a centralized French Church would be a less malleable Church, the Vatican opposed all efforts at centralization. This reduced the French Church to near impotence when its prerogatives were threatened by the French state, and affected its stances toward efforts to form Christian Democratic parties during the Third and Fourth Republics.

The nature of both these conflicts affected the way Catholics were politicized, and the instruments the Churches could use in their various battles. When, finally, the Churches seemed to have resolved their problems through Marshal Pétain's Vichy regime and Mussolini's Fascist regime, they also helped to construct the constraints and opportunities that they would face, and the lens through which they would view them, upon the advent of the postwar democratic regimes.

ITALY: CHURCH-STATE RELATIONS

The Italian Church's actions in the immediate post–World War II years, particularly its stance toward Communism, make no sense without reference to the fact that Rome became the center of Western Christianity in the fifth century A.D., and remained so until challenged by Martin Luther in 1517, after which it remained the central locus of Catholicism. The Vatican came to conflate its temporal location with its religious mission, which was to protect Catholicism from religious and secular infidels and to expand its influence and control.[2] Rome became the center of Christianity by a political act; popes have recognized that it is through politics that it will remain so.[3]

---

[2] The Church was convinced that the state and Church had to be linked. As Cardinal Schuster (Milan) said at the end of World War II, "God has so linked the political destiny of Italy to its religious conditions that, after so many centuries, it is no longer possible to untie the knot tightened by the very hand of the Almighty" (June 1946, in Durand 1991, 522).

[3] In 313, Constantine had declared Christianity the preferred religion of the Roman Empire, allowed churches to own property, and "bequeathed vast fortunes to them" (Vaillancourt 1980, 24, 26; Hatch 1972). Later, Constantine prompted further centralization, with the bishop of Rome coming to be recognized by the bishops of the empire's other major cities (Alexandria, Antioch, Constantinople) as their "bishop," or patriarch, hence "papa."

Implantation of Roman Catholicism

By the time of Pope Gregory the Great (590–604), the supremacy of the papacy was solidly implanted in the Christian Church. What had started as a democratic, nonhierarchical organization was now an authoritarian, hierarchical one.[4] After his father turned the Byzantines away from Rome (752), Charlemagne established the pope as temporal ruler over Rome and its territories; "in return, the pope consecrated Charlemagne and crowned him Holy Roman Emperor" (Vaillancourt 1980, 27). Thus began the uneasy, perhaps unavoidably so, relationship between secular rulers and the papacy. The powers of the one vis-à-vis the other have ebbed and flowed over time.

When Western European governments were becoming limited democracies, the Catholic Church was governed by Pius IX (1846–78), who was particularly adamant that the Church not compromise with secular governments. Rather than give ground, he issued the *Non expedit* bull (1868), barring Catholics from participating in Italian politics. It was under him that the First Vatican Council, attempting to increase the papacy's authority, declared the pope infallible in matters of faith and morals. It was he who rejected the unification of Italy, the choice of Rome as the new liberal state's capital, and who wrote the "Syllabus of Modern Errors" (Pius IX 1864), rejecting all tenets and corollaries of liberalism, including the view that temporal powers were not subject to the Church's jurisdiction. Influencing the outlook of the Italian Church, Pius IX, between 1871 and 1875, filled 135 of 298 episcopal sees with new, mostly intransigent, clergy (Clark 1984, 86).

Prior to the unification years of 1861–71, Italy had been ruled by disparate political systems. In the nineteenth century, the south was governed by the Kingdom of Two Sicilies, the center by the papacy, the north by the House of Savoy and by Austria. The Church was on good terms with the Kingdom of Two Sicilies (Jemolo 1960, 9); the Church in Piedmont, associated with the House of Savoy, was not. In contrast to France, the Italian monarchy (House of Savoy) was allied with the liberal state (Header 1983, 236; Jemolo 1960, 10; Webb 1958, 6), leaving the Church with few friends.

Church Structure

The Church's organizational history and structure also affected what the Church did after World War II. The Italian Church had several structural

---

[4] As Gregory XVI (1831–46) declared much later, "Nobody can be ignorant of the fact that the church is an inegalitarian community, in which God has ordained one group to

features that accorded the pope considerable powers to influence Italian politics, should he so choose. First, the geographical proximity of the Italian dioceses to Rome and the Vatican gave it a palpable presence throughout Italy. Second, its being in Rome, the "seat" of Christendom, gave the Vatican a past it could glorify and a moral authority the French Church lacked. Third, there was no episcopal conference at which bishops regularly met to discuss policy. Whereas in France the long absence of an episcopal conference meant the Church had no unified policy response to the secular state's actions, or means to articulate one, in Italy the conference's absence meant that the Vatican had no competitors to policy formation. France, of course, had no equivalent of the Vatican. Fourth, Italy had an absurdly high number of dioceses—as one Church historian quipped, there was "one bishop per campanile" (Falconi 1955 in Durand 1991, 180).[5] Based on medieval boundaries, the diocesan structure made interdiocese coordination difficult and prevented any one diocese from being strong enough to challenge the pope. A bishop's presence in all parts of Italy was thought by the Vatican to be "a major way of affirming the presence of the Church, and defending also Christian civilization" (Durand 1991, 215). Fifth, the pope was the recognized commander and spokesman of the Church—the French Church had no such officer. Italian bishops, in contrast to their French counterparts, were *not* independent in their own dioceses; they were directly under the pope's authority. In France, the bishops did not answer to any higher French authority. The pope also had control over all Catholic seminarians, so that he was able, should he like, as Pius XII did, to mobilize them in the political battlefield (Durand 1991, 650).

At the same time, the large number of dioceses did hinder the Church's religious and political proselytizing efforts. As the publicity director of the Italian Catholic Action Youth League said of his trip through a diocese in the province of Campagna (southern Italy), "Here also, as in other zones of Italy, the very unfortunate division of dioceses, which was based upon absurd historical criteria, disperses forces and gravely compromises the possibility of work" (in Durand 1991, 214).

Regional differences were noticeable and also affected the Church's influence and actions. The Church in southern Italy had a weak or nonexistent parish structure. Priests were largely independent of their bishops (Clark 1984, 85) and diocesan governance but were beholden to various lay patrons. Southern Church patrons financed the ecclesiastical orders, the management of which was given to a specific number of priests in the

---

govern, and another to obey" (Vaillancourt 1980, 35). The papacy has long seen Italians "as essentially levitical people," there to serve it (Falconi 1967, 292–93; cf. Reese 1996).

[5] Italy had 320 dioceses, with 257 bishops; France, about 90 dioceses.

area. In a sense, the Church was "privatized" (Malgeri 1977, 311). Since the southern Church relied heavily on ecclesiastical properties for financing (Clark 1984, 85), when the new liberal state dissolved the orders and confiscated their property, the Church was dissolute (Durand 1991, 221). Considering that the southern Church had never welcomed "papal and intransigent Catholicism" (Malgeri 1977, 311) and was linked with the successive southern monarchs, southern bishops and clergy were not predisposed to welcome ancillary Church associations, such as Azione Cattolica, which were controlled by the Vatican.

In the north, on the other hand, generous donors financed the parishes directly. The latter thus were not affected economically by the banishment of ecclesiastical orders. Since the Vatican did not have a wealth redistribution program, the southern Church lagged behind the north and center in terms of resources it could utilize to proselytize, and in the prestige it could command. Its ancillary organizations—Azione Cattolica, missions—and its press were less rooted and extensive than those in the north. Other organizations, such as the Mafia, provided authority and roots for the DC (Gambetta 1994; Stille 1995). Establishing the Church's dominance in postwar southern Italy, including its control over politics, proved harder than in the north.

In terms of "infantry," the Church's resources in the south were limited. There had been, since unification in 1871, a sharp decline in the recruitment of clergy. Allum's study of Naples shows that in the 15 dioceses where in 1885 there were 6,714 clergy devoted to lay work ("secular" clergy), in 1962 there were only 1,985, a decline of two-thirds (1973, 265). The population had, in the interim, more than doubled, straining the priest-to-population ratio. The result was overpopulated, underfunded parishes. In such circumstances, the clergy had little time to proselytize. The paucity of priests and financial resources in the south was compounded by a relative lack of structures fostering a sense of community; creating a Catholic political *identity* would be harder where outlets for the social interactions that inculcate identities were scarce or monopolized by rival organizations (e.g., the Communists in Emilia-Romagna [Kertzer 1980]). Priests were compelled instead to use coercion, ensuring that at least individuals did not associate openly with something else. Numerous reports from Azione Cattolica workers in the south noted the lack of resources, and how that hindered their sociopolitical efforts.[6] One wrote, "The activity that one can carry on in a diocese in the Veneto [a northern region], for example, one cannot carry out in one in Puglia."[7]

---

[6] AAC, PG, VI f. 81, Calabria, questionario e relazioni 1946, Statistici, 1947, Mar. 20, 1947.

[7] He added that "the population is illiterate, so newspapers are ridiculous" (AAC, PG, VI f. 18, Meridionale, Visite alle diocesi, May 22–30, 1949).

Another commented that, for lack of Catholic newspapers, the priests were not following (indeed, could not follow) national directives.[8] Ill-educated to boot, many priests in the south lacked the most basic of clerical resources: a Bible.

The north was better armed for clerical work: the decline in recruitment had been far less severe.[9] In the northern regions in 1947 there was one priest for 861 people (in the center there was one for every 894, and in the south, one for every 1,285) (Durand 1991, 226). These figures indicate that, structurally, the resources of the Church in the center and particularly the south would hamper the Church's efforts to become hegemonic nationwide and to control political outcomes.

Nevertheless, the Church's structure enabled the Vatican to exert more control over its bishops and clergy, and it affected the Church's influence in different regions of Italy. For example, at the 1948 election, cardinals and archbishops could gather their bishops and clergy, instructing them on precisely what to tell their congregations about how to vote (Durand 1991, 649). Furthermore, the Church's structure facilitated its ability to monitor and sanction noncompliance. This was complemented by the DC's control of the Ministry of Interior, whose prefects reported on priests' departures from the DC line (Durand 1991, 653–54).

"Liberal Italy" and Church-State Conflicts

Italy, once merely a "geographical expression,"[10] became a unified state in 1871. The Kingdom of Italy had been declared in 1860, but the Papal States, separating northern from southern Italy in a belt running approximately east-west across the center of Italy, interfered with the realization of unity. These states were forcibly pried loose from Pius IX, and the capital of one of them was designated the capital of Italy: Rome. In September 1870, when Camillo di Cavour's troops defeated those of the papacy in Rome, the pope became, technically, a mere citizen of the secular Italian state.

[8] AAC, PG, VI, Visite nel Mezzogiorno d'Italia, Oct. 5–15, 1947, Sig. Rossati dated June 25.

[9] From 31,004 priests in 1881 to 23,872 in 1947. For the same time, the center went from 17,565 to 7,839 (55.4% loss); the south from 36,265 to 13,629 (62.4% loss) (Durand 1991, 225). For Durand, the north includes the dioceses of the conciliar regions of Piedmont, Ligurgia, Lombardia, Veneto, Emilia, Romagna; the center includes Tuscany, Marches, Umbria, and Latvia; the south Abruzzo, Benevento, Calabria, Campagna, Puglia, Salernitano-Lucania, Sardegna, Sicily.

[10] The phrase is attributed to the Austrian foreign minister, Prince Klemens von Metternich.

The government set about trying to release Italy from the clutches of the Catholic Church. Cavour, as the first prime minister, pitched the secular state's policies as "a free church in a free state" (Jemolo 1960, 23), but Pius IX would have none of it. The Papal States were annexed by the new Italian state (without compensation), the pope stripped of his sovereignty (and humiliated with an annual allowance), and priests made subject to military conscription; the income on which the episcopal sees and parishes depended was now subject to royal decree. The state renounced control over new ecclesiastical laws and acts of ecclesiastical authorities, but the monarchy retained the right to appoint southern bishops (Clark 1984, 81–84; Guasco 1997, 77; Jemolo 1960, 49–50). To further add insult to injury, religious marriages were not recognized by the secular government, and divorce became legal. The so-called Roman Question (i.e., the issue of the Church's status) was born.

Nor was it one easily resolved: as Leo XIII stated in 1887, "It is not enough, as it would be elsewhere, to make certain concessions to the Church, to modify or repeal hostile laws, to abolish contradictory regulations. It is necessary, in addition and above all, to regularize the position of the Supreme Pontiff" by bestowing upon the office "true sovereignty" (Jemolo 1960, 77). The Church, seeing itself as the center of Roman Catholicism, demanded complete freedom of action. An additional problem with the separation was, in the Church's eyes, that it would "give the state complete control of the law and of the external life of the people, leaving the Church to keep watch over men's consciences and denying it any authority other than that voluntarily conceded to it by the Faithful" (Jemolo 1960, 19). Some Catholics, on the other hand, thought reconciliation was necessary and theologically possible. They realized that no pro-Catholic monarchy was anywhere on the horizon (Jemolo 1960, 51).

The Vatican lacked powerful allies, making it difficult to gain political concessions. Worse yet, a new political enemy had appeared: Socialists. Whereas liberals at least believed that the Church could have some place in society, Socialists believed it had none. Some laity organized defensive movements on their own initiative (and sometimes obtained papal blessing).[11] In 1882, Leo XIII issued an encyclical, *Esti nos,* which "called Cath-

---

[11] One example was the Opera dei Congressi e dei Comitati Cattolici, founded in 1874. Not surprisingly, given the structure of the Italian Church, it was strongest in northern Italy (993 parish committees), and weakest in southern (57 committees). The movement did not want to participate directly in party politics, though it sought to counter Socialist organizations, and it staunchly defended the pope on the Roman question (Clark 1996, 87). As late as 1897, the movement had not accepted the permanence of republican Italy. It was, however, disbanded by Pius X in 1904 just two weeks after its progressive president, referring to the Church-state conflict, declared that Catholics were "anxious that the work of the living should not be impeded by dead issues" (in Clark 1996, 147). It and other lay movements

olics to form lay organizations throughout the country" (Kalyvas 1996, 217). The *Non expedit* (see above) was gradually transgressed—by the pope. In June 1905, Pius X let each bishop decide whether the Catholics in his diocese should vote in the upcoming legislative election in order to prevent the election of a Socialist (Mack Smith 1969, 225; cf. Baget-Bozzo 1974, 1:28; Kalyvas 1996, 219). The Vatican was suspicious of a nascent Christian Democratic movement and concerned about Catholics misrepresenting Catholicism in social and political fields. With democracy conflated with the source of the Church's troubles, the Church could hardly foster a party that accepted democracy. Doing so would legitimize the liberal state, the major source of its problems. Seeking to rein in the various new Catholic movements, both Leo XIII and Pius X had a stated policy that "the public action of Christians is a specifically ecclesiastical action and thus falls under the competence of the hierarchy" (Baget-Bozzo 1974, 1:29). This made the formation of any moderate Catholic party rather difficult.

The Church and Catholic Party Politics

The liberal-dominated parliament extended suffrage just prior to the 1913 elections; in order to prevent a Socialist victory, the Church had to revoke the *Non expedit* and find politicians supportive of the Church's goals. It found a number of liberal politicians willing to strike an electoral deal, the so-called Gentiloni Pact (named after a Count Gentiloni, president of the Catholic Union of Electors). In return for their agreeing to protect the Catholic Church, Catholics would vote for them (Jemolo 1960, 134–35). The Church gave tacit approval; the Pact candidates won a large victory. The malfeasance issue arose immediately, as many of the Pact politicians disregarded their pledge. Lay Catholics were not satisfied with the results; contracting out the defense of Catholicism had not solved their problem of getting the right policies delivered. The more progressive of them eventually founded, in 1919, the Italian Popular Party, or Partito Popolare Italiano (PPI),[12] Italy's first large Christian Democratic party. It was led by a southern priest, Don Luigi Sturzo (secretary of the national Azione Cattolica office), though mainly supported by "the small peasant proprie-

---

were reorganized and put directly under the control of their diocesan bishops (Durand 1991, 79).

[12] Kalyvas makes the odd claim (1996, 221) that the PPI's November 1919 electoral victory (actually 18%) "firmly established the new party," but only five years later, the party was easily destroyed by the Church and the Fascists. Data on PPI from Giusti 1922 and Chassériaud 1965, 376. Both authors take their data from Ministry of Interior publications but disagree on the PPI's 1919 results; Chassériaud claims 20.5%.

tors and tenants of Northern and North-Central Italy." It was "anxious to win over the Southern peasantry, [so] naturally backed the peasants' land and rent agitations, and indeed often organized them" (Clark 1984, 211).

The Vatican itself did not organize the new party, though many priests and Azione Cattolica organizations became its chief animators. In Naples, Salerno, and Potenza, for example, the "Catholic Circle," born in 1891, became regional sections of the PPI (Guasco 1997, 167). In many northern regions, priests and Catholic social or charitable organizations likewise assisted the party (Corsini and Porta 1985; Vezzoli 1965; Pollard 1996, 71; Guasco 1997, 164–69). Pope Benedict XV (1914–22) neither condemned nor blessed the party (Mack Smith 1969, 326). He explained to a politician, "I have not recognized [the PPI] as a party and do not want to recognize it as such in order to be free to disavow it when I want to" (Falconi 1967, 146–47). Benedict XV tacitly accepted that his clergy were investing Church resources in a political enterprise. Whether the creation of the PPI was an unintended consequence of the Church's earlier actions, or whether it was a deliberate strategy, the result was that the Church had a stake in its success. Suffrage had been extended to all adult males, World War I had mobilized and then demobilized millions of (now unemployed) males, and the Socialists and, soon, the Communists recruited many of them. In the face of such a threat, the Church was looking for a capable ally. The PPI was, in the words of Cardinal Pierre Gasparri, merely the "least worst of all" (Falconi 1967, 147). The conservative elite of the Catholic laity had not developed a party of their own, and if they had, it is unlikely it would have had the necessary popular appeal to compete with the parties of the Left.

The PPI, though constructed with Church resources and apparently popular with many Catholics, did not follow Church wishes, sometimes refusing to ally with anti-Socialist coalitions in local and national governments. While the party won 18% of the vote in its first election, it slid to 9% after the Church disavowed it at the 1924 election. Benedict XV's successor, Pius XI (1922–39), acted quickly to shut down the party. When presented with a more attractive organization, sunk costs were not an obstacle to breaking the link between the Church's clergy and the PPI. The Church hierarchy, however, was unwilling to put in resources to construct its own party,[13] and it was unlikely to do so under Benedict XV, who, in contrast to his predecessor (Pius X) and successor (Pius XI), did not see himself at war with the Italian state (Falconi 1967, 146). The effort, to him, did not appear worth the cost.

[13] The electoral system instituted in 1919 was not an obstacle to the creation of new parties. It was proportional representation, with "fifty-four huge constituencies" (Clark 1984, 212). That combination made it easy for new parties to gain entrance to parliament.

Pius XI found fault with the PPI for two reasons: first, its 1921 electoral showing gave it only one-fourth of the seats in the parliament, making it too small "to steer the solution of the Roman Question through Parliament" on its own (Falconi 1967, 186). Second, the Fascists, not the PPI, appeared to be tougher on Communism[14] and more amenable to the Church's demands (Clark 1984, 223). The PPI did not look to be worth the investment of the Vatican's organizational support.

The Impact of the Fascist Regime

Benito Mussolini founded his Fascist Party early in 1919 (the Fasci di Combattimento; later the Partito Nazionale Fascista). He became prime minister in November 1922, soon after the parliament voted him extraordinary powers. He was unopposed by most parliamentarians and major social institutions—the Church, the military, and the monarchy.[15] Mussolini promised to give Italy "peace and quiet, and to get on with its work" (Mack Smith 1969, 385).

Though he technically had come to power by democratic means, by 1925 Mussolini was running an authoritarian regime. Italy's democratic polity was no match for high unemployment, war reparations, the need and demand for land reform, the uncompromising stances of the newer political parties (PPI, Socialists, Communists, nationalists, veterans, Fascists), and was unable to control the social upheavals and violence attendant to its post–World War I travails (often fomented by the Fascists).[16] Mussolini shut down rival media outlets, took over the key posts in the Ministry of War, banned "secret associations," such as the Freemasons, restricted freedom of movement, dissolved municipal governments, and in various ways eliminated his political opposition.

The new regime was a boon to the Church. As early as 1924, Mussolini appointed chaplains to the Fascist Party, exempted clergy from military service, and gave government financing to repairs of Church buildings damaged in the recent war (Smith 1969, 440). He replaced the anticlerical Minister of Education with a devout Catholic. Reversing the laws the liberals had put into place in the 1870s, Mussolini increased state contributions to clergy stipends.

[14] Pius XI went so far as to laud Hitler for being "the statesman who first, after the Pope, raised his voice against Bolshevism" (in Falconi 1967, 194).

[15] The Church's preference for Mussolini was shaped partly by his threats: the dictator argued that if the Vatican did not depose Sturzo as the PPI's leader and did not get the party to desist in its opposition to the Fascists, he would turn the Fascists on the Church (Falconi 1967, 187). The PPI did not advocate violence as a means to win Church support.

[16] On the rise of Mussolini and the Fascist regime, the classic work is Lyttelton 1973. See also Whittam 1995; Payne 1995.

The nature of the Fascist regime affected the Church's position in Italy. Here, the Italian Church had significant advantages over the French, enabling it to come out of the Fascist years and World War II in a relatively uncompromised position. This may seem surprising, given the warm welcome that Fascism received from the Church. Pius XI indicated his sympathy for the regime and his "horror of liberalism and socialism," which he saw as leading to anarchy (Delzell 1961, 97). Prior to becoming pope in 1922, he had praised Mussolini as "a man . . whom Providence has caused us to meet." As pope, he complimented Mussolini for being "a man who does not have the preoccupations of the liberal school, of the men to whom all laws and regulations . . . were like fetishes—and the more ugly and deformed the fetishes, the more stubbornly to be worshiped" (in Delzell 1961, 100; cf. Mack Smith 1969, 441). Due process of law was not high on the pope's list of priorities. He and the rest of the hierarchy praised Mussolini's regime for its corporatist policies and for having "turned Italy more toward the Christian conception in its social orientation" (in Miccoli 1976, 374–75). Some of this was done through the manipulation of symbols: crucifixes reappeared in classrooms and courts (Falconi 1967, 185). In return, the Church acted at times as an apologist for the Fascists. When Mussolini demanded an oath of loyalty from teachers and university professors to the Fascist regime, the Vatican convinced them to comply by telling the professors that they really were only swearing loyalty to the "Government of the State" (Delzell 1961, 92).

Adding to the Church's potentially compromised position was the fact that the clergy, and Pius XI, had supported Mussolini's actions in the Spanish Civil War and Italy's invasion of Ethiopia (Delzell 1961, 175). Not condemning Italy's entry into World War II, some in the hierarchy focused on upbraiding Italians for their moral failings (Traniello 1988, 338). Others described the war, with some enthusiasm, as the "gigantic battle with which it is intended to give a new order to the world" (*Civiltà Cattolica,* July 6, 1940, in Magister 1979, 6). Pius XI saw the Nazis as a means to conquer the Russian Orthodox Church and the other Slavic Churches; training schools for Jesuits (the Russicom) were set up, preparing missionaries to follow on the heels of German soldiers (Falconi 1967, 255). Though many sources indicate Pius XI opposed Mussolini's anti-Semitic policies and actions (Delzell 1961, 176; Clark 1984, 257–58), he never condemned those policies in other states (Falconi 1967, 186). His successor, Pius XII, neither acted to stop the deportation of Jews from Rome and elsewhere in 1943 nor condemned the Nazi regime until the act of doing so was a moot point: June 2, 1945. The Vatican actually congratulated itself that the Nazis had said the Church had remained strictly neutral (Magister 1979, 35; Malgeri 1985, 97).

Despite these compromising endorsements, the key difference between the situations of French and Italian Churches is contained in the Lateran Pacts. These pacts, signed on February 11, 1929, with Mussolini, included a treaty settling the Roman Question, a religious concordat, and a financial settlement (Delzell 1961, 99). The Vatican was declared sovereign over its 44 hectares of land and compensated for the expropriations of its lands during the unification of Italy. The pacts made Catholicism the official religion of the Italian state, guaranteed religious (Catholic) instruction in public elementary and secondary schools, granted state recognition of Catholic university diplomas, and validated Church weddings (an additional civil ceremony was no longer required). The state paid clerical stipends, while the Church retained control over clerical appointments (Webb 1958, 7; Clark 1984, 254–55). The Church was given not only privileges in Italian society, but considerable freedom from state intervention. Azione Cattolica, a potential rival to the Fascist youth leagues, was to remain autonomous from the Fascist regime, and firmly under the pope's guardianship. Mussolini went further, banning Freemasonry and exterminating the Socialists (Clark 1984, 254). The Church saw these "rights" as being extremely significant; as having, in the words of Pius XI, who oversaw the concordat, "rendered God to Italy and Italy to God" (Durand 1991, 521; Baget-Bozzo 1974, 1:199; Magister 1979, 78; Clark 1984, 255).[17]

What is notable is that, in contrast to the French situation during Vichy, the Lateran Pacts separated the Church from the Fascist regime, enabling the Church later to distance itself from Fascism without also incriminating Catholicism, or appearing to reverse itself. When Fascism was defeated and repudiated, the Church's position remained strong. The pacts gave the Church firm control over Azione Cattolica, something Vichy did not do for the French Church. By 1939, the Italian Church could look like the defender of Western civilization against the "Totalitarian State" (Webb 1958, 9)—even though the concordat and the other agreements Pius XI signed with authoritarian or Fascist rulers exempted the Church from the treatment meted out to others by "the most inhuman oppressors of fundamental freedoms" (Falconi 1967, 204). Mussolini further made the Church appear as an opponent, or at least as a victim, by restricting its Azione Cattolica recruitment and by blocking ecclesiastical promotions (Mack Smith 1969, 442). Pius XI responded in 1931 with the encyclical *Non abbiamo bisogno*, stating that the Church was independent of "totalitarianism" (Mack Smith 1969, 443). The Italian Church also had the advantage that, in the final months of Fascism, Mussolini's Republic of Salò

---

[17] This is a typical bargain that was also struck in Latin America under many populist governments of the 1930s and 1940s (Gill 1998, 34).

lashed out at the clergy for being unsupportive. This only helped the Church's image and leverage in postwar Italy. Indeed, there was no outburst of virulent anticlericalism in the two years immediately after Mussolini's fall (Jemolo 1960, 278; Ginsborg 1990).

The final critical difference between Vichy and Mussolini's fascism was that the latter did not explicitly incorporate the Church into its political plans. Certainly Mussolini relied upon the acquiescence of the Church, but he did not claim to be reestablishing Italy's Christian heritage, nor did he give the Church privileged positions within his regime. Whereas the Church relied upon traditional morals, Mussolini denied their priority: "we will permit ourselves the luxury of being aristocrats and democrats, conservatives and progressives, reactionaries and revolutionaries, legalists and illegalists, according to time, place, and circumstances" (in Bobbio 1995, 122). While the Church might have agreed with the Fascists that "The greatest happenings of history—the Caesars, Christianity, the religious orders, war, fascism—are mystical movements, acts of faith," it could not have agreed that "the unique source of the mystique is . . . (sic) Mussolini, exclusively Mussolini" (Bobbio 1995, 132; Bobbio's *sic*). For the Church, the regime was worshiping false idols.[18] What the Church objected to was Fascism's "Cult of the State" (Durand 1991, 20). Some called it a "phase of the eternal battle between Christianity and paganism" (26). Not having been an integral part of Mussolini's Fascism, though clearly a significant prop, the Church emerged from the twenty years of Fascism and the war "with uncompromised prestige" (Scoppola 1988, 30; Webb 1958, ix). Its status at the end of the war was high, particularly in Rome, which had been abandoned by the king (Vittorio Emmanuele III), leaving the Vatican as the only national institution left to speak for Italians. Few bishops were accused of having aided the Fascists (Durand 1991, 168), in contrast to the extensive number in France (Latreille 1978, 31–32). On the day before D-Day, Pius XII, and not the Allies, was able to appear as the savior of Europe. A crowd of tens of thousands celebrated Pius XII in the piazza of St. Peter's; even Communist and Socialist flags waved greetings to the pope (Jemolo 1960, 280; Durand 1991, 165–68). So well positioned was the Church that the United States, in 1943, asked the Vatican its opinion on the postwar government's nature, and who should lead it (Magister 1979, 3; Scoppola 1988, 46).

In sum, two factors facilitated the Church's relatively uncompromised status at the end of Mussolini's reign, allowing the Church to claim the moral high ground after the war. First, the institutional arrangements ne-

---

[18] For Fascism, religious principles were "incompatible with the notions of the state's possessing its own gods, and hence of religion as *instrumentum regni;* with the conception of the country as the highest good, as the arbiter of moral values" (Jemolo 1960, 285).

gotiated between Mussolini and Pius XI allowed the Church to remain separate and distinct from the regime. Second, because Italian Fascism had not made the Church an integral part of its sociopolitical blueprint, the Church was able to avoid being compromised by its behavior during Mussolini's tenure.

The Church during the Demise of Fascism

With Allied troops storming southern Italy in 1943, the king, at the behest of military advisors and others on the Fascist Council, used his remaining constitutional powers to depose Mussolini. The Germans then set him up as puppet ruler of the Republic of Salò. The Vatican, sensing which way the wind was blowing, refrained from recognizing the Republic (Magister 1979, 33–34). Mussolini, pursued by the Resistance, was captured, shot, and hanged in April 1945. Organized Catholicism was looking forward to its triumph after Mussolini's demise—expecting, in the words of a Fascist police informant, that "Italy will find its unique salvation in a Christian social government headed by groups from Azione Cattolica."[19] In the 1942–43 years, ecclesiastics heavily stressed that the pope was the sole guide and norm of conduct (Miccoli 1976, 375). Not until his Christmas message of 1944 did the pope admit that democratic governments might be desirable.

Catholic views toward Fascism's fall and the Resistance were mixed (Durand 1991, 14–16). The hierarchy in the north feared "tubercular bolshevism" and a revolution (Webster 1960, 163–64), while some of the lower clergy welcomed Mussolini's demise and participated in the Left-led Resistance (Delzell 1961, 298; Webster 1960, 163–65; Morelli 1985, 65–66). Catholic activists did not play a large role in the Italian Resistance (Webster 1960, 166–67; Bianchi 1971; Miccoli 1976, 378), and that fact significantly affected the character of the Christian Democratic party with which the Church would later try to work. The gulf between the Church and Catholic politicians, chastened by the Church's earlier rejection of the PPI, was not wide (Webster 1960, 172). The institutional arrangements of the Lateran Pacts and papal directives gave the Vatican a tight hold on Azione Cattolica and restricted it to (technically) nonpolitical activity and a weak contribution to the Resistance. That meant, in direct contrast to the French situation, that many future DC activists, including those who

---

[19] ACS, MinIntPS, Affari generali e reiservati, 1920–45, cat G. 1, b. 146, f. 22 "Azione Cattolica," sf. 3, Nov. 30, 1939 (in Scoppola 1988, 45).

had been socialized in AC, were not determined to carry on in the spirit of the Resistance.[20]

The Church's position as the center of Roman Catholicism, its experiences under liberal governments, and its institutional and ideological distance from the Fascist regime made the Church particularly sensitive to threats to its autonomy and survival, gave it a strong dislike of democratic governance, yet shielded it from anti-Fascist reprisals. Fascism also left Italy with a set of Christian Democratic politicians and activists willing to work with the Church. These features of the Church's recent historical legacy partly shaped the outlook of its postwar leadership, its evaluation of costs and benefits, as well as the resources available and contexts in which choices would have to be made. The legacy thus not only affected the "choice set," or market conditions in which the Church, as an interest group, would try to find a policy supplier, but also the prices religious entrepreneurs would attach to those choices.

FRANCE: CHURCH-STATE RELATIONS

The French Church had long been accustomed to seeing itself as a counterweight to the Vatican, "not in any way inferior to Rome in theological substance" (Gough 1986, viii). If anything, the French Church thought itself superior: it regarded its Italian coreligionists as "Machiavellian" (viii). This independent streak and high self-esteem eventually affected its activities as an interest group after the war. The French Church's struggles with temporal powers had an additional angle—its relations with the Vatican. Various popes' efforts to curb the French Church hindered the Church's ability to act as a unit, and the ability of French politicians to form a significant Christian Democratic or clerical party.

The French Church's independence and importance were embodied in the notion of Gallicanism, a crucial historical feature of the French Church, which affected the Church's relations with the papacy, and with the French state. Of long lineage, Gallicanism was summarized by the French clergy in 1682, in the "Articles of Gallicanism."[21] The first article draws a sharp division between temporal and spiritual powers: "S[t]. Peter and his successors, vicars of Christ, and likewise the Church itself have received from God power in things spiritual—but not in things temporal

---

[20] The issue of the extent to which the Italian Church's action was an opportunistic decision or a sincere one is complicated. A careful, well-documented study finds that the decision "corresponded to a profound sentiment" (Durand 1991, 9–33, 123–63, here at 33).

[21] Some argue Gallicanism began with the alleged conversion to Christianity (hence Catholicism) of Clovis, king of the Franks and ruler of "France" in 496; others argue that it did not begin until Charles VI, in 1408 (Martin 1978, 35–38).

and civil. . . . Consequently kings and princes are not by the law of God subject to any ecclesiastical power . . . with respect to their temporal government" (in Phillips 1967, 4; his translation). Gallicanism predisposed the clergy to see the temporal and spiritual worlds as distinct, that the one should not become enmeshed in the other. Well before the French Revolution did so, the Church was seeking to delineate spheres of authority. If the French Church saw the world from that perspective, direct intervention in party politics would logically appear out of line. Moreover, it emphasized the link between the monarchy and Church, with the former protecting the latter, and the monarchy receiving, in return, the absolute loyalty of the clergy (Martin 1978, 39).[22]

The Second and Fourth Articles temper the authority of the pope: "The Pope has the principal place in deciding questions of faith and his decrees extend to . . . all Churches: but nevertheless his judgement is not irreversible unless confirmed by consent of the Church" (in Phillips 1967, 4). Gallicanism "keeps the pope at a distance" (Martin 1978, 38). The Third Article, again noting that the pope is not the absolute authority, invokes the autonomy and unique history of the French Church and its institutions. "Hence the exercise of the Apostolic authority must be regulated by the canons enacted by the Spirit of God. . . . The ancient rules, customs and institutions received by the realm and Church of France likewise remain inviolable" (Phillips 1967, 4). In essence, Gallicanism meant that whenever it appeared that the French Church was about to strengthen its alliance with the French state (in whatever guises), the pope would be inclined to clip the French Church's wings. Indeed, various French Catholic social, spiritual, and political movements became religious footballs between the French Church and the Vatican.[23]

Gallicanism had an influence over the hierarchy and clergy in the latter half of the nineteenth century, predisposing bishops to maintain good relations with the state "at all costs" (Phillips 1967, 238), both to retain some independence from Rome and to sustain the collaborative nature of Church-state relations. Accustomed to its status as the state's advisor, the Church was slower to mobilize opposition to the secularizing actions of the Third Republic.

[22] Cardinal Richelieu's role in Louis XIV's reign (1661–1715) is a notable example of that collaboration.

[23] Dansette argues that by 1905, if not earlier, Gallicanism was a moot point; the French Church had become submissive well before then (1965, 626). Yet evidence of submissiveness is uneven; the 1801 concordat signed by Pius VII and Napoleon Bonaparte concerning the Church's status gave the pope the opportunity to dissolve the entire hierarchy and replace it with his appointees, but the French Church also evinced an independent streak at times. For instance, it persisted for some time, despite papal pressure, in utilizing local dialects rather than Latin in the liturgy and mass (Phillips 1967, 20–21). The first diocese to switch to the Roman liturgy was Langres in 1839, the last was Orléans in 1875.

The polar opposite of Gallicanism, Ultramontanism, needs an introduction. The latter was an ideological and religious movement favoring the direct control by the pope of national churches. The conflict between the two perspectives, Gallicanism and Ultramontanism, was "in essence, a conflict between the belief that the challenges of the post-Revolutionary society could be met only by a centralized Church, uniform in doctrine, style, and discipline, controlled by an infallible Pope and a vigilant Roman administration, and the contrary belief that the Church would lose all influence in modern society unless it had deep roots in national character and local institutions, and a looser, federal, collegial structure" (Gough 1986, vi–vii). For the Gallicans, the Vatican's "franchise mentality," with national Churches being duplicates of the Roman Church, was a blueprint for failure; for the Ultramontanes, it was a recipe for survival.

Ultramontanism in the hierarchy and laity weakened the belief that the Third Republic might be acceptable, and it undermined the Church's will to decide, independent of papal directives, to support a political party. The Ultramontane view held itself apart from the temporal world, putting "trust in the idea that they were bound to prevail in the end because of the semi-divine powers of their leader" (the pope) (Gough 1986, ix, 236). French Catholics, politically mobilized but by diverse groups, were split between Gallican and Ultramontane perspectives.

These views divided the French laity as well as the hierarchy and clergy throughout the nineteenth century. The balance among the laity favored the Gallicans, as the laity resented the imposition of the Roman liturgy in place of their dialects, the Gregorian chants, and the loss of local feast days. Resentment was so high that when, in 1860, parishioners were asked to contribute to a fund in defense of the besieged pope and the Papal States, most refused. As one group told the French Ministry of Cults (i.e., religions), "the priest bores us with his pope" (Gough 1986, x). The pope was foreign to them; their loyalties lay with the French Church.[24]

Church-run public schools became one of the victims of the Gallican-Ultramontane division, as well as the centerpiece of the conflict between the Church and state in France. Until the Revolution of 1789, public instruction had been in the hands of the Church. The faith was perpetuated by religious teachings in "public" schools. The First Empire nationalized the entire school system yet allowed the Church to continue to provide most instruction in the state (public) schools; its services were paid for by the state. Since the government controlled the appointment of bishops and clergy, it could control who taught. Private schools, at first illegal (save in a few approved cases), were gradually legalized.

[24] The contrast between popular and religious piety has generated a large literature, pointing out that practices of French Catholicism varied extensively across regions, even within regions (E. Weber 1976; Badone 1989; Tackett 1977, 1986; Ford 1993; Lambert 1985).

The 1801 concordat between Napoleon Bonaparte and the pope rees-tablished Church control over education. During the nineteenth century, primary education was largely in the clergy's hands (Ford 1993, 136). One might think that the French Revolution would have impelled the French Church to unify, but before the Church could regroup, the new pope, Pius VII (1800–1823), took advantage of Napoleon's rule, and the pope's position as supreme ruler of the Church, to "dissolve the entire French hierarchy" and appoint, after consulting with Bonaparte, 60 new bishops. Since Pius VII was able to appoint more pliant bishops, the con-cordat thus "proved lethal" to the French hierarchy's independence from the Vatican (Vaillancourt 1980, 34).

Church Structure

In notable contrast to the centralized structure of the French state, the French Church was decentralized. The Assembly of Cardinals and Arch-bishops (Assemblée des Cardinaux et Archevêques, ACA), created under Benedict XV in 1919, had no "judicial" powers over the French hierarchy or clergy. The directives and statements from the bishops' plenary sessions and the ACA were not binding; as Cardinal Liénart said, "The decisions which we shall take in common will not have the force of law, because our assembly is not a Council and each of us remains the judge of what should be applied to his own diocese" (in Bosworth 1962, 67, 63–64; Chaigneau 1955, 49). Coercive powers and authority rested with the Vatican.

Because of that, precisely at the time when the French Church was under anticlerical attack, it had no organization that could speak for it as a whole. Both popes and French rulers had "worked together to restrict any institutions of the Hierarchy above the diocese level," in order to prevent a reemergence of Gallicanism (Bosworth 1962, 16). If a bishop needed help in his diocese, he had to address the Curia in Rome (Chai-gneau 1955, 43). After the 1801 concordat, each diocese "jealously guarded its independence in social and temporal matters. Bishops accepted superiors in Rome, but not in Paris" (Bosworth 1962, 66–67). This meant that the only "organization" to speak for the French hierarchy on the eve of the Separation Law[25] was the pope himself. The consequences of this structure were significant for the fate of the French Church. The bishops did meet in three "plenary" sessions on the eve of the Separation Law (1905) to discuss strategy but did not meet again until 1951 (Chaigneau 1955, 42–43). While most of the hierarchy was willing to accept some compromise (if Church rights were guaranteed), the Vatican forced it to

---

[25] This law formally disengaged the state from the Church. See pp. 65–67.

take an intransigent position (Bosworth 1962, 20; Dansette 1965, 333–72),[26] thereby hardening anticlerical hostilities.

As to why the Church was decentralized, popes had fought hard to make it so in order to prevent a resurgence of independent thinking and acting (Gallican) bishops. To counter the pope and to persuade bishops to give up their local autonomy would require a strong leader and a fair degree of unanimity among the bishops. Yet the Church itself had no central leader, and the popes certainly did not want a centralized French hierarchy that, like the Gallican Church, would challenge the pope's authority. By keeping the French Church decentralized, the Vatican was able to ensure that local bishops could not mount a coordinated effort to counter Rome.

Pius X reorganized France's social Catholic movements under the hierarchy (Durand 1995, 79; Chaigneau 1955, 46), but it was not until 1931 that the ACA established Action Catholique as a national organization. The local clergy and bishops rejected the operations of Action Catholique's national branches; they wanted only diocesan groups (Chaigneau 1955, 44, 46) that would be directly under their control. Due to the lack of authority of the ACA to compel cooperation, local control prevailed.

Differences in institutional relationships across regions of France also affected the Church's political activities. In some "Catholic" regions the lower clergy promoted Christian Democratic parties, and their efforts had a noticeable effect on the success of those parties (e.g., the PDP in the 1920s and 1930s; the MRP in the Fourth Republic). In other "Catholic" areas, the clergy leaned, or were compelled by their paymasters to lean, toward the more traditional, conservative candidates. These differences had institutional roots.

The south central part of France, the Massif Central, is an area where religiosity traditionally has been high. One department, Aveyron, was named the "Brittany of the Midi" by Pius IX, invoking its similarity to the Catholic departments of Brittany (Bretagne) (Jones 1985, 285). Its inhabitants are, like the Bretons, descendants of the Celts. Both have a cult of the dead (Jones 1985, 134–37; Badone 1989). Both areas have similar agricultural lifestyles, the *bocage*. Yet the social Catholicism that formed the basis for Christian Democracy never took hold in Aveyron; it did in Brittany. Why? One clue may be in how parish priests were funded during the nineteenth century and later. The 1801 concordat had restored state salaries for priests but at a level far lower than of priests in other parts of Western Europe (Ford 1993, 84). In the Massif Central and elsewhere, a priest was "entirely dependent upon the local nobility, who supported him financially and put him entirely at the mercy of his bishop" (Ford

[26] In 1945, a Secretariat of the Episcopate was set up in Paris to help link "individual bishops more closely to the national activities of the Church" (Bosworth 1962, 70).

1993, 85). The bishops, in turn, were financially "at the mercy" of the local nobility (98–99). Jones gives no information on clergy funding (1985, 305–7), but argues the peasants were converted to voting for republican candidates by the patronage dispensing state. Under the Third Republic, the state replaced the nobility and Church as the source of patronage. In Aveyron, the clergy, still financially dependent on the nobility, were most likely to ally with one of the Monarchist candidates (Jones 1985, 240).

A "rigid, intransigent, authoritarian" clergy was not likely to embrace social Catholicism; its Gallico-Jansenist background would, however, predispose it to question the absolute authority of the pope (Tackett 1986, 7).[27] The consequence of this structure was that in Aveyron after World War II, Christian Democrats (the MRP) and their supporting clergy "ran into the intransigence of the hierarchy, which reproaches the young ecclesiastics [for] a tendency a little too advanced."[28]

In Brittany, priests were funded largely by their own parishioners, not by wealthy bishops or absentee landlords. Thus, they were able to break with the monarchists in the Third Republic, retain the loyalty or blind obedience of their parish, and support an effort to reconcile the republic with democracy. Indeed, it was in the peripheries where the Gallican tradition was weakest (e.g., Brittany) (Tackett 1986, 105). In many dioceses of Brittany the bishops were not able to control their own priests (Ford 1993, 87).[29] The Church and government could not retaliate effectively: salary withdrawal had little effect (88). Social Catholicism would provide motive, terms, and justification for a break with the Monarchists and the conservative hierarchy. It was a message the Breton clergy found persuasive.[30] As Ford (1993) notes of Brittany, Christian Democracy caught on best where the population was culturally and ethnically more distinct than in other regions, even those not incorporated into France until relatively

---

[27] Jansenists during the French Revolution had "leveled searching indictments against a wide range of ecclesiastical practices and institutions" (Tackett 1986, 7). A contemporary description of the Aveyron clergy during the period 1890–1910, when the first efforts at launching social Catholic movements began, reveals a conservative, staid lot, "immersed in its role, intransigent in its faith, still enclosed in questions of exegesis, authoritarian in its relations with the faithful, dominated by an ancient and powerful esprit de corps" (Cholvy 1979, 409).

[28] ADA, fonds Ramadier, dr. 52J 15, 1947.

[29] This may have had a long history. When Brittany was made part of France in 1532, the pope retained power to appoint at least three-fifths of the Breton clergy, the remaining posts being obtained through competitive exams. "The peculiarly Breton conjunction of traditions and institutions combined, in the words of one historian, 'to make the clergy of the province more Roman than Gallican in character' " (Tackett 1986, 107).

[30] Ford adds that, in contrast to most parts of France, social Catholicism was spread by a local seminary (in Quimper), so the clergy were indoctrinated (1993, 104).

late: Brittany, Flandres, Alsace, and the Basque area. Other Catholic regions, Franche-Comté, the Savoy, and Massif Central, did not host Christian Democracy.

The organizational structure of the French Church provided its bishops with more independence from the ACA, but not necessarily from the Vatican. The decentralized structure of the Church also affected, as the next section shows, the Church's ability to defend itself against the anticlericalists in the Third Republic.

The Third Republic: Anticlericalism and Christian Democracy

France had a variety of governing systems in the nineteenth century; the one that most concerns us now is the Third Republic (1871–1940). It was France's first experience with sustained parliamentary democracy, and a time when the Church's former political allies were on the defensive. Indeed, the Church's status came under attack at various times during the first part of the Third Republic. By the end of the nineteenth century, the Church had lost all connection to the French state, religious instruction in public schools was forbidden, and religious orders were forbidden to teach in private schools.

The French Church had the misfortune to be in a country with deep anticlerical roots, reaching back to at least Voltaire and the Encyclopedists, but certainly galvanized by the French Revolution. On occasion, and the Third Republic was one such "occasion," anticlericalism would seize the political day. In 1876, the premier, Jules Ferry, explained that the legacy of the French Revolution was "to have stripped the clergy of its political organization, its rôle as a State institution" (in Mayeur and Rebérioux 1987, 84). While the previous regime (the Second Empire, 1852–70) had restored to the Church many of its privileges, Ferry and other Third Republic politicians wished to carry on with the French Revolution's secularizing goals. To that end, working on Sunday was legalized, funerals and cemeteries could not be restricted to Catholic rites, and crucifixes were removed from classrooms. The educational system was also secularized; in 1882, primary education was made free and obligatory, with attendance counted only if at secular (public) schools (Dansette 1965, 422–25).

The Church sought some support from politicians grouped under existing political "parties." While most in the hierarchy preferred the monarchist candidates who were in the Union de la France Chrétienne (Dansette 1965, 455–56), some supported the moderate republicans. Save for a few local clergy, the Church steered clear of Christian Democratic politicians. A major work on the subject (Kalyvas 1996) argues that the Church did not sponsor Christian Democracy because Catholicism proved to be a failed electoral issue. For Kalyvas, Catholicism failed as an issue because the Church, thinking the Third Republic would collapse, failed to mobilize Catholics in Catholic ancillary organizations. After this prediction proved false, the Church could not get the bulk of politically mobilized Catholics to support Conservatives espousing clerical principles. With the Church thinking that the Third Republic would soon collapse, and that the monarchy (and Church privileges) would be restored, the Catholic mobilization (or, "organizational strategy") assumed higher costs in France than in the other countries where Christian Democratic parties did form. In those other countries, the Churches were allegedly convinced the liberal regimes were "rock-solid" (Kalyvas 1996, 141). To the contrary, the Church had good reason to believe the Third Republic would endure, and indeed, in 1890, French Cardinal Lavigerie astonished the public by exhorting Catholics to adhere to the Republic, provided "the form of government" was not contrary "to the principles by which civilized nations can live" (in Mayeur and Rebérioux 1987, 151; Darbon 1953, 126). Leo XIII, in 1892, urged Catholics to reconcile themselves with the Republic (Bosworth 1962, 17). His and Lavigerie's views were not shared by the cardinal archbishop of Paris, a convinced monarchist and Gallican, nor by most others in the hierarchy.

Since the Church did *not* expect the Republic to fall at any moment, why did the Church not bother to mobilize Catholics to counter the Liberal governments' attacks on the Church? First, the Church was divided on the appropriate response. In some areas, the lower clergy rallied to Christian Democracy. In general, those areas were where the clergy was not monarchist, and where there were more distinct regional cultures, that is, Brittany, the Basque area, and, after World War I, Alsace-Lorraine. Many priests had their own *cahier de doleances* (list of complaints) against the French episcopate (Gough 1986, 22–33). Second, in 1885, just prior to the anticlerical attacks, Pope Leo XIII condemned a nascent Catholic-monarchist party because he wanted to break the alliance of French Catholics with the monarchy, since the latter tended to espouse Gallicanism (in which the French monarch appointed the bishops and the pope merely gave his consent; see below). No pope wanted another party linked to the crown (Vaillancourt 1980, 40–41), but many defenders of French Catholicism were also monarchists (Brown 1974). Further hindering links to Christian Democracy, Leo XIII's successor Pius X, and many in the French hierarchy, opposed it as an alternative.[31] In 1890, when the French hierarchy appeared ready to sign a public declaration opposing the Third Republic's policies, the Vatican refused its approval (Ward 1964). Whatever its

---

[31] Witness their demolition of the Christian Democratic organization, Le Sillon (see p. 67), despite its popularity.

motives, the Vatican had, again, undermined the hierarchy's unity—this time by blocking its presentation of a united front. Third, French Catholics were split in ways that militated against a cohesive response to the pope's interference, and against the formation of an umbrella party.

Dreyfus Affair

France's failure to produce one large Christian Democratic party at the end of the nineteenth century was partly due to what is sometimes dismissed as "exogenous events" (Kalyvas 1996, 14). One of those events was the Dreyfus affair. In 1894, a Jewish military officer, Alfred Dreyfus, was court-martialed for treason (for allegedly leaking military documents to the Germans that, supposedly, led to France's defeat in the Franco-German War of 1870) and sentenced to life in prison on Devil's Island. After the French intellectual Emile Zola's famous "J'accuse" article in 1898, and much agitation, the case was reopened (1899), only to have Dreyfus convicted again. (He was later pardoned.) Church actions in the Dreyfus affair, in which it sided with the anti-Semitic, nationalist military, unhinged Leo XIII's efforts "to get French Catholics to accept the Republic" (Sedgwick 1965, vii; Dansette 1965, 559, 631) and undermined the efforts of social Catholics to broaden their appeal. The Dreyfus affair, by heightening the antirepublic spirit of many Catholics, drove a wedge between the social Catholics, who were not anti-Semitic, and the more conservative bourgeois and monarchist Catholics, the Jesuits, and the army, all of whom supported the conviction of Dreyfus (Dansette 1965, 546–47, 560; Mayeur and Rebérioux 1987, 200). Since the army recruited its officers from the upper middle class and aristocracy, and those groups tended to be traditional Catholics, the Church became implicated in the Dreyfus affair (Dansette 1965, 553). Although eventually Leo XIII sympathetically compared Dreyfus's position (as wrongly accused) to that of Jesus (Dansette 1965, 554; Phillips 1967, 257), the French Church hierarchy was compromised by its silence. When it finally broke its silence, it only compounded its apparent complicity with Dreyfus's accusers: a statement by the archbishop of Toulouse in 1898 lambasted the "harmful campaign" against the army by the Dreyfus supporters (Dansette 1965, 555).

In this complex situation, to be anti-Dreyfus (think him guilty) was to be antirepublican, proarmy, promonarchy, and anti-Semitic. To be pro-Dreyfus (believe in his innocence) was to be the opposite, that is, prorepublic, antimilitary, and antimonarchy. Since the monarchy and the army were Catholic traditionalists, being anti-Dreyfus became conflated with being pro-Catholic (which by association was antirepublican). The ramifications of the affair were thus significant for the Church and Christian

Democracy: since Catholics were branded as antirepublican, despite the efforts of some to reconcile Catholicism with the democratic tenets of the Third Republic, the Dreyfus affair ensured that the important electoral alliance that occurred in Italy in 1913, between republicans and Catholics, became impossible in France.

It is no surprise that in such circumstances, Catholicism was not a successful electoral focal point. The problem was not that the Church failed to implement an "organizational strategy" of mobilizing Catholics to vote for a Christian Democratic party. Catholicism was indeed politicized, but via the nationalists and monarchists, not the Christian Democrats (Durand 1995, 72). As Action Française and the Fédération Nationale Catholique would show, the Dreyfus affair had promoted the mobilization of Catholics on the side of the nationalists and monarchists rather than on the side of Christian Democrats.

Separation Law

The division over the appropriate response to anticlericalism hindered a coordinated defense and meant that any Christian Democratic movement would not be backed by a cohesive Catholic Church. In 1901, the Law of Association required all religious orders ("congregations") to obtain authorization from parliament or face dissolution. They were forbidden to run primary or secondary schools. In 1905, the French government made formal a separation of the state from the Church by abolishing religious education in public schools, and state payment of wages to priests (Mayeur and Rebérioux 1987, 230–31). The parishes running many of these schools could no longer afford to offer free private (religious) education to children no matter what the family income. Surprisingly perhaps, Church attitudes toward the Separation Law were not unitary. On the one hand, some in the hierarchy saw the law as inflicting severe damage on the Church's ability to perpetuate itself. On the other hand, some in the hierarchy saw the law as liberating the Church—no longer would it be subject to state control.

The Separation Law further facilitated the papal exercise of power over the French Church. With its implementation in 1906, Pius X had a free hand to appoint bishops, and the bishops to appoint clergy. He took advantage of this to appoint intransigent non-Gallican clergy. Not surprisingly, the French hierarchy became increasingly opposed to collaboration with the Republic through political means. Education also put a papal stamp on the hierarchy. Whereas between 1871 and 1905 only 5 bishops had been trained in Rome, between 1906 and 1919, 17 had been to the French seminary of Rome (Dansette 1965, 628). In fact, the Vatican developed numerous colleges and seminaries in Rome where clergy were to be "denationalized" (628). When the first episcopal conference was held (in May 1906), Pius X strictly controlled it, forbidding the bishops to discuss matters pertaining to the French Church's relations with the Vatican, the nomination of bishops, and the tenure of clergy. The conference's deliberations "were submitted in secret to the Holy See" (626–27). After Benedict XV, Pius XI, as conservative as Pius X, placed his men in key French positions. Rome, not Paris, became the "place of legitimacy" for French Catholics. When the next round of anticlerical attacks came, in 1924 under the Heriot government, the French hierarchy did not rally to the social Catholic party (Lebrun 1980, 420–23). Ironically, in an effort to defend the Republic, secular politicians had let a foreign power (the Vatican) acquire the means to strongly influence the French population.

Though the Separation Law freed the Church from state interference in religious and ecclesiastical matters (Chaigneau 1955, 52), the law's educational provisions limited the Church's capacity to cultivate the next generation of Catholics. In other words, the interest group was granted autonomy, but had its ability to recruit new members circumscribed. Worse, it ended state "recognition of the Catholic hierarchy. The church in France could now claim legal recognition only as an aggregate of *associations cultuelles* [cult-type associations]," which Catholics in their local parishes were expected to form to administer "the property left to the church" (Larkin 1964, 298). The law directly challenged the Church's hierarchical structure by turning it into a congeries of locally organized and run parishes. Moreover, the French Church had lost its ability to protect itself, via the French state, from Vatican control. Pius X, refusing to allow any undermining of the hierarchy (and perhaps fearing other countries would adopt similar laws were the Church to permit the formation of such associations), forbade French Catholics to form those associations, a move that angered Catholics who thought that they had no alternative.

The timing of leadership in conjunction with events was important. Where Leo XIII's appointees viewed the separation as something to live with, his successor, Pius X (1903–14) and his appointees condemned the law and any concessions to it (Bosworth 1962, 18–19). The fact that Pius X could appoint the French bishops "resulted in a new intransigent generation of bishops" (Larkin 1974, 3). Pius X urged Catholics to unite in one Catholic party to protect the Church, yet he wanted it to be an intransigent party, not one reconciled to the Republic or willing to compromise. Pius X had undertaken a concerted effort to eliminate moderate, prorepublican bishops—those most likely to support a Christian Democratic party. Intransigents were appointed to the most important dioceses of France: Paris, Rennes, and Lyon (Arnal 1985, 50–53).

A small social Catholic political movement, Le Sillon ("The Furrow"), begun in 1894 by Marc Sagnier, dramatically increased its membership after 1905. Yet to the conservative episcopacy and Pius X, Le Sillon seemed to be a threat to Catholic unity: it refused to ally with other Catholic candidates who did not share its progressive social and economic ideology (Breunig 1957, 238). Further, the hierarchy was not yet ready to accept Sagnier's proposition that in political matters, Catholics could think for themselves.[32] Persecuted by the Vatican, by French royalists and Ultramontane bishops, the social Catholics disbanded after official papal condemnation in 1910 (Arnal 1985, 53–61; Breunig 1957). Thus, when Pius X later urged Catholics to unite, there were no national level organizations in the Church around which to do so. The Christian Democratic political identity was a failed electoral issue not because the Church had not mobilized Catholics for it, but because all efforts to create one were deliberately derailed.

The leader of the Church makes a difference: whereas Leo XIII probably would have accepted it, Pius X demolished Le Sillon, denouncing it for trying to escape ecclesiastical authority (Durand 1995, 70). Leo XIII tended to be noninterventionist, counseling the bishops to decide for themselves about how to respond to law on congregations that taxed their property (Phillips 1967, 238). In contrast, his successor Pius X told the archbishops and bishops of France: "one cannot build society if the Church does not pour the bases and does not direct the work" (Durand 1995, 71). Rome, not the independent French Church, was to control the French institution.

The Separation Law and papal machinations were not the end of political Catholicism in France. In 1919, over 200 Catholics were in the Bloc National that won the majority in the legislative election. When the Left (Cartel des Gauches) won the 1924 legislative elections, a French general, sponsored by much of the French hierarchy, founded the Fédération Nationale Catholique (FNC) (Arnal 1985, 95, 133–140; McMillan 1996, 42). It was not a political party but nevertheless rallied Catholics to defend their faith by opposing France's anticlerical laws. The FNC's version of political Catholicism was integrist (i.e., demanding that politics and society be thoroughly Catholicized) and monarchist, not Christian Democratic, and therefore quite appealing to much of the hierarchy.[33] Also in 1924, several social Catholics founded the Parti Démocrate Populaire

[32] Sagnier thought bishops could "require only respect for dogmas, for religious discipline and also for the moral and social teachings of the Church" (in Breunig 1957, 240, his translation).

[33] An older nationalist party, both authoritarian and Catholic, Action Française (1898), led by an agnostic (Charles Maurras), collaborated with the FNC (Weber 1962; Arnal 1985).

(PDP), the Christian Democratic party that survived the Third Republic (Delbreil 1990). But the Dreyfus affair, Gallicanism, Ultramontanism, and Pius X and Pius XI had done or would do their damage. The Church, now divided between the hierarchy and clergy, supported Catholic candidates and their parties only on a case-by-case (diocese by diocese) basis. An uncoordinated, decentralized French Church did not give Catholic politicians any incentive to coalesce into one party, if indeed Catholics ever could have overcome their ideological differences. The PDP's electoral showing was negligible.[34] Further, the Gallican conflict with the Vatican resurfaced as the FNC and Action Française gained prominence: Pius XI reprimanded the FNC for its nationalism and condemned Action Française in 1926 because he feared the party was winning over the French hierarchy by tying the party's nationalist and monarchist platform to a strident defense of Catholicism (Arnal 1985, 143–45; Dansette 1965, 760–94).[35]

Catholicism, in the multiple interpretations assigned to it by the French, clearly had not expired as a fuel for political movements. The French hierarchy showed diverse preferences and did not support one movement to the exclusion of others. Policy disagreements and a decentralized institutional structure undermined the likelihood that the French Church could or would, collectively, support a party, Christian Democratic or otherwise. Gallicanism and the papacy's efforts to quell it had altered the Church's ability to evaluate, as a unit, the utility or ideological acceptability of supporting *any* political party. When the Vichy regime failed, the Church was ill prepared to influence the construction of a party to its liking or to work with the "Catholic" party that swept into prominence in 1945.

Impact of the Vichy Regime

On June 14, 1940, German troops marched into Paris. On June 17, Marshal Philippe Pétain asked the Germans for an armistice, which came into effect on June 25. It divided France into two zones: occupied—the northern half and west coast of France, and unoccupied, the remaining southern portion. On July 10, the French parliament (National Assembly) voted itself and the Third Republic out of existence by giving full governing powers to Pétain. While the Germans ran the occupied zone from Paris,

---

[34] France's single-member district electoral system (at the time) may have aggravated this tendency to look at politics on a case-by-case basis. My thanks to Susan Scarrow for pointing this out.

[35] Action Française's leader, Maurras, was convicted in 1945 of "treasonous collaboration with the German enemy." His response was, "This is Dreyfus's revenge" (Arnal 1985, 11).

Pétain's government moved to the resort town of Vichy. Only General Charles de Gaulle argued, from London, that the Occupation, the armistice, and the Vichy regime were invalid. The Catholic Church, and many Catholics, welcomed the new regime, with its promise of "work, family, country." In the face of collapse—military, political, even social—the Church was tapped to play an important role in the "moral regeneration" of the country.

For the hierarchy, and even for some prominent social Catholics, Vichy represented an opportunity to return France to its putative Christian origins (McMillan 1996, 55). Vichy, a self-declared "Catholic" state, promised to eliminate Communism, Jews, Freemasons, and other rivals to Catholicism and authoritarianism, and to restore Christian morals to public life. Catholicism was to be an integral part of Vichy's "national revolution." Liberal democracy had merely elicited "the animal" in man (in Duquesne 1966, 65). Pétain seduced the hierarchy with his language and with specific acts: restoring crucifixes to public schools and city halls, the death penalty for abortionists, and upgrading the status of congregations (Duquesne 1966, 85–87). In 1942, Archbishop Maurice Feltin of Bordeaux[36] expressed the belief that "Christian principles" were in harmony with the National Revolution of Vichy (in Halls 1995, 375). The Catholic newspaper *La Croix* welcomed Pétain's actions in favor of Catholicism and said "our gratitude toward the government of Marshal Pétain can and ought to be expressed without reserve" (in Duquesne 1966, 43). Some priests denounced public school teachers who did not put a crucifix in their classrooms (Weitz 1995, 272). Pétain's views of replacing the liberal order with a corporatist one resonated with the hierarchy's corporatist doctrine. Even Emmanuel Mounier, a social Catholic, saw Vichy as the opportunity to recruit new lay Catholic leaders and promote a Catholic vision of society. Cardinal Gerlier, archbishop of Lyon, welcomed and legitimated the Vichy regime when he said, "Pétain is France and France, today, is Pétain" (Latreille 1978, 33).[37]

The Church's resistance to the Occupation and to Vichy is more difficult to evaluate. Some clergy joined the *maquis* (armed resistance), and, in 1944, some exhorted the hierarchy to "switch sides before it was too late" (Halls 1995, 366). Some convents and monasteries sheltered Vichy fugitives (Weitz 1995, 220). As in Italy, what resistance there was to the war, to the Germans, to the regime, seemed mostly the activity of a minority among the lower clergy (Bédarida 1992; Fouilloux 1992; Duquesne 1966).

[36] On Suhard's death in 1949, Feltin succeeded Suhard as cardinal archbishop of Paris.
[37] The presiding priest at an anniversary ceremony celebrating Vichy's defeat of de Gaulle's forces at Dakar stated, "You are, Marshal [Pétain], the way, the truth, and the life

During World War II, the locus of the Occupation affected the Church and its public role and image. In the nonoccupied zone of southern France where the Vichy regime had its headquarters, Catholics "found a position that they had thought lost: priests and bishops became notables, even official *personages*." Catholic Action movements became influential (Duquesne 1966, 83). The Resistance, of which MRP founders were distinctly a part, was, at best, a nuisance. The Aveyron clergy's weekly newspaper, *l'Union catholique*, was ardently pro-Vichy (Duquesne 1966, 78) and the bishop of Rodez was later condemned by the Christian Democrats for having told young men to accept "as a duty of conscience" forced labor in Germany (Halls 1995, 369). This put the MRP in Aveyron on an uneasy footing with Catholics, the lower clergy, and the hierarchy. In contrast, in Brittany the lower clergy had fought on the side of the Resistance, though during the *épuration* (the purge of Vichy collaborators) many Catholics and their clergy closed ranks around their bishops (Halls 1995, 372–73).

One crucial difference between Italy and Germany, on the one hand, and France, on the other, is found in the Vichy regime and its antithesis, the Resistance. Neither in Italy nor in Germany did the Catholic Church figure into the core of the Fascist regime's moral order. In both those countries, the Church was instrumental in controlling Catholics and identifying Jews but was never embraced by the Fascist government. This is not to downplay the Church's complicity with certain features of the Nazi or Italian Fascist regimes. The French Church, however, was undeniably an integral part of the Vichy order. Pétain's government declared itself inspired by "Catholic principles" (Berstein and Milza 1991, 325, 328) and quickly put forth "legislation that lifted restrictions on [the Church's] activities as well as giving it considerable advantages" (Halls 1995, 87).

The Church condemned the Resistance, saying it was "disloyal" to the Church (Halls 1995, 383). While the Italian Church had also welcomed the Fascists (reasoning it was the lesser of the three extant evils: Communism, democracy, and Fascism), it more clearly distanced itself. This the French Church never did. Moreover, it never clearly supported the liberation effort.[38] Perhaps worse for the Church's postwar political standing, the Church had earlier condemned Charles de Gaulle, the one leader at the war's end most respected by the French, and de Gaulle made clear his view that the Church was compromised (Duquesne 1966, 413–16; Halls 1995, 383).

---

of the country" (in Duquesne 1966, 59). For Suhard, Pétain was the "unimpeachable Frenchman" (in Halls 1995, 45).

[38] This is not the place to discuss or assess the French population's acceptance of the Vichy regime and German Occupation. For a solid introduction to the Church, Vichy, and the Liberation, see Duquesne 1966 and Latreille 1978.

The Church, of course, gave organizational survival as the rationale for its behavior during the war. To quote the French Assembly of Cardinals and Archbishops, "the bishops had fulfilled their prime duty of sustaining the Church and its religious life" (in Halls 1995, 366). That they had done so by explicitly or tacitly collaborating with the occupiers and Vichy circumscribed the Church's opportunities for political influence and alliances after the war. The problem for the Church was that the party that came to be labeled as Catholic and Christian Democratic in the Fourth Republic had been launched by Resistance activists, while the Church's formal incorporation into the Vichy "revolution" had linked it with that regime and made it impossible to deny complicity. In the powerful myth that de Gaulle established in the post-Vichy period, France was liberated, saved, not by the Catholic Church, not even by the *résistants* (and certainly not by the Allies), but by "eternal France" (Rousso 1991, 16). Henceforth, the Church would no longer be viewed as the guardian of things eternal, and certainly not of France.

Thus, the Church's actions during the Vichy regime limited its possibilities for action after the war. The failure of Vichy, moreover, compelled the Church to see that collusion between Church and state, with the Church in a privileged position, was no longer an acceptable goal.

CONCLUSION

The historical experiences of the two Churches bequeathed organizational cultures with different orientations. Critically, the Churches' ideological and institutional distance from the previous regime created opportunities for, or constraints on, the types of alliances the Churches could make after the war, affecting how the Churches could act (blatantly or surreptitiously) in politics and whether each one would find a sympathetic political party ally, or a party that wanted the Church as a supporting interest group. The question was partly answered by the Church's relation to the previous regime.

The Italian Church, including its ancillary organizations, remained institutionally and ideologically distinct from the Fascist regime; the French Church was incorporated into the Vichy regime. The Italian Church emerged dominant, the French chastened. The Lateran Pacts heightened the Italian Church's control over Azione Cattolica at the same time that the pacts delineated separate spheres of action for the Church and the Fascist regime. Nor was the Church an integral part of Fascist ideology: the pacts had removed Azione Cattolica from the political sphere (the Fascist regime not wanting it as a competitor) and firmly placed it in the

Church's hands. The Church thus was able to cultivate and control AC activists.

A different situation obtained in France. The French Church was made an integral part of Vichy. However, Vichy did not formally put Action Catholique under Church control. Action Catholique had been, owing to the structure of the French Church, a decentralized organization; some branches supported Vichy, others did not. With Action Catholique not firmly under the control of the hierarchy, it was often in conflict with the hierarchy and, in contrast to the situation in Italy, did not become a tool for training political elites sympathetic to the hierarchy.

The historical legacy also left the Churches with different structures. The Vatican's position at the center of Roman Catholicism and its putative authority over the national Churches seems to have heightened its sensitivity to anticlerical affronts and its determination to control the actions of hierarchies in other states. Its internally centralized structure facilitated control over its clergy, though that structure was itself constructed (i.e., the Church before Italian unification was not a unified entity with homologous structures in each diocese). The French Church tried at times to create central coordinating organs; these were always subject to disruption by the pope, who feared a cohesive, confrontational, and Gallican Church. The French Church's comparatively decentralized structure meant that when severe threats to its status occurred, it had no authoritative central organ to coordinate a response. Because of that, the Church (as an interest group) supported a variety of parties in the Third Republic, depending on the preferences of each bishop. The Church as a whole thus could neither compel nor provide an incentive for Catholic politicians to coalesce into one party.

Institutional structures can be changed, but effecting change requires resources, external shocks, new coalitions. Institutional inadequacies, like mechanical flaws in automobiles, do not repair themselves. The failings of institutions do not contain the sources of their own transformations, though they may provoke suggestions and pressure for change. Depending on circumstances and existing arrangements, the threshold for change may be quite high (Pierson 1997). The institutional structure may well block it, or block *timely* change, resulting in a missed opportunity. These characteristics of institutional structure influenced the Catholic Church's interaction with the Italian and French states, and with the Christian Democratic parties.

The varying policies of the different popes indicates that leadership is a significant factor in an organization's history. By virtue of their power to appoint bishops, popes have at times staffed the national Churches with hierarchies that impeded the policies of later Vatican rulers and national Church hierarchies. In conjunction with particular events and organizational structures, popes have altered the probabilities that Christian Democratic or other types of Catholic parties would succeed electorally, or even survive as organizations. Whereas Leo XIII and Benedict XV were less interventionist in the affairs of other national Churches and in national politics, and slightly less sensitive to the anticlerical policies of the new liberal governments, Pius IX, Pius X, and Pius XI had a managerial style that was controlling, and that viewed any anticlericalism as a mortal threat to the organization. The popes thus varied in the costs they attached to particular choices. Leadership has systematic and long-term systemic effects.

The argument here is that the Churches arrived at the dawn of the new republics encumbered with assorted baggage that impeded some strategies and facilitated others. The French Church was in a disadvantaged position. Though it had many faithful followers, to the new political entrepreneurs of the Fourth Republic it looked tainted and contaminated with Vichy. The Italian Church entered the new Italian republic in a strong position as an organization that commanded the respect and attention of political elites. The historical legacies produced different working conditions for the two religious organizations.

With these two religious interest groups, as with other interest groups, the subsequent political alliances pursued by the Italian and French Churches can only be understood by taking account of their prior structure, critical experiences, and recent history of institutional and ideological linkages with major political actors.

CHAPTER 4

Interests, Identities, and Role Definition

ONE OF the arguments of this book is that the extent and durability of interest group–party linkages vary according to solutions to contracting problems, and to organizational definitions of "self-interest." This chapter concentrates on the latter issue. Interest groups vary in their nature, priorities, methods, and goals. To understand the choices they make about political parties as suppliers of policy products, we have to look beyond the structure of the political market to the groups' preferences. We can make some basic assumptions about preferences, based on the fact that the subject in question is an interest group, and on the type of interest group. There are, however, variations in how interest groups define survival, in how they define membership, in the types of structures they establish to gain their goals, in how they interpret their environment and what they must do to be successful therein, and in their political motivations. These differences lead to different behaviors in the face of the similar problem of finding political party allies to further the interest group's goals. Thus, along with specifying the basic incentives and constraints a group has in trying to find a political supplier, we must also ascertain how each group views its role in society, and how it defines its key interests. These particularities help to account for why similarly situated groups act differently. While the previous chapter indicated that variations in the context bequeathed by history have a role, this chapter concentrates on the group's self-conception.

The reader might object that it is impossible to know the intentions of an interest group; the best one can do is make basic assumptions about preferences and constraints. What actors say about what they are doing may be propaganda, or it may be that they misunderstand their own behavior and thus misrepresent it; public pronouncements also may be only for public consumption. These points are well taken, yet it is worth checking our own assumptions about intention against what the actors, who are likely more familiar with what they are trying to do, say. Moreover, I do not use behavior as the sole indicator of an actor's intentions. Even agreeing that the words of actors cannot always be taken at face value, it is still important to ask, how does the group's leadership market the organization? What image are they seeking to live up to, to operate by? Whether the leaders were cynical or sincere, their behavior would be guided by the effort to promote a particular image (to capture a market segment, protect market share, etc). What criteria are they using to measure their own success? More acolytes, more Church buildings, more conversions, more "true believers," more priests, preferential treatment from the state? Those images, concepts, and criteria have an impact on their behavior.

This chapter shows that the Church marketed itself differently in Italy and France, had different views of what it should and could be doing, and had different views of what constituted survival and success. It first reviews the basic assumptions about Church preferences, then the contexts the two Churches were in, and the differences to be explained. The following section analyzes the Italian Church's view of its role, showing that it had a broad definition of legitimate action, was highly sensitive to threats, and saw itself as not just the foundation of Italian civilization but indeed of Christendom. The analysis then turns to the French Church, which had a much more limited conception of its position, and strove to present itself as an institution that empathized with its members. Although it earlier had claimed to be an essential element of French civilization, it no longer took that position for granted. Its view of how to reclaim lost ground even differed from the Italian Church's: the French Church emphasized missionary work, the Italian pedagogy, politics, and pageantry. These differences help to account for the differing levels of investment the Churches made in the postwar parties (but that is the subject of the next chapter).

In general, the Catholic Church has several priorities in common with other interest groups; among these one would have to include, as two of the most important, survival and increased influence. Further, it presumably wishes to exercise some measure of control over its members, increase its membership, maintain or increase its revenue and its capacity to influence its environment. The Church, however, may be differentiated from most if not all other groups in the fact that it claims to be universally authoritative; that is, its position, priorities, and goals are said to be universally applicable. It has, in its own view, literally a God-given right to the (broadly defined) spiritual allegiance of all persons. Its ideology (and the political consequences thereof) is not restricted to a specific or limited field, such as economics, agriculture, or the environment; its values and priorities are (asserted to be) eternal and absolute, and apply to political, social, economic, cultural, and other fields of human activity.

The limitations of the market analogy are evident in the actions and policies, even in the structures, of the postwar French and Italian Churches. In a broad sense, both Churches faced the same sort of market: both had to grapple with societies that had become, almost overnight, true mass democracies—systems very different from those that had existed prior to the war. They faced well-organized parties on the left, fledgling Christian Democratic parties that the public might mistakenly think spoke for the Church, competition from the traditional liberal and generally anticlerical elements, and a political Right that was not subservient.

Those similarities did not produce Churches following the same course. What this chapter shows is that, in part, different "market strategies" were due to a divergence in the roles the two Churches defined for themselves, and in those that were defined for them by their respective societies. In short, the Churches' motives and goals diverged. The Italian Church, which saw itself as the axis of Christendom, had an ambitious program for the Italian state, and its society, deviation from which was held to be a mortal sin. The French Church, on the other hand, adopted a moderate program, one that sought to cope with the new arrangements at the same time that it sought to bring more of the French population back to Catholicism. Before being able to analyze the actual selection of political party allies, it is crucial to understand what the two Churches understood to be their interests and role definitions. That is the task of this chapter.

The Italian Church sought to dominate Italy and to assert its supremacy over all national Churches; its position within the state was reasonably well established and recognized, and it could, therefore, be more aggressive in its efforts to attain its goals. The French Church, in contrast, rather clearly exhibited a weaker organization's concern over loss of membership and staff attrition. It viewed its survival as hinging on Catholic education, and therefore on state subsidies to private schools. Far more than the Italian Church, it was prepared to recognize a "truce" with a secular regime and avoid the anticlericalism that it had been forced to deal with several times since the French Revolution.[1]

The Italian Church after the war was on better ground: the Italian Communist Party acquiesced to putting the Lateran Pacts into the new constitution (Ginsborg 1990, 101)[2] and only the Liberals insisted on a separation of Church and state (Webb 1958, 42). The Left's compliance on the separation issue enabled the DC to collaborate with the Socialists without the latter throwing the red herring of Church status into coalition politics at every opportune moment (which is what happened in France). The DC, through no merit of its own, was in a position to provide the Church with what the latter regarded as an essential service—constitutional recognition of the Church as a fundamental part of the Italian sociopolitical order.

---

[1] I write as if the Church were a unitary actor. For this period, the hierarchy of the Italian Church had a common vision of a Christian state, though there was some disagreement on how to arrive at that state. It should be noted that much of the scholarly work on interest groups views them as unitary actors as well.

[2] The Communist philosopher Antonio Gramsci (1891–1937) had understood Christian Democracy as a "necessary phase in the process of the adhesion of Italian workers to communism" (Webb 1958, 24), and the PCI's leader, Palmiro Togliatti, recognized that Italians could not immediately be detached from Catholicism or the Church.

The French Church faced large and hostile Communist and Socialist parties (a combined total of about 900,000 members in 1946 [Warner 1994, 292a]), public skepticism about its role in Vichy, and a Christian Democratic party hesitant to work with a tainted ally. These factors impinged on the Church's view of what was possible (the collapse of Vichy had shown that the secular-clerical divide was permanent), contributing to the Church's more modest definition (virtual denial) of its contemporary political role, and to its focus on "re-Christianizing" the country. If bridging the secular-clerical divide were not possible, the Church would instead try to gather more people on its side of the crevasse.[3]

In France and in Italy at their respective first postwar regular elections, the correlation of Catholicism in a given electoral district with vote for the Christian Democratic parties was strong. In France, however, by the second regular parliamentary election, that correspondence had weakened considerably (Warner 1994, 154–60; 1998, 563). Why did French Catholics, who once voted for the MRP at the same rate that Italian Catholics voted for the DC, quit doing so? I suggest it had much to do with the interests and identities of the two Catholic Churches and their subsequent efforts to influence the political choices of Catholics.

ITALY

The main postwar political task in Italy was to write a constitution for a new representative democracy. Elections were held in 1946 to elect a Constituent Assembly, and a referendum was held to determine whether Italy would retain its monarchy (the republic won, with 54.2% to 45.8%). The Christian Democratic party (DC) and the Communist Party (PCI) were the two largest and, with the Socialists (PSI)[4] and (secular) Republicans (PRI), formed the first postwar governing coalitions.

Preferred by the Allies and the Vatican, the DC, founded in Milan in 1942 by a steel magnate and Catholic university intellectuals, soon became a major player in the postwar transition. The Communist Party, established in 1921 and in the 1940s led by Palmiro Togliatti, successfully competed with the Socialists for the votes of agrarian and rural workers.

---

[3] Numerous studies of the PCI and PCF exist; the standard work is still Blackmer and Tarrow 1975.

[4] The Partito Socialista Italiano (PSI), led by Pietro Nenni, was voluntarily subordinate to the PCI. In 1947, the party split, with Giuseppe Saragat forming the PSLI that soon became the PSDI (Social Democratic Party), to act autonomously from the PCI (Ginsborg 1990, 104). The PSI was temporarily known as the PSIUP, or Partito Socialista Italiano di Unità Proletaria (or Social Proletarians).

TABLE 4.1

Italian Parliamentary Election Results, 1946–1958, by Party

Party	1946[a] % of Vote	1946[a] % of Seats	1948 % of Vote	1948 % of Seats	1953 % of Vote	1953 % of Seats	1958 % of Vote	1958 % of Seats
Christian Democrats (DC)	35.2	37.2	48.0	53.1	41.1	44.6	42.0	45.8
Communists (PCI)	19.0	18.7	31.2	31.9	23.4	24.2	22.1	26.3
Socialists (PSI)	20.7	20.7	—	—	12.7	12.7	13.6	14.1
Splinter Socialists (PSDI)	—	—	6.7	5.7	4.4	3.2	4.1	3.7
Republicans (PRI)	4.4	4.5	2.8	1.6	1.9	0.8	1.5	1.0
Liberals (PLI)	6.8	7.4	4.5	3.3	2.9	2.2	3.0	2.9
Monarchists (PNM/PMP)	2.8	2.9	2.4	2.4	6.4	6.8	4.3	4.1
Neofascists (MSI)	—	—	1.9	1.0	5.9	4.9	4.6	4.0
Uomo Qualunque	5.3	5.4	—	—	—	—	—	—

Source: Calculated from *Istituto Centrale di Statistica e Ministero dell'Interno; Elezioni per l'Assemblea Costituente e Referendum Istituzionale (2 Giugno 1946)* (Rome: Istituto Poligrafico della Stato, 1948), *Elezione Politiche del 1948. Elezioni della Camera dei Deputati*, vol. 2, *Elettori, votanti, voti di lista validi, voti non validi in ciascun Comune della Repubblica* (Rome: Tipografia Fausto Failli, 1949), *Elezione della Camera dei Deputati, 7 Giugno 1953*, vol. 2, *Voti di lista e voti di preferenza-candidati ed eletti* (Rome: Istituto Poligrafico dello Stato, 1956), Elezione della Camera dei Deputati, 25 Maggio 1958, vol. 2, *Voti alle liste e voti ai candidati* (Rome: Istituto Poligrafico dello Stato, 1960).

[a] Constituent Assembly election.

The final years of the war seemed to have reinforced regional differences: the south had not served as an industrial base for the war and saw far less fighting. After 1943, the north was essentially occupied by the Germans, its industrial base and workers the target for Allied bombing, and it was in the north that the Italian resistance, dominated by the Communist Party, was born. The war ended without effecting major changes in Italian society; the impoverished agrarian south, only marginally involved in the war, returned to the status quo ante. The transformative potential of the northern resistance, with factory strikes and cross-party activity, was halted by the Italian political elite and by the United States (Ginsborg 1990; Hughes 1965). Moreover, the Communist strategy had been not revolution, but leading a united, national resistance to the Nazis and Fascists (Ginsborg 1990, 43). The result was that Italy's major problems were left unsolved: the vast discrepancy in wealth and industrialization between north and south; the bureaucracy (national and local) staffed by patronage appointees under the Fascists and earlier, clientelistic political practices more widespread in the south than the north; and Fascists and *mafiosi* left in positions of local political power by the Allies.

While the DC was trying to position itself as the dominant party in the government and electorate, obtain U.S. loans, qualify for Marshall Plan aid, quell strikes, and negotiate the Church's demands, the PCI and Socialists initially tried to work with the DC on behalf of the immediate needs of labor and the poor. Significantly, Togliatti (PCI) misread the DC as a "potentially progressive force in Italian society" and so put off for a few years the demands for complete transformation of the economy and polity (Ginsborg 1990, 83). Those years were crucial, enabling the DC to consolidate its position without having to yield to PCI and PSI demands. Only in late 1947 did the PCI try to gauge when to start the revolution, and how to keep the Church from blocking it.

Vatican Motives

Like the French Church, the Italian Church feared secular, particularly Communist, control of the national government. Such a government might ban religious instruction and lay religious organizations such as trade unions or social action groups, require priests to do military service, and adopt and permit social policies (such as divorce) contrary to the teachings of the Church. With the Soviet Union as its image of a Communist-led state, the Church concluded that an atheistic government might banish the Church altogether.[5] To prevent that from happening, it needed to rally politicians and citizens to its cause; it may not have wanted to sponsor a political party, but given its view of the circumstances and the meaning it attributed to events, the Church thought it had to. It was always politics that had saved Roman Catholicism in the past.

The Church's strategies were underscored "by a simple ideological analysis: reconstruction [of Italy] occurs by recalling a basic principle, the sacred role of Rome, the civilizing mission of Catholic Italy, and by a high-priority objective: saving Christian civilization from the dangers that were menacing it" (Durand 1991, 360). The Jesuit newspaper, La Civiltà Cattolica, was among those that conflated Italy with the Church (Magister 1979, 84). The Church believed it was only doing what was within its rights—taking defensive action and trying to structure society on its own, and universally applicable, terms. In 1948, the Church had the opportunity for which it had long hoped: building the Christian state. At a celebration in Rome, before a crowd of three to five hundred thousand, to conse-

---

[5] This view seemed to be derived from events outside Italy's borders. In the 1947 Constituent Assembly, the PCI, while it did not repudiate its Communist (i.e., atheist) ideology, was remarkably conciliatory toward the Church. See Bocca 1973, 442–44; Ginsborg 1990, 101; Falconi 1956, 74–75.

crate Rome to the Sacred Heart, a priest declared, "France gave the world liberal civilization, Russia the Communist civilization, Italy will give the world the great civilization awaited for centuries, that of Jesus Christ" (in Durand 1991, 647). Pope Pius XII saw Rome and Italy as the defenders of Western civilization; Communism was not part of that civilization, hence could not be part of the government of Italy. A sampling of public statements by Italian bishops and cardinals shows that, for the Church, "Christian Rome" was opposed to "atheist Moscow"; "to be anti-Catholic implies for us being a traitor to the country" (Durand 1991, 366). Such thoughts and fears were not merely for public consumption; they were expressed privately as well (Durand 1991, 368–99).

Pius XII (1939–58), born Eugenio Pacelli (1876–1958), was an astute political strategist, a "flag bearer of doctrinal integralism" and anti-Communism (Falconi 1967, 269; cf. Holmes 1976). He had been, under Pius XI, secretary of state and papal nuncio to Germany during Hitler's rise to power. Like Pius XI, he seemed to fear Communism more than Fascism. His failure to condemn the Nazis or apologize for the Church's "neutrality" has given him his critics (e.g., Falconi 1970; Hochhuth 1963) and his apologists (e.g., Chélini 1983; Woodward 1998). What is of relevance here is that Pius XII stubbornly sought to make the world conform to the Church, and to further centralize its structure in Italy (Alberigo 1986).

Pius XII, in contrast to his successor and to the French hierarchy of the 1950s, saw his role as that of preserving Catholic orthodoxy. The laity was to be under the strict control of the hierarchy in any activity that involved Catholics and Catholicism; the clergy was to adhere to the Church's authoritarian teachings and methods and mold the laity to Catholic orthodoxy (Riccardi 1985a, 40–43; Falconi 1967, 281–92; Chélini 1989, 220–24). Pius XII and an influential bloc within the Church, known as the "partito romano" for its base in the Vatican and in the Jesuit (Roman) newspaper *Civilità Cattolica,* found the somewhat innovative French Church their bête noire. Fascism's failing was not due to its authoritarianism, its violence or denial of democracy, but to "its refusal to found itself on the Church and to profess itself Catholic" (Riccardi 1985a, 42–43). The narrow view of the position of the laity and the clergy in the Catholic Church meant that the means to dominate society would have to be organized in military fashion, to avoid any deviations, innovations, or loss of control.

Pius XII saw no limits on the Church's role or tutelage of society, culture, and politics. Regarding politics, he asserted, "The power of the Church does not limit itself to strictly religious questions, as some say, but has authority over the entire object, institution, interpretation, and application of natural laws, as regards their moral aspect" (in Malgeri 1985, 113). While the priority was on religious correctness and dominance, the Church encompassed the political—as Pius XII reminded DC politicians and citizens in a 1951 Christmas radio message: "The Church cannot forget, not even for a moment, that its role of representing God on earth does not permit it to remain indifferent, even for one instant, to the good and the bad of human things" (in Malgeri 1985, 113).

For Pius XII and the Italian hierarchy, Italy, and Rome in particular, was the moral, religious, and civilized center of the world (Durand 1991, 363). Cardinal Salotti argued that, for those reasons, it was necessary "to remake Italy, an Italy wiser and more conscious of its immortal destiny, and to remake Italians, reconstructing in them an integrally Christian conscience" (in Durand 1991, 364). The Vatican was quite sensitive to the fact that "the whole world watches us in Rome" (in Riccardi 1988, 55): what the Church did, or what happened to it, would have repercussions throughout the world. In October 1946, Cardinal Ruffini of Palermo practically threatened Italy with missing the Second Coming should Italy not follow the Church in political matters.[6] "Christian Rome" and the special religious mission Italy had to fulfill gave the Church, with Catholics beneath it, a "right of hegemony" in Italian society (Stabile 1986, 371). Politics could not exist in a separate sphere, merely informed by Catholic premises; it was an inherent part of the Church's plan and should be directed by the Church: "It is necessary that our politicians be convinced that Religion is not at their service; but rather they must see themselves as humble servants of the Church in the social realm" (in Stabile 1986, 370)—not humble servants of *Christ* but of *the Church*. The organization had priority over its spiritual founder.[7]

This attitude was not a mere reflection of the circumstances of 1946–48. It went beyond getting a foothold in society, or of preserving gains made during Fascism; it was a call for complete Catholic dominance. Just before the 1958 legislative elections, the Italian Episcopal Conference stated that "the electoral programs should affirm the full sufficiency of the Catholic doctrine for the solution to social problems, excluding every implied or explicit need to integrate part of the Marxist or whatever foreign doctrine into Christian thought" (Tassello and Favero 1983, 65–66).

The Church was unyielding, and successful, in its requirement that the Lateran Pacts become part of the Italian constitution (Durand 1991, 523). Nothing less would do. Indeed, the Church's independence and privileged position was guaranteed by the constitution adopted in 1947. Further, the Church wanted to have its social teachings made an integral

---

[6] "Too great is the destiny of Italy, too necessary her mission in the world that she can miss the resurrection, the life. Christian Rome, vital center, Catholicism irreplaceable and indestructible, there is the most reliable guarantee" (in Stabile 1986, 371).

[7] Cf. "The Grand Inquisitor" segment in Dostoyevsky's *Brothers Karamazov.*

part of the constitution (thereby providing it with additional mechanisms to guarantee that Italians would be good Catholics).[8] The Church also wanted to maintain its religious monopoly. The alarm it expressed over the advance of Protestantism in Italy was as great as its alarm over Communism and the Masonic movement (Durand 1991, 373–404; Casella 1992; Falconi 1956, 299–314).[9]

In the year preceding the first regular postwar legislative election (April 1948), the Church, though now constitutionally protected, still believed that its very survival was at stake. Azione Cattolica leaders compared the Communists to the Ottoman Turks; they ranked the electoral battle in significance to that of the Viennese Christians fighting off the Muslim hordes (Durand 1991, 644). Despite PCI leader Palmiro Togliatti's conciliatory stance and his recognition that the Italian people were very attached to Catholicism (Falconi 1956, 74–75; Ginsborg 1990, 101), the Church argued that if the Communists were to win a legislative majority, then Church altars "would be burned and ravaged" (in Durand 1991, 643).[10] Prior to the aforementioned election of 1948, the pope rallied a group of Catholic youth to arms, telling them to display "personal courage" in order to save Italy for God.[11] The embattled perspective persisted: at the 1954 beatification ceremony for Innocent XI, Pius XII drew a parallel between the situation of the Eastern European Churches under Communist rule and the Christian Churches during the Islamic expansion of the seventeenth century (Riccardi 1985a, 69), praising the new saint for having "led the resistance of Christian nations against Islam" (in Riccardi 1988, 109). The Church, as the self-proclaimed center of Christianity, felt the threats to other national churches as corporal assaults. Whatever the actual events, the Church's position at the center of the Catholic world— a position it, with political assistance, fashioned—magnified their impact.

That being the case, the Italian constitution seemed merely a paper shield against the perceived threats. Though the Church had been strident about constitutional guarantees, it did not think that its provisions could

---

[8] While the Church failed to have marriage made explicitly indissoluble, by virtue of the Italian constitution's recognition of the concordat's validity, divorce was illegal. It took the 1974 referendum to make divorce legal (Ginsborg 1990, 101; Clark 1984, 381–82).

[9] AAC, PG, X 26, fondo corrispondenza con le diocesi 1926–72, Catanzaro, survey of Mar. 4, 1949.

[10] Togliatti, for his part, lamented in January 1947 the Church's "exercising a terror using spiritual methods against a party like ours" and noted that "we don't want Italy [to be] lacerated by ideological and religious conflicts. We'll leave that responsibility to the Church, if it wants it" (Falconi 1956, 75, 80).

[11] Speech of Dec. 8, printed in *Osservatore Romano*, Dec. 9–10, 1947.

guarantee the Church's status.[12] As an Azione Cattolica publication stated, "The new Italian constitution, recently in force, has saved by judicial means many Christian values. . . . But it offers also many erroneous interpretations, many applications contrary to our faith and our Christian social principles" (in Casella 1992, 85). The Church, in its own view, would have to be protected by political and social means as well, arguing one of the points this book makes—that institutional structures and provisions do not in and of themselves determine how they will be utilized.

The Vatican justified its political intervention by arguing that such was legitimate when morals were at stake (Magister 1979, 20; Webb 1958, 44); indeed, Pius XII asserted that the Church's jurisdiction extended to *anything* that could possibly affect morality (in Scoppola 1988, 57). Since the Church viewed itself as the rightful religious power in Italy, it had no compunction about persecuting rival sects, or asking the state to do so. In 1952, Cardinal Ildefonso Schuster, archbishop of Milan, publicly complained that whereas earlier Italian clergy had "the great advantage of the aid of civil power in the repression of heresy," the Italian Church currently did not. It, instead, was "impotent" (Falconi 1956, 311) and merely sat by as the Protestants penetrated the population. Schuster (perhaps deliberately) underestimated the Church's power to harass infidels and to compel Italians to give up one faith for another. In Treviso, in 1949, the city turned off the potable water supply of a family who rented a room to a Protestant. In Novara, a secretarial school expelled a Protestant student. Priests refused burials in village cemeteries to those who were Protestants, even exhuming some (Falconi 1956, 304–5). But Protestants were not the only concern of the Church hierarchs. Secular rivals posed equal if not greater threats.

The Italian Church and Communism

Pius XII was a staunch anti-Communist; under his leadership, the Church saw itself as a fortress, protecting Italy from unspeakable (though highly publicized) evils.[13] As Cardinal (archbishop of Florence) Elia Dalla Costa

---

[12] The constitution read that "the state and the Catholic Church are, each in its own sphere, independent and sovereign. Their relations are regulated by the Lateran Pacts" (in Clark 1984, 321).

[13] Pius XII temporized until Hitler's demise; thereafter his doubts about the Allied alliance including the USSR were publicly expressed. The USSR's treatment of the Russian Orthodox Church, and the fate of the Eastern European Churches, gave Pius cause for concern and fuel for his view that Communism was the greatest evil to emerge in the twentieth century (Riccardi 1985a, 66–70).

asked rhetorically in his 1945 Christmas message, "Do you want an irreligious, atheist, Masonic government, which then would progressively try to eliminate from Italy every trace of faith and Christian morality?" (in Magister 1979, 62). He went on to emphasize other horrors that would obtain should the "enemies of the faith" enter the government (63, 65).[14] A Capuchin monk from Calabria (southern Italy), alluding to the red in the Communist flag, declared, "Our flag is white, and if it must become red it will be only after the civil war has stained it with the blood of future Christian martyrs."[15] The Church evoked the specters of civil war, free love, poverty, and chaos. It was a rhetoric that those repeating it, if they did not already, came to believe.

Pius XII saw an opportunity to bring straying souls back to the "Father Church" (Magister 1979, 135; Prandi 1968, 199–200) but used a stick (excommunication), not a carrot. His priorities and traditional attitude toward the laity and toward the industrialized world were evident in his dealings with the worker-priest movement, which had started in Paris in 1943. Pius XII was skeptical, saying, "If one has to choose between apostolic efficacy and sacerdotal integrity, I choose sacerdotal integrity" (Riccardi 1988, 67). He effectively ended the movement in 1954 by reorganizing it in a watered-down version (Dansette 1957, 300–303; see also chap. 7).

Pius XII's view of Italy's political problems influenced the Church's approach. The problem was, in a nutshell, that the Communists threatened the end of Christendom. Postwar elections were thus a matter of being "for or against Christ," not of choosing between two political programs (Durand 1991, 362; Riccardi 1988, 90). His 1947 Christmas radio message rephrased Hamlet's famous query: "To be with Christ or against Christ; that is the whole question" (Falconi 1967, 266). The Church, since the "threat" was not merely political, had to mobilize self-conscious Catholics to occupy all parts of society. It therefore put extensive efforts into rallying Italians against the "false prophets" of liberalism and Communism (Durand 1991, 370–404).[16] That Pius XI had had a similar attitude helped: Pius XII did not have to struggle to mold a recalcitrant hierarchy to his outlook.

---

[14] See also the assessment of Sergio Paronetto (a close friend of Monsignor Montini), *Il communismo visto dal Vaticano,* Dec. 8, 1944 (in Scoppola 1988, 272–77).

[15] ACS, MinIntGab, 1944–46, b. 26, f. 1982, rapporto del prefetto, July 8, 1945.

[16] Magister argues that the Church's stance toward the Allies was pragmatic, accepting the U.S. alliance with the USSR (while angry at the bombing of Rome); and that its later, uneasy tolerance of the PCI in the first postwar government had its roots in that pragmatism (1979, 10–11). Yet it certainly did not tolerate the rise of the Catholic Communist Party (1938–45) (1979, 11) and by 1948 was condemning the United Nations and its "Great Power Unity" (Falconi 1967, 267).

Politics took on an apocalyptic aspect; in his address to the crowds in St. Peter's Square after the 1948 Easter mass, Pius XII did not reflect on the Resurrection, as popes traditionally did, but stated, "The great hour of the Christian conscience has struck." The Church and Italy were at the crossroads, and Italians were exhorted to consider what that meant "for Rome, for Italy, for the world" (Riccardi 1988, 90). The Church's sense of importance was displayed in its view that the Italians' choice would affect political outcomes throughout the world for years to come, not just in Italy until the next election.

Given actual conditions, the Church's response may not have seemed appropriate or strictly rational. Public opinion polls in the month before the 1948 election revealed that 45% intended to vote for the DC, versus only 27% for the Socialist/Communist list ("Popular Front"). Pius XII himself, on April 6, 1948, told U.S. diplomat Myron Taylor that he expected the elections to renew the existing DC-led government from which the Communists had been expelled (Durand 1991, 645–46). As early as December 1947, at the same time Pius XII was exhorting Catholic youth to defend the faith, the Church was convinced the DC was in good shape. Moreover, the government was prepared, in the event of a Communist insurrection, to repress it. It had reinforced the prefects' powers, stashed armaments, and purged the police and army of leftist sympathizers (Durand 1991, 646–47). Where was the massive threat that motivated the Church to undertake organizationally costly campaigning for a political party? An explanation that does not take into account how the Church itself defines a situation is incomplete.

One might argue that circumstances compelled the Church to reason as it did, that is, to stress the Communist threat. While there were disagreements about the appropriate strategy in regard to Communism, the preoccupation with it "was common in all the Vatican." Even the relatively progressive secretary Montini was suspicious of Communist Party intentions (Riccardi 1988, 72, 88). Yet organizational leadership matters—to both the assessment of the "threat" and to the choice of strategic response. Pius XII maintained his obsessive anti-Communist stance after Stalin died, when, under Khrushchev, there was a temporary easing of tensions (Falconi 1967). He did not do as his successor, John XXIII, did: precisely when the Cold War was "heating up," John XXIII sought an easing of tensions, in Italy and elsewhere. Montini, while serving Pius XII at the Vatican and later (1954) as archbishop of Milan, suggested that Communism not overwhelm the Church's other concerns. He argued that the Church's position as leader of world Catholicism should not lock it into one particular, narrow strategy.

Under Pius XII, the Church's motives and goals, and its view of its role in society, gave it a high tolerance for the organizational costs it would

TABLE 4.2
French Parliamentary Election Results, 1946–1956, by Party

Party	1946 (Nov.)		1951		1956	
	% of Vote	% of Seats	% of Vote	% of Seats	% of Vote	% of Seats
Christian Democrats (MRP)	25.3	29	11.1	15.1	10.4	13.1
Communists (PCP)	26.7	30.5	24.3	17.8	24.8	16.2
Socialists (SFIO)	17.6	16.5	13.2	17.3	13.4	16.2
Gaullists (RPF)	—	—	19.8	19.7	—	—
Conservatives	7.5	—	9.3	—	13.8	—
Radicals	11.7	10.1	10.0	14.2	8.7	10.2

Source: Calculated from Raoul Husson *Elections et Referendums des 21 octobre 1945, 5 mai et 2 juin 1946. Résultats par département et par canton* (Paris: Le Monde, 1946); Ministère de l'Intérieur; *Les Élections Législatives du 17 juin 1951* (Paris: La Documentation Française, 1953); Ministère de l'Intérieur, *Les Élections Législatives du 2 janvier 1956* (Paris: La Documentation Française, 1958).

have to incur in order to reach even some of its goals. The French Church, with a rather different perspective, had a lower threshold.

FRANCE

When General Charles de Gaulle later wrote that he had "a certain image of France," it was clear that the Fourth Republic had not fit that image. De Gaulle's government, formed in opposition to Vichy in 1943 (in Algiers) gradually won recognition by the Allies and became the first government of liberated France. De Gaulle remained as the head of state until his resignation in January 1946.[17]

Elections to the Constituent Assembly in liberated France were held in 1945. The Communist Party (PCF), Socialists (SFIO), and Christian Democrats (MRP) split the results, making the constitution a battleground between those three political forces.

This time it was the Christian Democratic party's turn to be naive, thinking that the cooperation achieved in the Resistance by the three parties could be carried into the new (Fourth) Republic. The party made concessions in a number of areas in order to maintain harmony. The Radicals, blamed for the failings of the Third Republic, and the old Right,

[17] On the motives for his resignation, see Charlot 1983, 18–39; Lacouture 1985, 225–49; Williams 1964, 22.

blamed for Vichy, were (temporarily) discredited. With de Gaulle's resignation, the PCF, SFIO, and MRP formed a tripartite governing coalition and fought about the constitution, the first version of which was rejected by voters in May 1946. The second version, approved by a disaffected electorate that October, provided for a bicameral legislature with a powerful lower house, a weak executive branch, and a proportional representation electoral system. The Church was not given subsidies for its schools, but freedom of "educational choice" was guaranteed (Wright 1970; Williams 1964, 20–25; Rioux 1987). In the fall of 1947, the PCF began actively opposing the Fourth Republic and the other two major parties. De Gaulle, railing against the institutions and parties of the Fourth Republic, reentered politics with the launch of his party, the Rassemblement du Peuple Français (RPF). Since de Gaulle's party was immediately popular with many voters, the Republic now had two large and popular parties opposed to its very existence.

French Catholic Church Motives

A priest will act wisely—the man of all, who
is sent to save all souls—not entering any
[political] party, at least not as an activist; . . .
a party would separate him from those who
belong to another party.
(*French clergyman, 1945*)

The French Catholic Church had several concerns that influenced its inclination to only briefly engage in party politics. The first was to "re-Christianize" the country. It viewed with alarm survey findings that in many parts of France, less than half the population attended Mass regularly; in many areas, particularly the worker *banlieus* (suburban ghettos), no more than 1% of the residents were practicing Catholics (Dansette 1957, 66–67). The Church wanted to reverse the decline of Catholicism and make Catholics aware that they needed the Church for more than just burial rites, and that no substitutes (in the form of Protestantism or Communism) were suitable.

The second concern derived from the first: it was to protect religious schools (primary and secondary) by maintaining state subsidies to these private schools. Church schools were seen as the crucial means of stopping Communism (in contrast to the Italian Church, which demanded a variety of political mechanisms) and of ensuring a supply of future parishioners.[18]

---

[18] Religious beliefs and the knowledge associated with them can be costly to acquire; that investment raises the opportunity costs of defecting to agnosticism or to another religion.

It worried, as Cardinal Feltin, archbishop of Paris, said, that "even those who say they are still well disposed toward the Church" think that "religion is nothing more than an ensemble of aesthetic or archaeological considerations." Worse, there were those who saw the Church as "nothing but a perpetuator of petty, annoying prescriptions" or "a commercial administration of gestures and pious rituals" (in Dansette 1957, 76). Complicating its plans was its goal of retaining some independence from Rome, primarily by responding to perceived national needs with national methods, not those dictated by the Vatican.

The Church's definition of its goals and its decision on tactics were affected by its relations with the new state. The bulk of the governing parties' leadership had been Resistance members. Given the Church's record under Vichy, those parties did not look sympathetically at the Church's interests (or leadership). The Church was constrained from pressing hard for what it felt were essential arrangements.

The subsidies to private schools that had been restored in 1941 by the Vichy regime were immediately challenged by the Communist, Socialist, and Radical parties at the outset of the Fourth Republic. So too was the liberty to choose "freedom of instruction" (Wright 1970, 139–40, 158–59). In the final versions of both the First and Second Constitutions liberty of instruction (i.e., the parents' right to choose public or private schooling for their children) was not guaranteed.

From 1939 to 1949, the French Church's most prominent office, archbishop of Paris, was held by Cardinal Emmanuel Suhard (1874–1949). Suhard's concern as he rose in the religious ranks seemed to lie with the apostolic, proselytizing work of the clergy. His emphasis as cardinal, first at Reims and then at Paris, was on missionary work, not in the French colonies but in France. Cardinal Suhard, in contrast to Pius XII, noted that the French Church could not afford to be hidebound; "The Church, despite the presence of buildings and priests, is no longer visible for a certain number of men . . . and it is good that priests become witnesses again" (1949, in Riccardi 1993, 67). He conceded that the Church needed the world as much as the world needed it: "the world needs the Church for its life; the Church needs the world for its growth and achievement" (in Vinatier 1983, 356). Unlike Pius XII, Suhard seemed reluctant to draw the line on where Christians should stand politically. He recognized intricate patterns and thought that a "Catholic synthesis" could overcome the strictures of integralism and the failings of the modern secular world. That synthesis let Catholics "fully engage" in temporal tasks while not forgetting "the primacy of the spiritual" (Vinatier 1983, 360).

Thus, the more individuals had been educated in Catholicism, the less likely they were thought to quit practicing (Gill 1998, 210–11; Iannacconne 1995).

Suhard was followed by Maurice Feltin (1883–1975), who held the Paris archbishopric from 1949 to 1966 and was cardinal from 1952 to 1975. Feltin was nearly indistinguishable from Suhard in his attitudes and actions.

Rather than responding aggressively to the anticlerical parties, as the Italian Church did, the French Church tried to adopt a modus vivendi with the Republic. The failure of Vichy seemed to have convinced it that Catholic hegemony in France was not possible. It tried to present a low profile, knowing that, "despite all [the Church's] clarifications," some would "continue to brandish before the masses the hackneyed specter of 'clericalism.' "[19] Though many French citizens had openly welcomed Vichy and did not see the Church's actions as reprehensible, the Church hierarchy needed to overcome the opprobrium of having acquiesced to, indeed been a supporter of, the Vichy regime. It did so by arguing its innocence and seeking to protect its hierarchy from prosecution and removal. Yet it could not give up politics: education law was controlled by the parliament. As the Church explained, since politicians' actions had serious repercussions on moral, family, and educational issues, it had to be concerned with politics.[20]

Why did the French hierarchy behave this way when in Italy it gave no ground on the schools question? The main answer is that the French Church, in contrast to the Italian, drew a line between spiritual and other matters. It recognized a separation of Church and state and so placed limits on its own intervention into political matters. The Church reminded Catholics that it had "the right and even the duty to state which part [on public policy] to take." However, it noted that it "does so only rarely, and when spiritual interests are directly and gravely at stake, but it does so while in full consciousness of fulfilling its mission and it estimates highly its opportunity for intervening" (Suhard, in Deroo 1955, 181).

The hierarchy, however, was divided. Some in the Church were reluctant to press the Church's claims for fear of stimulating a harsh anticlerical attack. Monsignor Elchinger said of the Barangé law of 1951, which restored a minimal level of state subsidies to private schools, "that law wound up poisoning the political atmosphere" (in Lecourt 1978, 57). Others were adamant that the Church not compromise: in 1950, the bishop of Luçon (in the Vendée of western France) advocated that Catho-

---

[19] *SRP,* Jan. 19, 1946, 41–42.

[20] Along these lines, the Church stated, "It [the Church] has never imposed on them [Christians] a rigid method of conquest. Always realistic, it knows to respect the inclinations of its faithful. . . . but Catholics cannot conduct themselves without limits, anywhere, always, and in all directions of thought, of worship, and of the apostolate; then, yes, there would be no agreement." The author then indicated that "anarchy and despotism" of thought could be the result (*SRP,* Apr. 13, 1946, 251–52).

lics not pay their taxes until Catholic schools were given subsidies (Williams 1957, 339). Cardinal Feltin reminded voters in 1951 that despite other pressing problems, "school choice" was of "primordial" importance (Charlot 1957, 132). Two days prior to Feltin's statement, Cardinal Liénart of Lille told the press that given the importance of other problems, and in the interest of peace, the hierarchy was avoiding emphasizing the school question. In the department of Morbihan (Brittany), the bishop of Vannes, Monsignor Le Bellec, denied the sacraments to a family that sent its children to public schools.[21] Some in the hierarchy, although declaring, "For a Christian only the Christian school is fully satisfactory," accommodated themselves to the anticlerical culture of France. Monsignor Chappoulie noted that "in a country of divided beliefs the formula of a neutral school" is the only workable solution in many cases (Bosworth 1962, 286). There was no consistency in political positions across dioceses. The contrast with Italy is striking: the Vatican would not accept that Italy could have "divided beliefs," that Catholicism could peacefully coexist with other beliefs.

Some of the Church's struggles for presence involved maintaining the trademark, in other words, sole distribution rights to the "product"—salvation and the sacraments. The French Church exhorted Catholics to use its product instead of a generic (Deroo 1955, 223). Having Catholicism declared the religion of the state was the optimal solution; so too was having rival cults banned. This is one reason Vichy was so attractive to the Church—with competitors outlawed, all rents accrued to the Church. After the war, the Church had to continually remind Catholics that it was a relevant institution and necessary for "civilization": French bishops declared, "Whatever the external successes of modern civilizations constructed outside the Church, one must affirm that they cannot be authentic civilizations unless saved by the Church" (Dec. 24, 1953, Deroo 1955, 220).

France's Action Catholique felt the effects. The hierarchy viewed Action Catholique as "the incarnation of the spiritual in *all [aspects of] human life*," not "the incarnation of the spiritual in *the temporal*." Action Catholique was seen as a means to Christianize institutions and social life, but "it must respect the autonomy of temporal institutions" (March 1949, in Deroo 1955, 191). Action Catholique "should not engage the Church in the realm of other questions, on which the Church does not want to speak. It must, like the Church, respect the autonomy of the state in its proper domain. It [Action Catholique] does not direct the temporal, but ani-

---

[21] On Liénart, see Charlot 1957, 132–33; on Le Bellec, Bosworth 1962, 287. Bosworth (79) notes that the statements of bishops and archbishops on the school question were not correlated with the number or existence of Catholic schools in a diocese. A department is the major territorially bounded administrative division of France; there were approximately 95 of them under the Fourth Republic.

mates it" (ACA, March 13, 1946, in Deroo 1955, 192). While some might argue that this perspective was an inevitable result of the Church's diminished status and possibilities in the twentieth century, it should be recalled that the Gallican Church of the sixteenth and seventeenth centuries acknowledged such a distinction—at a time when the Church's influence was high.

The Gallican Church resurfaced in the hierarchy's articulation of the Church's relations to the state after World War II. Bishop Blanchet noted that the Church was a part of history: "The Church is in history, without being submerged nor carried by it." The Church would not judge "always and immediately" the legitimacy of existing governments (Deroo 1955, 341). In the mid-1950s, Monsignor Emile Guerry, the secretary of the Assembly of Cardinals and Archbishops (see below), argued that papal pronouncements could be treated with "respect, prudence, delicate and docile attention" or a "favorable predisposition" (in Bosworth 1962, 50 n. 12), while the Vatican was arguing, "No Catholic is permitted to consider a Papal document out of date because the circumstances that fostered it have changed. Only the Church can make such a judgement" (50 n. 12).

Nevertheless, the shame of Vichy and the defeat of the pro-Catholic state prompted the Church to examine its balance sheet. The Church was worried about losing the working class, if it was not already lost, to Communism: its "apostolic action had to be centered on the working class" (Suhard, Sept. 1945, in Deroo 1955, 196). But its means of bringing the proletariat to the Church were essentially mere proselytizing; it thought that by converting France to Christianity (the Catholic version, of course), justice would prevail, "abolishing all painful oppressions," and there would be the "fraternal love without which there cannot be true social peace" (cardinals of France, Feb. 2, 1945, in Deroo 1955, 197). These were platitudes that may have seemed more far-fetched than the program of the Communists. The Church frequently lectured capitalists about being greedy but did not exert any political pressure to change capitalists' ability to exploit workers.[22]

When several clergy published their research on the decline of Catholicism as a practiced faith in much of France, other clergy and much of the hierarchy concluded that the Church's concern should be on re-Christianizing the country, not on politics. The "delicate problem" was to "Christianize a modern society that is not pagan but de-Christianized, that is to say, which turns itself in large part from the Christianity that it believes to be an outdated religion."[23] The Church's worries were not so much

---

[22] ACA, Apr. 28, 1954 (Deroo 1955, 176–77); ACA, Feb. 28, 1945 (Deroo 1955, 157–58 and 295–96); cardinal of Bordeaux, June 19, 1953 (Deroo 1955, 303–5); Pierrard 1991.

[23] CCR, Mar. 1945, 17 n. 68. The first report, by Henri Godin and Yves Daniel, La France, pays de mission? was released in 1943 (Paris: La Cerf, 1950). Ferdnand Boulard's

political as religious: "The present hour demands that we do not tremble, but act. And act quickly. Because if, as Pius XI said, the grand scandal of the Church of the nineteenth century was to have lost the working class, in the future one could say that the great sin of the baptized of the twentieth century was to not have been Catholics."[24] The contrast with Italy is striking. While one could also have said that Italy was a country needing missionary work, the Italian Church's preoccupation was not with individual conversion but mass subjection to Church political directives.

The call to arms in 1945 was for priests to re-Christianize France, not to ensure that a particular party win office—for the French Church, that was largely irrelevant to the problem (cardinals of France, Feb. 2, 1945, in Deroo 1955, 197). This perspective is significant. For the French lower clergy, and to some extent the hierarchy, the real problem of the Church was that France had become a *pays de mission*—a country needing missionary work. Large regions of France were no longer Catholic; the Church could neither presume membership nor subservience. Since a de-Christianized France enabled the Socialists, Communists, and other anticlericals to win elections and influence public policies, the Church would have to reconvert the French to Catholicism.

Although the French Church was more constrained, relative to the Italian Church, from political intervention, it is clear that the Church was still a potential ally of the MRP. It was determined to be active in French society. Invoking Marshal Foch's principle, a clergyman noted, "The best defense is a good offense."[25] It did not abandon its efforts to direct sociopolitical, economic, and cultural developments in France, nor its efforts to remain a viable organization replacing its deceased membership and retaining primary control over its activities (as opposed to letting the Vatican gain such control).

The French Church clearly struggled to define the appropriate realms of action of the Church and state. Where Pius XII and the Italian hierarchy took it for granted that the Church held sway over "the city" (temporal government), writings of the French episcopate indicate that the issue was a major preoccupation. Unlike the Italian Church, the French Church approached politics cautiously, striving to justify actions that the Italian Church took for granted as its prerogatives. For the Vatican, the question of Church and state authority had been settled; the issue at hand was to use the Church's power to ensure that the Vatican had the advantages

---

many studies were published in various issues of the *CCR*. Perhaps the report that most disturbed the Church was Boulard's map of the percentages of practicing Catholics (see *CCR*, Nov. 1947). The map is reprinted in Le Bras 1955, 324+. See also Le Bras 1945.

[24] "Le Sens de l'Eglise," *SRP*, Feb. 10, 1951, 134.

[25] Père R. P. Carré, director of *Revue des Jeunes* at the conference of Sacerdotales des Oèuvres, Dec. 17–18, 1946 (reported in *SRP*, Mar. 22, 1947, 462).

that were, in its eyes, rightfully those of the Church. Distressed by "the temptation [of "modern man"] to put his confidence exclusively in his own abilities and to not await his salvation except from himself" (bishops, Dec. 24, 1953, in Deroo 1955, 219), the French Church struggled to explain why it should not be relegated to private affairs and "mystical speculations" (Feltin, in Dansette 1957, 76).

The French Church and Communism

The Church perceived Communism as a severe threat, and the conflict with it as a battle between the City *with*, and the City *without* God.[26] Although the Church made it clear which party Catholics could *not* vote for, its battle tactics confused Catholics about which party they could or should support. In contrast to the Vatican, the French Church argued that the *péril marxiste* was to be handled primarily in the moral and intellectual realms, not political. Even though the Communist Party had been pushed out of the government in 1947, the Church still considered Communism a threat (as in Italy)—yet a threat on a level more fundamental than that of politics: thought and belief.[27] By proposing a doctrine, a new conception of the world and of life, Communism was a "pseudoreligion," a spiritual problem (Pierrard 1991, 155). Thus, "one doesn't bar the route to a current of thought by political measures. That would be as effective as damming a river with a filet of fish" (Boulard 1946, 38). The institutional barriers, such as might be provided by a confessional political party or by legislation, could not, in the Church's eyes, alter the very interests of those encapsulated by the party or affected by the legislation. In the clergy's view, because Communists analyzed events and provided a rationale for their occurrence, it was incumbent upon Catholicism to do the same—responding "to the present needs of the intellect." On the "moral plain," it was necessary to be a zealous missionary, even a martyr for Christ (Boulard 1946, 38).

Cardinal Liénart warned Christians not to be deceived by the PCF's campaign for peace: Communism "has a very singular way of conceiving of peace and freedom; it does not at all correspond to that which we have in mind when we speak those same words" (in Deroo 1955, 182). The barrier to Communism would instead be provided by Christians, many in Action Catholique, taking action in a "Christian way." The rural clergy's

---

[26] In 1944, just after D-Day, Cardinal Suhard (then archbishop of Bordeaux) indicated he thought the Communists, not the Nazis, were the barbarian infidels. He praised the German fight against the Soviets as "a European crusade" (June 7, 1944, in Halls 1995, 186); also Duquesne 1966, 92.

[27] Ferdnand Boulard, "Reflexions sur le Péril Marxiste," *CCR*, Nov. 1946, 36–38.

view of Catholicism denied class and other divisions: with a near monopoly on charity and the union of all in the village, "we are unbeatable" (Boulard 1946, 38). Catholics were to participate "everywhere," as the "yeast" or "rising agent" of society.[28] Thus, organizational efforts were meant not primarily to counter anticlerical political threats but to re-Christianize France. Political influence would come from the renewed dominance of Catholics in all areas, as well as from lobbying, attempts at associating with a political party, and creating interest groups. The Communist threat was not confronted head-on in politics. Church energies were directed to the social milieu.

The Church, however, often hedged. It is not always clear why the French Church was not the aggressively anti-Communist organization that the Italian Church was. It is perhaps owing to the Church seeing a disjunction between thought and politics that Cardinal Suhard could say in 1949 that it was possible for Communists and Christians to cooperate to a small extent if the two political parties had "precise and limited objectives" (in Bosworth 1962, 49 n. 9), while Monsignor Guerry (secretary of the ACA) could declare that "even if Marxism were perfect from a worldly standpoint, even if it assured peace and prosperity to men and nations, even if it suppressed all earthly injustice, the Church would maintain its absolute condemnation" (in Bosworth 1962, 49, his translation).

Significantly for Church actions vis-à-vis politics, the rural clergy were willing to admit pluralism in agrarian unions, cooperatives, and mutual societies and suggested that if these bodies were pluralistic, all should unite in one organization recognized by the state for administration, reconciliation and adjudication, and consultation with the state. Communism should neither be feared, nor reviled; "if collaboration [with the PCF] is necessary for the good of the country, it should be done with openness and clarity."[29]

One obvious question quickly arises: if the Church in France realized by the 1950s what dire straits rural and industrial workers were in, why did it not try to approach them through the MRP, a party that had as a declared aim that of preventing workers from leaning toward Communism by improving their conditions? Skepticism of method is one answer: the Church did not see party politics as having the capacity to change the moral state of workers. Second, the hierarchy gave lip service to impoverished workers, but its distaste for the political solutions offered (Communism, nationalizations) deterred it. Finally, those clergy who were deeply disturbed by the actual conditions of French workers, primarily the

---

[28] *SRP*, Mar. 22, 1947, 395–96.
[29] *CCR*, Jan.–Feb. 1945, 32.

worker-priests, became convinced that Communism, not Christian Democracy, was the political solution. The latter had never shown a willingness to put itself into the trenches, as the priests had.

CONCLUSION

One of the most striking differences between the French and Italian
Churches was that the Italian Church under Pius XII would not consider
any form of collaboration between Catholics and Communists in postwar
Italy. One possible explanation is structural, stemming from differing positions in Christendom. The Vatican, as the self-proclaimed seat of Christianity, would see Communism in its "homeland" as a direct threat to
itself as an institution and as an ideology. Since the Vatican was responsible
for the national Churches in the East bloc, and the French Church was
not, the Vatican could easily develop a greater distaste for Communism.
Further, it would, due to its position and its relations with East bloc governments, see that *politics* was responsible for the Eastern Churches' situation. The Vatican's hierarchical structure ensured that all "sensations" of
Communism were transmitted to, or focused on, the center.

In contrast, the French Church, while it could argue for a Catholic
interpretation of France's heritage, was not the focal point of Christendom. Nor was it directly involved in the issue of the Churches' treatment in the East bloc. The French Church's decentralized structure also
diffused its reactions to Communism. There was no central organ that was
the repository of reports on Communist Party action, or the focal point
for anticlerical activity. The French Church's less political interpretation
of the Communist "threat" was not due to a less active Communist presence in France (as compared to Italy); for it, Communism was more of a
moral, not political, problem. The French Church had no reason to feel
secure: it had often come under attack from secular governments. Differing structural positions led the two organizations to view the role of
politics differently.

No matter what the structural positions and associated incentives, perceptions are a critical factor. In the cases here, Church leaders' views of
their role in Christian civilization were important. The Italian Church
saw, in the way postwar politicians were organizing, an opportunity to
control a party that, if backed by the Church, had the potential of controlling the Italian government. The French Church, knowing the history of
French Church-state relations, saw no such possibility. The French Church
faced a spiritual contest and reasoned that were it to be heavy handed, the
results would backfire. Its actions were often more indirect than those of
the Italian Church: by re-Christianizing France, the Church would create

voters who would vote for Christian parties.[30] The reader might object that these perceptions are merely derivative of the context in which each Church found itself. Certainly, I have indicated the key environmental factors; yet the environments still allowed for choice. The French Church perceived Communism as a threat to itself and its followers, and it could have responded in ways similar to those of the Vatican. It did not. I suggest that the reason is partly due to leader perceptions.

While the Catholic Church is unlike other interest groups in several respects, particularly in its claims to universality and authority, its strategies are, like other interest groups, affected by several similar factors. Those include the group's perception of its role and of what it is trying to accomplish, the institutional and ideological distance from the previous regime, public legitimacy, and available party allies. Organizations do not all react effectively or quickly to threats and new situations (e.g., the sudden loss of political assets, prestige, membership, funding opportunities, influence). The experience and actions of the Italian and French Churches illustrate these differences, as well as highlight some of the similarities in how organizations deal with a changing political environment. Having been repudiated at Liberation, the French Church saw itself as compelled to justify its presence in, and relevance to, worldly affairs. In contrast, Pius XII took the Church's relevance for granted. Where the French Church had to *ask* for recognition, the Vatican could *demand* it.

Church traditions have been invented, culled, and revised over the centuries. Popes, based on their predispositions and their political and spiritual goals, select among them when their control of the Church gives them the latitude to do so. Pius XII preferred to emphasize the hierarchical and orthodox aspects of Catholicism at the expense of proselytizing. Cardinals Suhard and Feltin responded to the perceived "de-Christianization" of France with less orthodox methods, using their leadership to encourage missionary work in France and to discourage political ties.

The policies on which the Churches would not give ground reflected their ideas of what to accomplish in the new postwar societies. The very fact that the Churches existed in temporal society meant that their choices would be made under constraints. What set the context was the institutional and ideological distance of the Church from the previous regime, the structure of the Church, and the political entrepreneurship of the Churches' leaders. Not all of their preferred options were available; the Churches had to take into account the sociopolitical limits imposed on their behavior. Those limits differed in France and Italy, leading the Churches to set different agendas, even as they defined their overarching tasks differently.

---

[30] Cardinal Suhard, "Essor ou déclin de l'Eglise?" *SRP*, Feb. 22, 1947, 245.

CHAPTER 5

Selecting an Ally: The Catholic Church and Christian Democracy in Italy and France

One of the issues facing an interest group, especially in a fledgling democratic system, is whether to ally with one political party, many, or none. Affiliation with parties, however, entails risks and costs for an interest group. The French Church, which needed far more help than the Italian to recover lost ground after the war, linked only superficially and briefly with a political party. The Italian Church, emerging unscathed from the war, needed little help, yet forged strong connections with a party. Why did the French Church not expend resources when it needed to, while the Italian Church invested heavily when there was little reason for it to do so? And why did both Churches choose, for whatever links they established, Christian Democratic parties when there were others more willing to be explicitly pro-clerical? Why did the Vatican, with all its resources, not create its own party, but instead ally with one that refused to subordinate itself completely to the Church? There were and are distinct advantages to *not* allying with just one party. Why did the Churches forgo those benefits? It is easy enough to say that "the structure of incentives," in conjunction with their perspectives, determined their choices, but that evades the questions of *which* incentives, and how those incentives interacted with interest group identity to yield particular outcomes or similar choices despite differences in perspective and in context. What were the elements common to the process of ally selection by the French and Italian Churches? What elements differentiated the national Churches?

First, both faced roughly similarly structured states: parliamentary democratic political systems. Political parties, not a dictator or authoritarian regime formally independent of the masses, were the key to public policy formation. Second, both desired to establish or expand their influence, and that influence would be affected, as they well knew from prior experience, by government policies. Public bureaucracies could not be discounted, but the access points to them were either guarded by the parties or off-limits. Third, early action was crucial: the first election(s) would select members to the parliament that would write the new constitution; the next election would decide which parties would enter the legislature. Because the results would have a lasting impact on the Church, it, like other interest groups, had a strong incentive to mobilize effectively, trying to ensure that its preferences would be favored by the electoral and institutional outcomes.[1]

Both Churches wanted a defense against what they perceived to be an impending sociopolitical and economic revolution led by the Marxist Left; hence, they sought political parties capable of resisting that threat, parties that could and would use the state apparatus to eliminate Communism. In the early years of the new republics, the Italian and French Churches both chose to support the nascent Christian Democratic parties. By way of a market model, this chapter reviews the logic behind an interest group's choosing to support one or several parties. The opportunity costs of each choice are weighed against the group's preference for the "product" being sold by the party and the party's ability to deliver it.

Interest groups vary in the extent and nature of support they give to political parties. They may endorse candidates or the party as a whole, or supply campaign workers, organizers, logistical support (including office space and facilities for rallies and meetings), and financing. The Italian Church did all of those things, while the French limited itself mostly to endorsing a party. That divergence can be explained with reference to the Churches' respective status in their societies and to the perspectives of the leadership.

THE MARKET MODEL

Because an interest group searches for a political party supplier of policy, I begin with a simple supply-demand model. According to that structure, when there exists a demand for a good or service, suppliers compete with each other to sell, while customers shop for the best deal, competing with each other by offering more for the scarcer goods. The supply-demand relation is a competitive one—not just between the suppliers and between the consumers, but between supplier and consumer. Second, nonmarket preferences may interfere with the operation of supply and demand, leading to rejections of apparently rational transactions. The model needs to be applied with caution: while there may be a demand from an interest group for a particular type of party, due to institutional and political relationships under the prior regime or to organizational ideologies and electoral systems, there may be no suppliers.[2]

---

[1] On the importance of founding elections, see Bogdanor 1990; Munck and Leff 1997; O'Donnell and Schmitter 1986.

[2] The supply-demand phenomenon is also characterized by competition between the supplier and "demander." Consumers seek the help of product safety commissions, of antitrust and "truth in advertising" legislation, of price regulation and product liability rules; suppliers seek market protection through preferential taxation and government subsidies, the forma-

Interest groups and political parties are in a mutually dependent (or symbiotic) relationship. The party needs group support for votes, organizational infrastructure, and activists; the group needs the party for legislation. The interest group, unless it radically transforms itself, cannot become its own political supplier, and, excepting perhaps authoritarian political systems, the party cannot provide itself its own votes. For the interest group, the supply of parties is less than perfect. Parties come into being for a variety of reasons and to meet different interests; these may not match the profile of the interest group. Politics often has high barriers to entry: institutional, organizational, and ideological. Parties require substantial organizational resources (inputs) to become established and survive (Panebianco 1982; Scarrow 1996); some electoral systems can make it difficult to gain office, thus reducing the ability to enter the market; and there may be a limited number of themes that resonate with the voters. Existing parties attempt to restrict rivals and to monopolize the policy arenas (Greenberg and Shepsle 1987). With an imperfect supply, the interest group must either turn itself into a party or create one, either way expending inordinate resources and altering its own organizational purpose and activities; or it must entice some suppliers to offer the desired "product" (policy). To do the latter, the group will have to commit resources to the supplier, which can then use "the business" to pursue its own interests, perhaps diversifying to other "products" (interest groups, demographic categories, ideological preferences). Indeed, the party wants interest group "investors" not in order to build the groups' desired product, but rather the party's product.

Vertical Integration of the Representation Function

The question then is: why doesn't the interest group just vertically integrate, that is, cut out the middlemen (the party politicians) and supply its own politicians? Politics is a specialized field that requires specialized organizations to mediate between state and society. While interest groups (e.g., the Church) have an incentive to influence policy, for several reasons it is not cost effective to form a party. First, the rules of the market may prevent it. In the case of the European Catholic Churches, while they may have had a demand for a certain type of party, supplying it themselves would have elicited outrage at clerical intervention in politics (more so

---

tion of cartels with other suppliers, the establishment of a monopoly, and lobbying to block proconsumer legislation. Consumers however, are dependent upon suppliers to provide what they want at an affordable price, and suppliers are dependent upon consumers to buy what they sell at a profitable price. By definition, consumers cannot be their own suppliers and suppliers cannot sustain themselves by being their own consumers.

in some countries than in others). Second, start-up costs may have been prohibitive: again in the case of the Churches, they would have had to expend enormous organizational resources. This is particularly the case in new political systems (new markets) in which the negative effects of the market's being taken over by another party (i.e., the Communists) are perceived to be high. If the interest group wants an immediate and substantial policy voice, it must corner a large part of the political market right away. The Churches could not just start off with running one or two of their own candidates in secondary (e.g., local) elections.[3] Third, the effects on the organization itself are a factor: creating a party probably would alter the very nature of the interest group and force difficult internal reorganization.

Fourth, there may be high barriers to entry into electoral competition, especially after the first or second elections, when incumbency advantages kick in for the existing parties. Fifth, the range of issues for any one particular interest group is probably too narrow to justify the ongoing costs of organization incurred by becoming a party; and, if it is successful in obtaining its goals, it is even less rational to maintain a permanent organization. Sixth, there are unlikely to be enough "single or limited issue" voters to give specialized interest groups much chance at winning election unless they broaden their appeal. This, however, runs the risk of diluting the credibility and reputation of the interest group. Finally, a party must serve multiple constituencies and therefore prefers that interest groups compromise their demands. Interest groups themselves have an incentive to play brinksmanship and not compromise, thus creating complex bargaining dynamics. Thus, for narrowly defined interest groups (it is debatable how "narrow" the Churches were), it is more cost effective to *not* organize a party. While it is true that a narrow issue party could participate in a coalition government, such parties usually do not make good bargaining partners because they do not have much to give up when it comes to logrolling. Of course, there are some incentives in proportional representation systems for small parties to form, but if these parties do not find a broader constituency, they are likely to fold. Given these costs, we would expect that, unless the Churches could not immediately find a party amenable to promoting their interests, they would not create their own.[4]

---

[3] The latter has been the strategy used by the "Green" or "ecology" parties entering established political systems (Kitschelt 1989, 75).

[4] I thank Tony Gill for helping me to sharpen these points. The electoral system affects how votes are aggregated into seats for political office: this affects the ease with which new parties can become viable, and thus the potential party allies an interest group has. The electoral system has a strong influence on how many parties, what types of parties, and in what numbers they will be able to gain office and influence outcomes, as well as affecting the relative difficulty of getting a new party into office. For example, in postwar Italy, the

The Churches had difficult decisions. Political parties were not all clamoring to fulfill the demand. Each had distinct marketing preferences and capabilities. The Churches could try to shape the supply available, enticing with their own resources (especially influence over the Catholic vote), but had to deal with, from their perspective, less than perfect suppliers. Only if the Church could give the party enough business would the latter possibly agree to supply what the Church wanted; yet that business could also be the key to enabling the party to expand its own enterprise, branching into other fields, cultivating other customers perhaps at odds with the demands of the Church, and raising the "price" the supplier can charge the Church.

The interest group runs the risk that it will lose sight of its primary purpose. The interaction with a political party could turn the interest group into a more political organization. As the Italian Church discovered, the problem was that the priests conflated the party's success with their success: DC victory was equated with "success of the faith," seemingly obviating the need for proselytizing. As the Calabrian Vito Giuseppe Galati complained, "How many times did we have to recognize that the parish had become the electoral market?" (in Malgeri 1985, 118). If it becomes involved in politics through its own party, the Church may have its success in the secular realm (economic policy, public health) cast a shadow of noncredibility or disrepute on the Church's overall goals. Being a poor performer in government may signal that the organization is run poorly, does not have the interests of its constituents in mind, or is just plain wrong, thus casting doubt on the spiritual message and mission of the Church and driving away adherents.

The question for the Church, as with many businesses, becomes whether to contract out to several suppliers (parties) to ensure competitive pricing and an alternative source should one or two of the suppliers fail, or give its business to one supplier (party) that it can presumably better monitor, and that might be more inclined to retool for the quantity of business the Church will bring. Further, frequent party switching may hurt the interest group's credibility among its followers and potential suppliers.

---

electoral system was characterized by relatively large constituencies, no vote threshold for qualifying for seats, with seats distributed proportionately to vote percentages. These features reduced the resources and popularity necessary for a new party to organize and take office—even if its support was concentrated in a small area of the country. In France, on the other hand, although the basic system was also one of proportional representation, the size of the districts and vote aggregation mechanisms produced a bias toward larger, widespread parties (Williams 1964, 504–5; Campbell 1965). Because of this, one could have predicted higher new party survival rates in Italy than in France, and, thus, more opportunities for an interest group to create its own party or sponsor a new one, should the existing ones be judged unsatisfactory. The Italian Church did not take advantage of those opportunities; to

Why Multiple Parties?

These effects put the interest group in competition with others for that
party's political capital; the group now runs the risk that its "supplies"
will not arrive when needed (to sustain membership, fend off a rival). If
the group cultivates several suppliers, its "buying power" with any one of
them is diluted, but it avoids vulnerability to supply bottlenecks. Another
risk of using only one supplier is that if "business" (or votes) is sufficient,
the party may be able, through the exercise of its acquired political power,
to establish a virtual monopoly. The group will be stuck with whatever
product the monopoly cares to supply, and at whatever price. Unless the
interest group is willing to fund the party in full, the party needs to get
other investors. Yet, since the party's use of support is not easily measured
(noise from electoral system, competitors), the investor has difficulty assessing the expected net benefit, and of seeing whether the party is fulfilling its end of the bargain. It may be the case that the politician/party can
exploit the interest group; that is, the party's costs are less than what it is
charging the group, such that it diverts the difference to its own uses.

One risk for a consumer when high-ticket items are involved, or for a
business that has contracted out the supply of various goods and services,
is that the supplier will go out of business. Should there be a problem
with the product, the consumer has no recourse; should the consumer
need more of that product, again, the consumer has no recourse. The
effort that went into finding and arranging a contract with a particular
supplier are sunk costs, including the forgone opportunities of using alternative suppliers. Interest groups face a similar risk. Parties fail. When they
do, their supporting interest groups are unable to recoup organizational
investments and must expend additional resources if they wish to cultivate
another party. Other parties, however, because of prior commitments
(they too have sunk costs, organizational rigidities), may be unable to
"retool" for the new demand.

Another risk, with a different set of consequences, arises because, in
allying with a party, the Church appears partisan or abusive of its spiritual
authority. This latter drawback was argued by one branch of Azione Cattolica (Magister 1979, 127), but proved unimportant in the Vatican's view
(see below). Last but not least is that when the party appears to be, or is,
a winner, it attracts not religiously motivated politicians, but sheer political
opportunists. In Italy, there were plenty, and many of unsavory character.
The Church found its preferred candidates competing with (rival) opportunists for standing on DC party lists.

---

understand why, one must look to other aspects of structure and to other variables discussed
in this chapter.

Why Choose One Party?

The arguments for choosing only one party as an ally depend heavily on notions of transaction costs and obligation. With only one party, it is easier to monitor compliance with group demands and, in theory, to sanction deviance (or at least identify who is responsible for it). Multiple parties may work at cross-purposes; the actions of one may vitiate agreements made with others. One party would, presumably, ensure uniformity of purpose: that party would be more dependent on its ally, feel more obliged to it for having been helped into a monopoly position. The costs of negotiating, of arranging policy positions, are also reduced when there is only one party with which to negotiate. Demands and instructions are easier to convey; messages need not be repeated to, and confirmed by, separate organizations.[5]

Transition politics does give an interest group the opportunity to test either strategy—typically, there are elections for local and regional governments, elections to a constituent assembly, and finally, elections to the regular legislature. During the parties' debates on the new constitution, and during their reign in interim governments, the group has a chance to observe the behavior of the party it selected. This aspect of transitions reduces the immediate opportunity costs of one strategy versus another. It does not, however, indicate to a group which choice to make at the outset. The advantages of one strategy or another are not, in the circumstances of the transition, clear as websterd cut. The parties' behavior and reliability in office have not yet been tested. Any strategy contains risks that could, by some calculi, appear greater than the benefits. In part what matters is the equation used, the values assigned to competing risks and advantages.

Which One?

The ability to procure "product" information is a factor in the group's decision to support a party. First, the group needs to know the specifications of what it might support; second, the group needs to be able to verify what is being supplied. For the first problem, the group must rely on past actions of the leaders and on ideology (Hinich and Munger 1994). It is providing support (electoral resources) for something that won't be deliv-

---

[5] These advantages are most likely to occur in contexts of high party discipline; if parties have little authority over the politicians who run under their name, the interest group may have reason to support several parties (or many politicians across party lines) to guarantee that when that group's issue comes up, it will be addressed.

ered, if at all, until later (when/if the party takes office). For the issue of monitoring supply, the group must rely on infiltrating the party, on establishing open lines of communication with party leadership, on government sources, and on press reports.

Unlike a pure market in which supplier and consumer are indifferent to the character of either (brand name should matter only if the quality is significantly better than another brand or the generic equivalent, or if its price is lower), in the party–interest group relation both actors care about who is who. The supplier may not want a particular interest group as a customer, no matter how much "business" the group promises to yield. The group may reject a party for reasons unrelated to the actual "product" being supplied.[6] Reliance on the market analogy has a serious shortcoming: in short, "there is no accounting for taste." The analogy cannot explain preferences; it merely provides a description of what happens to fill those preferences.

Only if the Church were to give a party enough "business" would the latter likely or even possibly agree to supply what the Church wanted.[7] Church leverage would come primarily in the form of votes and organizational resources. In fact, that "business" could enable a party, as it did the DC, to expand its own enterprises, branch into other fields, cultivate other interests (some actually at odds with the demands of the Church), and attract investors (political entrepreneurs) who had no interest in the actual product, only in profit. Church influence would also be dependent upon whether the party *wanted* or needed the Church as an ally, or agreed that the Church's priorities were worthy of commitment.

Turning to the Italian and French cases, ideology and interests figured strongly in each Church's interactions with the parties, its demands, the tensions that arose, and its decisions about whether or not to break the recently established alliance. We can analyze those decisions in terms of costs and benefits, risk-avoidance and risk-taking; to do so we must accept that the actual assigning of values to those elements depends on perceptions of interests and structures. If the organization has one goal or outlook as a priority, it may neglect secondary goals, it may be able to overlook occasional free-riding as a negligible factor, and it may not devote re-

---

[6] The market experiences these effects: consider the Greenpeace campaign against tuna companies using nets that trap dolphins; the (unsuccessful) boycott of grapes; the Denny's Corporation's alleged discrimination against non-Caucasian customers. These effects are not predicted by neoclassical economic theory. Advertising, of course, does not merely provide information about a product's existence; it is geared toward circumventing pure market logic by preventing consumers from being indifferent to the supplier.

[7] To extend the market analogy to the party concerned, the DC leadership feared a consumer revolution—an overthrow of the "market," with the Church supporting an authoritarian regime—if the Church did not get what it wanted.

sources to other problems inherent in interest group/party relations. Which party a Church saw as an acceptable ally was affected by the Church's priorities and its worldview, not just by the situation it faced. Its interests, influenced by its situation in each country, ruled out some options. When tensions arose, how the Church reacted depended on a mixture of political entrepreneurship and interests.

The Italian Catholic Church did not create its own party, but instead formed a partnership of sorts with the Christian Democrats, contributing resources and, from its ancillary organizations, candidates. When the Church decided it needed political allies to fight for its prerogatives and help it to dominate society, three questions arose: which allies, how many, and how extensive the support? The Church's siege mentality prompted it to view politics in military terms. It concluded that the need was for one large party, not an alliance of several parties, fearing that Catholics dispersed across various parties would permit easy infiltration and conquest by the Left. The decision was not made entirely independent of events—it was affected by the fact that there existed a Christian Democratic party of some popularity, many leaders of which were familiar to, and regarded as safe by, the Church.

Given the strong anticlerical streak in France, the French Church was even less likely to create its own party. It instead opted to support at a minimal level (i.e., party endorsement) the nascent MRP. The choice of party was relatively straightforward: the other parties with any sympathies to Catholicism and the Church could be considered parties only by a large stretch of the imagination, and they were small—they did not look capable of making a common front against the secular Left in the parliament. Since the French electoral system gave a slight advantage to larger parties, the Church had another reason to endorse the MRP: it was the largest and best organized of the parties not historically tied to the Left.

ITALY: THE VATICAN AND SUPPLIER OPTIONS

One or Many Parties?

In the period when the Democrazia Cristiana was getting organized (1943–44), the Catholic Church had not yet clearly decided on its preferred option, that is, whether it wanted numerous Catholic parties or just one (Magister 1979, 39; Durand 1991, 581–93). And, although the DC was receiving assistance from the clergy in some areas, it "was not born as the 'party of the Church' " (Scoppola 1988, 53). In other words, the link between DC and the Italian Catholic Church had to be forged. In fact, the Church was, at first, reluctant to support a party that had such obvious leanings toward the political center. Moreover, there were important actors in the Roman hierarchy (Domenico Tardini, Alfredo Ottaviani, and Luigi Gedda) who very clearly preferred to see a regime and political party that would produce a system more like the clerico-monarchist regime that ruled in Franco's Spain (Riccardi 1983, 51–55).

The Church temporized until its preferred authoritarian option had been ruled out. The Vatican wanted a conservative-monarchic government and showed no interest in Alcide De Gasperi's efforts to create a Catholic party (Scoppola 1988, 49, 53). While the Church still entertained hopes for a new authoritarian regime, it did not seek a democratic party ally. In 1943, when the United States asked the Vatican to suggest leaders for an interim government, Pius XII, through one of his secretaries, Monsignor Tardini, recommended two moderate Fascists (Luigi Federzoni and Marshal Caviglia) and a member of the pre-Fascist political elite (Vittorio Orlando) (Scoppola 1988, 49; Miccoli 1976, 376). After Mussolini had been banished by his own Fascist Council, the leader of Azione Cattolica, Luigi Gedda, told the new prime minister, Pietro Badoglio, that Azione Cattolica directors would be able to fill posts vacated by Fascists in the management of corporatist entities (Miccoli 1976, 376; Sala 1972, 530). Despite the king's subsequent flight from Rome and the collapse of the Italian army, the Church did not immediately start cultivating the DC nor any other parties. Only when the Church accepted that democracy was inevitable did it start looking for democratic party allies.

The decision to support one party was not an obvious one. The advantages of supporting a multiplicity of parties were significant. First, it would have prevented one party from acting as a monopoly, setting "prices" and not responding to group (Church) demands. Multiple parties would, at worst, form a cartel, defection from which would be easy for an interest group to encourage. Second, it would have enabled the Church to test the political waters, seeing which party or parties was or were most likely to be compliant with its demands and capable of meeting them, and which party, if any, was most popular (recognizing that any level of Church support would affect that popularity). Third, with a set of acceptable parties, it would have been easier to communicate to voters what to vote for—the target, constituted by several parties, was much bigger.[8] With only one party, the interest group (the Church) would have to exert considerable effort to ensure that its members understood that, despite the seeming

[8] The context is not one in which one party would be an obvious "focal point," in Schelling's sense (1990). Focal points work when two parties can communicate about where to meet and there is only one "high point" on the horizon, or when the parties have *no* contact. In the latter case, each guesses about the point the other would select.

acceptability of other parties, only one was to be voted for. The Church would also have to expend substantial organizational resources to actively eliminate prospective party rivals. Fourth, in supporting multiple parties, the Church would have avoided the risk that marginally observant Catholics would not like the Church's choice and therefore not vote (it did declare vote abstention a sin). Finally, there was no theoretical justification, in Catholic theology, for supporting only one of several pro-Catholic parties.

Some in the Vatican argued that Catholics could have diverse political preferences yet still be obedient to Catholicism. If so, a plurality of parties was acceptable. Others argued that the variety of Catholic views on politics could not, in practice, be contained in one party. It was inevitable that Catholics would disperse themselves across parties, so that Church should accept a variety of confessional parties (Durand 1991, 582–83). The Church, however, chose to support the DC.

In fact, there were influential leaders who were wary of the selection of the DC. In 1945, two of Pius XII's closest advisors, Monsignor Tardini and Cardinal Ottaviani, scolded De Gasperi, leader of the interim government, for not having tried, with agrarian reform and worker policies, to quell the "Communist bacillus" that the Church argued stemmed from discontent and poverty and hence could be countered with the proper programs. One of Azione Cattolica's key leaders, Luigi Gedda, accused the DC of three errors: "the fact of having taken a position in favor of the Republic instead of remaining neutral; having let the Left develop an unjust [anti-Fascist] purge [program] against men of good faith; finally, the feebleness of the anti-Communist campaign" (Durand 1991, 613). With those strikes against it, one might well ask why the Church chose the DC as its ally.

At the time, the far Right was pledging strong support for the Church, was obviously not interested in an anti-Fascist purge, and was stridently anti-Communist. In 1945–47, the Church's potential suppliers of desired policies looked suboptimal. One small grouping, Uomo Qualunque (Everyman's Party, hereafter UQ) could be negotiated with, but, as with Mussolini, might not put the Church as its top priority.[9] The DC, though widely visible, was poorly organized and seemed somewhat feeble in its anti-Communist resolve. The Church needed to make a decision: its con-

---

[9] Uomo Qualunque was a reaction against Communist agitation and a protest against miserable living conditions. It was also another repository for fascists. Since the UQ's leader had declared, "God is the only boss of the UQ; only to him and his laws [the UQ] declares itself unconditionally the subject" (Pallotta 1972, 141), Uomo Qualunque had the potential to siphon off a number of Catholic votes (Ghini 1968, 66–67). On Brescian priests' view of the DC, see ACS, MinIntGab, fondo Situazioni Politica ed economica della regione, Lombardia, f. 2493.42, Comando Generale dell'Arma dei Carabinieri, no. 200/I, Feb. 22, 1947, p. 4.

stitutional position and the status of the Lateran Pacts would be discussed in the Constituent Assembly debates of 1946–47.

Why the DC?

First, policy stance mattered. Other parties were dismissed as potential allies when serious doubts were raised about whether those parties would act "in service to the Church" (Durand 1991, 619–20; Malgeri 1985, 111–12). The Church's treatment of the Christian Left Party (PSC) was an early indicator that anti-Communism was going to be a litmus test for receipt of clerical support: in 1945, it condemned the PSC, saying that the principles of that party, "despite the Christian appellation," did not conform to the Church's teachings.[10] The Church wanted guarantees of influence and of anti-Communism, and it was beginning to appear that the DC would be able to offer both.[11]

The Church's essential reasoning was clear: it wanted not just a party that would respect the Church's privileges (as elaborated in the 1929 concordat), but also a party that would promote explicit guarantees regarding a Christian social program, as part of the Church's goal of obtaining "a hegemonic position of control over the life and orientations of the collectivity" (Miccoli 1976, 378; Falconi 1967, 264–75). The hierarchy demanded that the party protect Italy, and the Church, from Communism. To Pius XII and the Vatican establishment, these were the essential elements to the Church's survival (Riccardi 1988, 82–94).

Second, party coalition problems were important: the Church diagnosed the difficulties of the tripartite government (1946–47) as stemming from the DC's lack of an absolute majority in the 1946 Constituent Assembly elections. It therefore was determined to have the DC win an absolute majority in the April 1948 legislative elections (Casella 1992; Durand 1991, 641). If the DC had won that majority in 1946, the logic of parliamentary majorities meant that there would have been no need for the DC to compromise with the Socialists or Communists. In essence, the Church was making an informed guess about the outcome of the 1948 election given increased Church support, and about the DC's governing capabilities, also with increased Church support. It assumed (erroneously, as it later developed) that the DC would inevitably work in its favor should it have a parliamentary majority.

[10] *L'osservatore romano*, Jan. 2, 1945 (in Magister 1979, 50). The Catholic-based "direct cultivators" (independent farmers) union, Coldiretti, made scathing attacks on the Partito della Sinistra Cristiana, discouraging its members from voting for the Christian Left (Scoppola 1988, 275–76).

[11] Msg. Borghino, Azione Cattolica director, Mar. 14, 1946 (in Durand 1991, 600).

Third, political capability affected the decision of which party to support. In 1946, the DC seemed poorly organized and weak (Durand 1991, 613) and had yet to prove it could marginalize or control the Communists (Magister 1979, 53). The archbishop of Milan's daily paper admonished the DC two months before the municipal elections to raise "the weighty curtain of distrust that many have raised around the DC, accused of a dangerous acquiescence and of an organic incapacity to defend itself in a deceptive political game and fraught with unknown frights" (in Durand 1991, 612). The Church nevertheless gambled on the DC, halfheartedly for the 1946 municipal and Constituent Assembly elections, then wholeheartedly for the 1948 legislative elections. The alternatives to a feeble and ill-organized DC were worse. The Church could certainly imagine that with its investments, the party would become strong enough to supply the Church its desired policies. The Church waited until the DC gave a clear signal of its anti-Communist abilities before it swung all its support to the party (Durand 1991, 613–15). That signal came in mid-1947 when the DC forced the Communist party out of the government (Baget-Bozzo 1974, 1:153–60).

Fourth, familiarity may have increased the Church's confidence in the prospective policy stances of the DC. Many of its leaders came from Azione Cattolica or other Catholic ancillary organizations (Baget-Bozzo 1974, 1:54). The Church was familiar with these organizations, their leaders, and their political orientations. Particularly with Azione Cattolica, whose members became an influential part of the DC, the Church had been able, courtesy of the Lateran Pacts and its nominal independence of the Fascist regime, to nurture political allies. In the eyes of the Church, the DC was authentically Catholic, while other parties were not: "there may be parties which, even in saying they want to defend Catholicism and its institutions, limit themselves to an exterior defense, without occupying themselves by putting into concrete action Christian thought in the social and political sector" (in Durand 1991, 628). Ironically, many clergy would later make the same complaint about the DC. The Church reasoned that Catholic politicians in one dominant Catholic party would produce Catholic policies in a Catholic state.

Fifth, the views of the Church's leadership mattered: the Church's siege mentality tipped the balance scales. The one-party viewpoint, soon adopted by Pius XII, was that Catholic strength would lie in having the faithful united in one party. That justified the position of the hierarchy that the faithful should not have too many legitimate political options. Moreover, the opposing atheistic parties were large and well organized; *their* supporters were not dispersed across numerous parties. Indicative of the "Catholic unity" mentality of many in the hierarchy, Cardinal Ruffini, archbishop of Palermo, overruled a Sicilian bishop who had said in 1946,

"No theology can condemn a vote for the Monarchist Party, for l'Uomo Qualunque, etc." (in Stabile 1986, 374). Theology no, politics yes. To defend Rome and the Catholic Church, one army, united under one general (the pope), was deemed necessary.

The alliance with the DC was not a sui generis one. It had to be arranged, and its advantages and disadvantages were evaluated from the Church's perspective (and the DC's; see pp. 168–74). While historical events facilitated the alliance, they did not predetermine it. The Church could have made the choice of no alliance, or alliance with several pro-Catholic parties. That it picked the DC was partly a result of the DC's expected capability and of the Church's siege mentality.

Nature and Level of Support

The Church's mobilization on behalf of the DC in the election of 1948 has been rightfully compared to mobilization for war (Durand 1991; Casella 1992). The Church turned over its facilities to campaign rallies, had priests lecture not on theology but on politics in the weekly mass sermons, organized campaigns, staffed party headquarters, proposed and tried to implement party strategy. Its investment in the DC was phenomenal; however, the Church's support slackened somewhat for the 1953 and 1958 elections, when the party proved less capable and willing to fight than the Church demanded (see chap. 6).

THE FRENCH CHURCH AND ITS SUPPLIER OPTIONS

The MRP had been created independently of the hierarchy during World War II, and was therefore far from being an automatic extension of the Church in the political realm. Contacts between the party and the Church were not automatic, and any links between them were carefully forged and subject to scrutiny by both organizations.

After the war, it appeared that the MRP would be the largest, electorally most successful of the center and center-right parties available; it was setting up branches throughout France, and, as early elections confirmed, its popularity was spreading throughout the country. At the time, the Church faced a situation that strongly suggested the wisdom of supporting only one party, and that that party should be the nascent Christian Democratic party. In the aftermath of Liberation, the French political spectrum had, like the Italian, well-organized parties of the Marxist Left as well as several other secular parties. The difference lay in the center and the Right: there was the one large grouping of Christian Democratic inspiration—the MRP, and one ill-organized, small, pro-clerical conservative party—the PRL, plus a variety of insignificant other political organizations.

Why One Party?

The policy decision which the Church had to make was, however, influenced by some additional factors.

By relying solely upon one party, the Church could be risking political disaster because it might miss the chance to cultivate an alternative ally that might prove to be more suited to the Church's interests, and might even be more successful. If the support of one party did eliminate potentially suitable substitutes, then the party would have a monopoly on the Church's options, thereby reducing the Church's leverage and bargaining power. Exit would then lose its credibility as a threat, because the Church would have no alternative, and Church voice (complaints) could easily be ignored, precisely because the party would know that the Church had a limited exit option.

On the other hand, the French version of proportional representation slightly favored larger parties (Williams 1964, app. VI); this gave the Church an incentive to concentrate its support on one party. The alternative would have been to disperse Catholic votes (and influence) across multiple organizations (parties). In that case, the Left would likely obtain the highest percentage and the most seats in each district. Then, even if the pro-clerical parties did win a majority of the seats and subsequently could not agree to form a governing coalition, they would have (inadvertently) provided the well-organized and influential opposition with an electoral edge.

In the event, the Church chose the one-party option.

Why the MRP?

As in Italy, the Church was constrained by the need for an immediate ally: the question of state subsidies for education would be debated in the Constituent Assembly; so too other matters of concern and interest. It could not afford to wait for the conservatives to reorganize, and the MRP appeared to share many of the Church's concerns. On the policy level, the MRP espoused Christian social principles; moreover, most of its activists and leaders had been members of Action Catholique.[12] The two were also in agreement in their opposition to "the idea that the will of the State does not submit to any superior morality,"[13] as well as about trying to keep workers from the atheism of Communism.[14] Like the MRP, the Church claimed to downplay class differences. However, unlike the MRP, the Church could not ignore several other socioreligious issues; these were to become the point of fundamental divergence between the two.

Finally, a factor stemming from the nature of the previous regime and the Church's relation to it affected the Church's choice. The PRL was a party of discredited conservatives, most of them tainted with Vichy. Association with them would have hindered the Church's efforts to clear itself of the opprobrium of having been a willing partner in the Vichy regime; far better to ingratiate itself with the new Republic by allying with a prorepublican party such as the MRP. Since the Church had defined organizational survival partly as damage control, limiting the retribution exacted by Resistance-inspired politicians, the Church sought to hide under the guise of a noted Resistance party. The MRP was doubtless more progressive than the Church liked (Ravitch 1990, 147), but the Church had little choice.

Since supporting a political party is a decision that allows various levels of support, the Church could take a low-risk, low-profile approach to the MRP, instructing Catholics at mass and through diocesan bulletins, but refrain from creating new organizations to campaign for the party, or providing logistical resources, and then monitor the consequences. However, unlike the case in Italy, the French Church was not able to easily monitor the party's behavior. Since Action Catholique was not tightly controlled by the hierarchy, and the Church's role in Vichy was an issue, the Church was both less familiar with MRP leaders and less influential over them. The Church, operating on incomplete information, could have underestimated the MRP's determination to downplay the schools issue. It also could have underestimated the MRP's determination to pursue an alliance with the SFIO. This misinformation would have made the Church more likely to see the MRP as an acceptable ally, at least initially.

[12] Of the 152 MRP deputies elected to the 1946 Constituent Assembly, 66% were from Action Catholique, 75% of those on the MRP's executive committee. On the MRP, see Bazin 1981, 2; on its executive committee, see Irving 1973, 79.

[13] *SRP,* Jan. 19, 1946, 41–42.

[14] An MRP leader, Fernand Bouxom, stated that the MRP's mission was "to give hope again to the people, outside of communism and [outside] of sterile anticommunism" (AN, A-MRP, 350/AP/49, 2MRP2 dr. 20, Comité National, Mar. 19, 1951). Mr. Reille-Soult, June 21, 1951: "We must concern ourselves with not losing the worker souls, which would go to Communism" (AN, A-MRP, 350/AP/49, 2MRP2 dr. 20, Commission Exécutive). See also MRP 1946. On the Church, see Pierrard 1991; Wattebled 1990; *CCR,* Jan.–Feb. 1945.

The logic of alliance creation is evident in the transition period. The Church had some time to evaluate its choice of allies; it began by instructing Catholics to vote for the "Christian" party and encouraged Action Catholique to work for the MRP. In 1946, Cardinal Suhard, archbishop of Paris, stressed the election's "considerable importance for the future of France." Catholics were told to vote, to vote correctly, and to vote "usefully"; abstention, as in Italy, was condemned as a sin. The "useful" vote was for the religiously correct list that was most likely to win the most votes in any department. Catholics were to "group their votes around the list which, taking into account local conditions, seems to have the best chances of assuring the success" of family support, of morality, and of subsidies to private schools.[15] As in Italy in 1948, it was obvious to Catholics which list that was: that of the Christian Democrats. These instructions were reprinted in departmental newspapers around France and, more importantly, were read aloud to congregations at mass services in every parish. Where priests were not sure that the electorate understood, they made the point explicit, mentioning the MRP by name.[16]

However, a policy disagreement quickly emerged. At the Constituent Assembly, the MRP agreed to a compromise that would not restore subsidies to private schools and also avoided referring to education as a "public service" and thus open to state monopoly. The Catholic Church, of course, was adamant that church schools at least be guaranteed the right to exist. And, the small, conservative PRL (see above) supported and agreed with the Church's position. This created some second thoughts on the Church's decision to support the MRP.

On the other hand, the MRP and the Church were in agreement, and in opposition to the Socialists and Communists, with respect to numerous other provisions of the first constitution for postwar France. This draft failed to win public support, and a second draft was, shortly thereafter (October 1946), submitted to the French population for approval. Like the first draft, the second did not guarantee "liberty of instruction" but did avoid calling education a public service. The MRP, believing that no other alternative would win approval, supported the second draft; on this issue, in other words, it went against the Church (Wright 1970, 138–40, 158–59, 226). And, interestingly, the Church, while condemning the second draft, did not condemn the MRP on the subsidies issue, nor did it elect to switch its support to the PRL (French voters, by a slim margin and with low turnout, approved the second draft).

The Church evidently concluded that it would do better in the long run with the larger (and generally sympathetic) party, rather than with

[15] Cardinal Suhard, *SRP,* Nov. 2, 1946.
[16] AN, FI CII Morbihan, rapport du préfet, Oct. 10, 1946.

the much smaller, and thus less influential PRL; in other words, the latter was not a suitable substitute for the MRP. The party's capacity for being an effective advocate in parliament, and its policy sympathies, made a difference. In this instance, the MRP had a larger share of the seats in the National Assembly than all other groups sympathetic to the social and political goals of the Church. Exiting the MRP at this juncture would have stranded the Church. Observers of the political environment at the time seem to confirm this: "It is certain that the French Church does not want a rupture with the Mouvement Républicain Populaire and that the ecclesiastics will show patience, but will not give their approval to a laic tendency of the MRP"[17] This observer, however, notes an important fact: the Church had a core policy on which it would not budge; should the MRP challenge that, the alliance would be in jeopardy.

Level of Support

The French Church never supported the MRP to the extent the Vatican supported the DC. Doing so in the French context would have provoked an extreme anticlerical reaction; by 1944, with the failure of Vichy, the Church did not even consider it. Structurally, the French Church could not imitate the Vatican (and its actions in Italy). The decentralized hierarchy could not compel its members to follow French Church policy. The Church's ties to the party, while they lasted, were loose, informal, nonbinding, and varied across regions. The lower level of Church support is reflected in the MRP's electoral results in parliamentary elections, in which the MRP went from 25% of the national vote in 1946 to only 11% in 1951 and 10.4% in 1956. So, while the immediate postwar context gave the Church reason to seek a political party ally, it did not require the Church to support that ally in a manner that might have been more effective, in the short run, for the Church. In some ways, that is a moot point: the MRP did not *want* the Church as an integral part of its success, nor did it credit the Church with any part of the MRP's initial electoral victories.

CONCLUSION

The Italian and French Churches chose to ally with political parties because both had policy goals that required legislative support. Their preferences and the contexts in which they operated were not identical, and account for the divergence in levels of support the Churches gave the two

---

[17] APP, MRP box 278.247-2, June 27, 1945.

parties. Neither the French nor Italian Church faced an ideal set of potential allies; both had to deal with the existing supply of parties and tried to use their resources to mold the parties into more amenable organizations. Policy agreement and political capability were significant. A political party is a useless ally if it does not agree to pursue the core policies preferred by the interest group. It also is less desirable if it does not give the group's policies a high priority. If the party is politically effete, the interest group's efforts are wasted; if the party does not agree on key policy issues, again, the interest group's efforts ("investments," if one prefers) are wasted.

There clearly are limits on an interest group's ability to have its optimal supplier. The political market is far less flexible than the economic one. The French Church, hemmed in by its past association with the Vichy regime and by potent anticlericalism, approached the political scene tentatively. The Italian Church, emboldened by its separation from Fascism and its heightened reputation among Italians, came on full bore. Both Churches approached Christian Democratic parties not because they thought democracy was inherently a good thing, but because the alternative conservative, even authoritarian, pro-clerical parties were small and ill-organized. They most assuredly did not choose the parties out of habitual association with their predecessors. In fact, the Italian Church opposed a renewal of Luigi Sturzo's Popular Party (PPI), and the French Church had not supported the interwar Christian Democrats (PDP). The Churches chose the Christian Democratic parties because the parties' programs and capacities most closely matched Church preferences. In both instances the alliance had to be forged, and later actions and policies played a significant role in the nature and development of the alliance.

CHAPTER 6.

Evaluating the Alliance: Exit or Voice?

LIKE ANY marriage of convenience, conflict between an interest group and its chosen party always lurks in the background and occasionally becomes manifest. Relations between the French and Italian Churches and their respective Christian Democratic parties were no different. For example, during the 1948 electoral campaign in Italy, members of the Church hierarchy criticized a number of southern DC candidates, saying that their behavior was "unworthy" of Catholics.[1] In France, only a year after the Church had endorsed the MRP in the 1946 parliamentary election, priests in some regions were urging their followers to vote for rival, conservative candidates in the local elections. These are just two examples of the tensions that develop in the relations between an interest group and the political party(ies) it chooses to support. To avoid being taken advantage of, to ensure a return on its support, interest groups must monitor their parties. If the interest group delivers votes and/or organizational resources but the party does not deliver policy or other benefits in return, or if it sullies the group's reputation, what are the group's options?

An interest group, when faced with a party that displeases it, has choices somewhat analogous to a firm or consumer dissatisfied with its supplier. The situation is one to which Albert Hirschman's concepts of exit and voice apply (1970). In its original formulation, *exit* signifies that a consumer will switch brands if dissatisfied with the quality of the item purchased. This is most likely when suitable and/or equivalent substitutes are readily available, and the product costs little. *Voice* is the notion that, when faced with a decline in a specific product's quality, a consumer will not switch brands, but will instead complain. This is most likely to happen if the consumer estimates that the likelihood of positive response is greater than the effort of complaining, and also greater than the likelihood of finding a suitable substitute elsewhere.

Transposing this model to the interest group–party context, the key questions facing the group are these: Is there another party, a suitable substitute, to which it can turn? Can the investment be recouped with exit? Are there any tangible benefits to remaining? What is the likelihood that voice will have any effect on the party? The degree of control each

[1] AAC, PG, VI f. 35, f. Campagna, Feb. 11, 1948.

organization has over assets the other wants, and the extent to which each has invested assets in the other, weigh on the exit/voice decision. For instance, in dealing with a political party, an interest group has within its voice repertoire its influence over voters. If that influence is substantial, the interest group may find voice a better strategy than exit. If the political party ally has a near monopoly of one side of the political spectrum, that monopoly condition lowers the benefits to the group of using either exit or voice. Exit is not a credible threat, since there is no suitable substitute to which the group can turn; voice is not beneficial, because, as the only provider, the party can ignore it. The result is that the group has few options and is likely to conclude that the status quo is the most cost-effective one.

Another factor that affects the ability to use voice or exit effectively is that of permeability—of the party, and of the state apparatus. If it is easy for the group's activists and leaders to join the party and gain office in it, the group may enter into a relationship and mutual dependencies that cannot easily be dismantled: the group's assets then may not be redeployed without at least a temporary sacrifice of "productive value" (Libecap 1997, 719). This effect is heightened when the party has access to state resources (patronage) that can be distributed to party supporters. Paradoxically, permeability creates a barrier to exit: being extensively intertwined with the party raises the opportunity costs of exit, particularly if state institutions and agencies are involved.

Another factor that constrains exit options is perhaps more important to leaders of religious than of other organizations: consistency. Religion is a credence good, one "wherein the consumer cannot verify the quality of the product until a much distant point in the future" (Gill 1999, 71); it thus relies heavily on consumer trust and faith in those dispensing the good. A religious leadership that alters the political instructions it gives its followers may lead the latter to question the veracity of doctrinal instructions. Inconsistency is severely damaging to religious leaders, who need to remain credible for the sake of the faith.

But how does a group find out whether there is a problem with the "product" the party was explicitly or implicitly obligated to provide? In the event, the monitoring capability of the group becomes relevant. Conceivably, an interest group can have a centralized structure with one unit assigned to monitor external relations, or a decentralized structure in which each local unit monitors local and national party output and responds accordingly. In a hierarchical, centralized interest group, much of the information upon which a centralized unit relies comes from local organizations. More effective monitoring would likely come from members of the organization who are also members of the party. The drawback for the group is that the links created to facilitate monitoring may prove difficult to break when monitoring reveals that the party has deviated from the group's preferred course. The group, well informed that the relations with the party are problematic, finds that its own monitoring devices prevent it from acting on the new information.[2]

For a decentralized organization, monitoring of another organization becomes all the more difficult. Information flows are impeded by lack of vertical conduits, and by the multiplicity of horizontal linkages. Since there is no central authority responsible for processing and disseminating information, each segment of the organization is left to its own devices.

Whether centralized or decentralized, an organization may find that its own members, personally benefiting from a particular group-party link, will withhold information about party performance that might otherwise lead the group to reevaluate its links. Furthermore, in a multiparty legislature (and government), a party has innumerable ways of hiding its role in specific policy outputs. While a group may lack perfect information, one can assume it would not have allied with a specific party had it not been confident of some level of access to information, some ability to monitor its ally; the same is assumed for the party.[3]

Turning to the empirical cases, both the Italian and French Churches had reason to complain about their respective party allies. Both disapproved of the parties' participation in governing coalitions with secular left parties. Pius XII threatened several times to form his own clerical party, but only the French Church broke its links with its Christian Democratic ally. The key difference was that the DC did not fail the Church on the Church's core policy concerns; the MRP did. The comparison between the Italian and French Churches' situations shows that the Italian Church faced higher opportunity costs of exit than the French, and that, moreover, it had less reason to discount the exit costs than did the French

---

[2] Institutional arrangements serve multiple purposes. While membership overlap may facilitate monitoring, it may have developed as a way of supporting the party and of influencing its policies. Monitoring, then, is a subsidiary activity.

[3] One might ask if an interest group would be more or less tolerant of a party's policy deviance from the group's preferences at the beginning of interaction. Does uncertainty, lack of familiarity, play a role in this? If so, in which direction is its influence exerted: to increase or decrease group tolerance? There are countervailing pressures at the start of the group-party interaction. On the one hand, at the outset the group should be selective and uncompromising. In case of party deviance, since the group's investment in the party is still low, relative to what it would become should the group stay with the party, the group finds sunk costs less of a stumbling block to exit. On the other hand, the group may be more tolerant initially, expecting it will be able to exert greater leverage over the party as time goes on. In that case, the group would discount policy deviance, and use voice, not exit. Tolerance could also be a side effect of lack of good information about the party, with information being harder to obtain initially, before the group establishes monitoring instruments. The prediction seems indeterminate.

Church. The French Church, with a lower investment of personnel and campaign efforts, found exit a less costly way of resolving policy disputes and of expressing dissatisfaction with the party.

For the Italian and then French case, this chapter first addresses the Church's incentives to break links with its party, then explains the choices the Church made.

ITALY: CONSIDERING EXIT: WHAT WERE THE PROVOCATIONS AND OPTIONS?

There were numerous instances when the Church became dissatisfied with DC policies. However, Church leaders never seriously considered abandoning their alliance. The Church's failure to exit is due not to an inability to assess the situation nor to a lack of information. Instead, the Church's relative opportunity costs, the constraints of the various institutional arrangements, and its goals and outlook led the hierarchy to discount its level of dissatisfaction and maintain relations with the Christian Democrats.

Provocations to Exit

The lack of exit did not signal complete happiness on the part of the Catholic hierarchy with the relationship. Policy disagreements between the Italian Church and the DC surfaced early in their interaction. First, the Church was angered in 1946 by the DC's laxity in promoting the inclusion of a "sanctity of marriage" clause in the constitution, and by allowing the inclusion in the constitution of the right to strike (Durand 1991, 616, 642). Considering that marriage and divorce are positions on which Catholic doctrine allows no compromise, this omission was a serious issue. However, this was not the most contentious issue. Most egregious was the DC's very visible coalition government with the Communists and Socialists. The Church's irritation was mollified when De Gasperi reminded the papal deputy, Domenico Tardini, that breaking from the governing coalition would jeopardize the Lateran Pacts' constitutional status, that being the sine qua non of Church policy. The party held the greater bargaining position in this relationship, thereby raising the opportunity costs of exit for the Church.

Second, the DC, after gaining a majority of seats in the 1948 legislative election (with the Church's help), brought secular parties—the Liberals, Republicans, and Social Democrats—into its governing coalitions. The Jesuit journal *Civiltà Cattolica*, which shared its viewpoint with elements in the Vatican, argued in July 1953 that "a party that pretends to the label of Christian cannot extend contacts with the Saragat Socialists [PSDI] . . . in order to form a government without putting at risk the supreme principles and differentiations of its own program." Railing against the possibility that the DC would resurrect the coalition of May 1947–July 1951, which included the Social Democrats, the author, Antonio Messineo, argued that it would be "contrary" to the DC's electoral mandate and "would open the door to Communism" by way of a socialist "Trojan horse" (in Magister 1979, 184).[4] In his 1953 Christmas message, Pius XII criticized the DC's leftist leanings, those of Catholic Action, and "leftists" in the hierarchy, condemning them for being swayed by Socialist theory (Magister 1979, 188).

The third complaint was related to the second and is typical of interest group–party relations: the party does not adopt as allies ones that the interest group favors. In 1952, the Church wanted the DC to pursue an electoral alliance with the neo-Fascists and the Monarchists; the DC refused. The Church's intricate political maneuvers surrounding those municipal elections were geared toward ensuring the victory of a non-Communist, DC-led government, preferably a DC–right-wing alliance (Magister 1979, 167–68)—thus avoiding the arrival of "Stalin and his Cossacks" at Saint Peter's Cathedral (Jesuit Riccardo Lombardi quoted in Magister 1979, 169). Instead, the DC ran with several of the centrist secular parties (the Liberals, Republicans, and Social Democrats), and won that way.[5]

In the 1956 municipal elections, the DC flirted with an "opening to the Left," that is, bringing the PSI (Socialist Party) into the governing coalition at the national, provincial, and local levels. Pius XII personally told the DC mayor of Florence, running for reelection, that he was forbidden to negotiate with the PSI (Magister 1979, 213). In Venice, the DC ran a list of candidates supporting the opening to the left and, when elected, formed a one-party minority government relying on PSI support. The cardinal archbishop Angelo Roncalli condemned the act and admonished the DC that the Church's "authoritative opinion" was against it. "We find ourselves in front of a grave doctrinal error, and a flagrant violation of Catholic discipline. . . . we are either with the Church, and follow its directions and merit the name of Catholic, or we prefer to decide for ourselves, promoting division and secession, and the name of Catholic no

---

[4] Those coalitions had included the PRI (Republicans) and sometimes the PLI (Liberals), as well as the moderate Socialists (PSDI). See p. 77n.4

[5] The episode of the Rome elections is commonly referred to as the "Sturzo affair," a label that is something of a misnomer, as Don Luigi Sturzo had little to do with the maneuverings between the Church and the DC.

longer applies" (in Magister 1979, 215). Roncalli was supported by the bishops of the region, who declared that Catholics must not read the DC paper, *Il popolo del Veneto,* which advocated the opening. It is worth noting that the provincial DC leadership thereafter passed to the man preferred by Roncalli, indicating that voice *can* be effective.

Fourth, DC politicians often were involved in less than "Christian" activities (racketeering, adulterous affairs), and since the Church was tied in the public's eye to the DC, the Church sometimes feared its reputation may have been tarnished.[6] Fifth, the party leadership refused to fashion an explicitly clerical party; instead, it insisted on retaining some autonomy from the Church. In March 1954, De Gasperi discussed the work of the executive council of the DC, rejected the idea that the party should be "confessional, emanating from ecclesiastic authority," and denied that the Civic Committees (see chap. 7), "no matter how worthy for their efficient mobilization work," could "take on a function of political representation and responsibility" (in Magister 1979, 191). In an article edited by Pius XII, *Civiltà Cattolica* attacked De Gasperi for denying where the fount of morals and action lay: "The political Catholic, as regards moral and social principles, submits to the authority of the Church and follows the authentic teaching that emanates from the supreme organ" (Magister 1979, 191).

From the start, the clergy often complained that DC politicians did not favor them enough (Durand 1991, 614). Others complained that DC leaders were neither humble nor self-effacing, but rather were self-serving,[7] that not enough DC activists participated in the campaign against the anticlerical press (614), and that the party did not consistently seek clerical advice on the composition of its candidate lists (615). With so many points of serious disagreement between the Church and the DC, why did the Church not exit?

Exit Options

What were the Church's options? Was there a "suitable substitute" if the Church severed its link with the DC? After the 1948 election, there was not. The costs of an organization supporting a party are well illustrated

[6] For the rogues' gallery in various DC sections, see ACS, MinIntGab, 1944–66, fondo Partiti Politici–Democrazia Cristiana, Reggio Calabria, f. 165-P-66, b. 34bis, anonymous letter, "Per l'on. Amintore Fanfani," Apr. 19, 1958, p. 3; ibid., no. 1896, Feb. 6, 1957; ibid., Caserta, f. 165-P-21, b. 3, Oct. 8, 1958; ibid., Napoli, f. 165-P-60, b. 33, "Riservatissima," no. 3000/1407, May 7, 1957.

[7] AAC, PG, VI, Visite nel Mezzogiorno d'Italia, Oct. 5–15, 1947, Sig. Rossati dated June 25.

by the situation of Italy's Catholic Church. First, the threat of exit by an organization loses credibility when that organization has helped eliminate viable alternatives. Even after the 1946 Constituent Assembly elections, the Church's options had narrowed. Ironically, the Church, having concentrated its full support on the DC in 1948, gave the DC latitude to pursue policies the Church did not support. In the electoral campaign of 1953, for example, while the Church would have preferred a clearly proclerical, even promonarchy party, it was stuck with the DC. Taking the Church's support elsewhere would have, as both the party and the Church recognized, jeopardized the Church's chance of having its goals achieved. In other words, the Church had no alternative to the DC. Furthermore, the Church's defection from the DC would likely split the Catholic vote, making it easier for greater evils (the secular parties) to win legislative majorities. Thus, the costs of exit would be at least as high as remaining with the status quo.

Second, the Church had invested major resources in its alliance with the DC. If the Church shifted from the DC, some Catholics might see it as a signal that the Church no longer regarded anticlericalism as a threat, and that it was permissible to vote for any political party. Any serious diminution of the DC's strength would have given the Communists and their Socialist allies an entry into the government. Forming a pro-clerical government coalition would be difficult if one of the anticlerical parties had the most seats in the parliament. In fact, the Church's options had been narrowed as early as the 1946 Constituent Assembly elections: the DC was its only advocate of any size in the assembly (with 207 of 556 seats), and its leader had been chosen as prime minister.

The DC could and did argue that no other party was an effective barrier against Communism. One politician boasted that "the [Catholic] civic committees have no alternatives except to support D.C. candidates" (LaPalombara 1964, 337). In 1958, shortly before the legislative elections, the Vatican's daily paper, *Osservatore Romano,* commented that Catholics can only support the DC "because, in more than one occasion, sometimes grave and difficult, it [the DC] finds itself alone or almost [alone] in defending the rights of religion" (Magister 1979, 223). As De Gasperi's protégé, Giulio Andreotti, outlined to the pope when the latter pressed the DC to ally with the neo-Fascists and Monarchists for the May 1952 municipal elections in Rome, the DC as a centrist party was the pope's only "option"; all other alliances, or Church sponsorship of a separate list of Catholic candidates, would lead to ruin for the position of the DC as the bulwark against Communism (Magister 1979, 170–71). Exit had been blocked through the Church's own actions.

Third, the cost of exit was probably raised by side-payments. In contrast to the MRP and the French Church, some of the drawbacks to the DC's monopoly of Catholic representation and Church endorsement were counterbalanced by concrete benefits. As one northern DC activist commented, a number of positions on the DC electoral lists always went to "the people most representative" of the various Catholic groups. "The elections over, they divide the jobs in the administrations, the assessors' offices, and the presidencies of various agencies" (Bragaglio 1981, 184). An administration official explained, "Catholic Action can and does determine who will be the higher civil servants in many of the ministries" (LaPalombara 1964, 308). Furthermore, the Church's banks were clearly benefiting from financial arrangements with DC-awarded and DC-controlled construction contracts and other expenditures of public funds (Falconi 1967, 280–81; Caciagli 1977).

Moreover, some of the individuals who were monitors for the Church inside the DC, or in parallel organizations, such as Azione Cattolica, became co-opted by the discrete rewards of their positions. No longer monitors concerned with quality control, they competed with others in the DC for side-payments and power. This change in Church access to information is due to the very nature of interest group–party relations. The alliance creates new opportunities for each organization's members, any number of which might be seeking to better their own position, even at the expense of the organization.

Fourth, perceptions contribute to exit costs. Had Pius XII not been such a hidebound anti-Communist, the Church's estimate of the risk of leaving the DC in search of a more pliable political party would have been lower. So long as the Vatican leadership perceived a major threat to the Church, and that its defense had to be waged in the political arena, its assessment of the costs of abandoning the DC were higher than the irritations of continuing support. That leadership perceptions make a difference is evident in the fact that there were those in the Vatican willing to entertain the idea of a plurality of Catholic parties, in order to search for more amenable allies (Magister 1979, 222). That view had no powerful proponents.

Pius XII was, in addition, constrained by the anti-Communist positions of earlier popes. If he vigorously condemned and emphasized the Communist threat (as he did) and then later acquiesced to a DC alliance with any party of the Left, many Catholics would likely have begun to question the credibility of the pope as well as the Church's position on other social and political matters.

The absence of a suitable substitute, high investment costs, access to side-payments, and leader perceptions all combined to block exit. The cost of building a new party was prohibitively high. The case does not allow assessment of the relative importance of each factor, but it does show that the extent of structural involvement with a party and the ease of creating a substitute are the primary factors in an interest group's decision about whether or not to break its links with a party.

The Decision: Voice

As Hirschman (1970) points out, when exit is blocked, voice often becomes the only means of improving quality, even though it may be a weak tool. An interest group, when it perceives that exit is blocked, will likely elect to exercise its voice. But precisely how does it do so?

There are a number of ways. The first and perhaps most obvious is to intervene in a party's internal politics by supporting a specific faction. For example, the Vatican applauded and encouraged the formation of the Iniziativa Democratica faction within the DC, which declared its opposition to De Gasperi's policy of keeping the DC from becoming a clerical tool (Magister 1979, 162). With its control over the Ministry of Agriculture, it was able to exert considerable electoral pressure, proposing, with papal approval, alliances with the neo-Fascist party and the Monarchists. Clearly, a group's decision to discriminate between factions within a party is more likely (and more effective) when factional strength affects candidates' access to party, legislative, or ministerial offices.

The second obvious way to influence a party is through the use of powerful ancillary organizations. For example, in the central Italian province of Piacenza in 1953, the DC did not put the Church's preferred candidates at the top of the party list for the upcoming parliamentary elections.[8] The Church promptly threw Azione Cattolica behind its desired candidates. The Church viewed that action as necessary: it knew well that the DC was full of political entrepreneurs who were Catholic in name only, and in the DC because it could provide the most political and economic opportunities.[9]

Church discrimination between factions sometimes had the desired effect, in this example, that of hardening the DC's anti-Communist line.

---

[8] When in 1948 a DC/Azione Cattolica candidate lost votes to a nonclerical DC candidate, the Church investigated and charged the DC with corruption (AAC, PG, VI f. 19, corrispondenza con le diocesi 1947–52, Campobasso [in the south], May 25, 1948, letter from Avv. Giovanni Correra [?] to Rev. Monsignor Vittorio Longo, archbishop of Napoli). On Piacenza, ACS, MinIntGab, 1953–56, fondo Relazioni, Piacenza, f. 14861, b. 83, no. 688/2/1, Feb. 28, 1953. Other instances are noted in Chassériaud 1965, 239, and Manoukian 1968, 456.

[9] Examples abound. See AAC, PG, VI f. 18, Benevento, visite alle diocesi, corrispondenza diocesi, letter from Rodolfo Meomartimi (?) to Luigi Gedda [Azione Cattolica president], May 27, 1949; AAC, PG, VI f. 19, Sienna, corrispondenza con le diocesi, letter from Ezio Cantagalli to Sig. Rag. Renato Branzi, Jan. 15, 1950; on Catania, Caciagli 1977.

De Gasperi's party secretary, Guido Gonella, opened the Roman campaign for the municipal elections of 1952 with the familiar claim that the election was a choice between "Christian Rome and atheist Communism . . . morally and socially irreconcilable, irreducible" (in Magister 1979, 164–65). After those elections, in which the neo-Fascists and Monarchists won control of Naples, Bari, and Foggia, De Gasperi told his minister of the interior, Mario Scelba, "In the Vatican they insist on [carrying out] the tactical maneuver launched during the municipal [elections]. They are irritated by the MSI law [a bill outlawing Fascist parties]. . . . If we do not succeed at imprinting a more concrete, purgative, and resistant directive against Communism, every action against fascism will be considered an error and danger" (De Gasperi 1974, 1:209–10).

Like shareholders in a firm, an interest group may intervene in its party's internal politics to assure a return on investment. This is more likely when the group is a major "shareholder" in the party—both the shareholder and the interest group pay a commission when they divest stock. For interest groups, that loss comes in the form of forgone policies and influence over politics. Less like shareholders, the group may even undertake an advertising campaign on its own to rally support for the party: a party that repeatedly fails to win control of key government offices is useless.

The Church also weighed in on internal politics to keep the party from fragmenting, self-destructing, or from losing votes. In his pastoral letter for Lent, entitled "The Roots of Evil," the archbishop of Reggio Calabria launched a severe critique of the province's politicians. He noted their "ambition to be at the top positions" and their desire "to ascend higher and obtain large honors and riches."[10] The archbishop did not counsel voters to shift parties, nor did he himself threaten to shift support. It was a matter of voice, not exit; it was an effort at getting the DC to put its house in order for the next election, not in setting up a rival party house.[11] Even in the first years of the republic, local bishops and priests tried to quell internal party feuds and worked to convince or coerce voters to vote DC despite the party's governing record and some of the unsavory characters running as DC candidates. This costly aid was not altruistic; it was an effort to protect the Church's interests: a healthy DC was a protected Church.

Another method of exercising voice is by withholding support of some sort until the party capitulates or calls the group's bluff. This the Church did in 1947, when the Vatican tried to pressure De Gasperi into being the

---

[10] ACS, MinIntGab, 1957–60, fondo Clero, Reggio Calabria, f. 15326/66 b. 206, Monsignor Giovanni Ferro, "Alle Radici del male," n.d., 1957.

[11] ACS, MinIntGab, Partiti Politici–Democrazia Cristiana, 1944–66, Bergamo, 165-P-13, b. 31, Jan. 21, 1952.

Church's emissary (Magister 1979, 88). If the DC weren't forthcoming on policies, the Vatican threatened to break away and find a more suitable right-wing home, possibly even renouncing democracy (Scoppola 1988). Since this was a year before the critical first legislative election, and since party attachments had yet to be established, there was some credibility in the Church's threat. The DC could not yet know how far it could push the Church and still retain its support. When the party does "call the group's bluff," as De Gasperi did to Pius XII over the 1952 municipal election in Rome, the interest group can always retaliate by publicly embarrassing the party leadership. Pius refused De Gasperi and his wife an audience on the occasion of their 30th wedding anniversary, which coincided with their daughter Lucia's taking her vows as a nun. De Gasperi, reminding the Vatican that he was Italy's prime minister and foreign minister, protested (De Gasperi 1964, 1:335; cf. White 1999)

Particularly under the leadership of Amintore Fanfani, the DC appeared to many in the Church to be making political use of the Church without reciprocating service. Cardinal Ottaviani, on January 21, 1958, wrote a scathing, public attack on Fanfani's style of operating:

> There are even Catholics in seats of political authority who dare to take the part of those who not only offend but massacre the Church. And in the meantime everyone runs to the priests to make wire-pullers of them in regards to the powerful, and there results a weariness and boredom in the country regarding the men of eternity transformed into electoral agents. This is not the way in which to honor the Church. Rather, this way one dishonors it. This is not serving the Church, this is serving oneself of it. The bride of Christ not only should be defended from those who persecute her, but also from those who would muddy her, and compromise her.[12]

Ottaviani was not alone in his opinion, though the condemnation was undermined by an *Osservatore Romano* article (see below) reminding Catholics they still had to vote DC because the latter often was the only guarantor of religious freedoms.[13] The Church had a strongly felt grievance; it exercised voice and awaited a positive response. It was not forthcoming.

When a party does not respond to interest group pressure, the group has the option of diversifying its investments. Whether it perceives that

---

[12] Cardinal Ottaviani, prosecretary of the Holy See's Office, in Azione Cattolica newspaper, *Il Quotidiano*, Jan. 21, 1958. Ottaviano later became famous for trying to block Vatican II.

[13] The pitfall of voice is that the more a group exercises it, the more its members, seeing a high level of leadership dissatisfaction with the party, may decide to quit supporting the party, i.e., exercise the exit option.

exit is blocked, and what it elects to do, depends partly on leadership. While Pius XII's fixation on Church hegemony led him to tolerate a substantial degree of free-riding by the DC, he stepped up what one might call "Catholic pageantry" (White 1999, 6, 31; see also chapter 7 *infra*), and disbanded the Civic Committees, thereby reducing (slightly) the Church's organizational investment in the DC. "For the pope, the various branches of Catholic Action represented a more congenial and obedient instrument for advancing the Church's agenda in Italian society" (White 1999, 5). In short, to promote its interests when the DC did not, the Church tried to capitalize on its other assets.

FRANCE: CONSIDERING EXIT: WHAT WERE THE PROVOCATIONS AND OPTIONS?

In France as well, there were situations and policy disputes between the Church and its original choice of the MRP as an ally. As evidenced by their statements to their congregations regarding the school choice and electoral questions of 1951, members of the hierarchy had competing views of what policies were necessary to ensure Church survival; moreover, the diverse views of the bishops and cardinals did not necessarily reflect beliefs in their dioceses. Expressed opinions of the diocesan hierarchy had more to do with "the personality of the bishop" (Charlot 1957, 135): for Monsignor Elchinger, revived anticlericalism was the biggest threat; for the bishop of Luzon, it was the absence of state subsidies.[14] In part, then, it is incorrect to speak of the "French Church": the French hierarchy was not a unitary actor and there was no central Church office to coerce or cajole the hierarchy into some semblance of unity.

In France, when there were policy disputes, the Church chose the exit option. In fact, most of the French Church withdrew its support of the MRP rather soon after the affiliation was established. The MRP's continued laxity on the school choice issue, its refusal to be strongly enough anti-Communist, and its opposition to unconditional amnesty for Vichy collaborators are the major factors that drove the Church away.[15] The lack of a suitable substitute was constant in the Fourth Republic, so exit meant ending the opportunity for having a political voice in the legislative policymaking process.

---

[14] For the purposes of clarity, in this section the word *Church* represents the majority view of the Assembly of Cardinals and Archbishops (ACA).

[15] APP, MRP box 278.247-2, no. 622, Aug. 20, 1951; APP, MRP box 278.247-1, Mar. 11, 1948.

Provocations to Exit

In late 1944, the Liberation government, dominated by a tripartite coalition of resistance parties (the PCF, the SFIO, the MRP), called for the
resignation of more than 30 of France's approximately 87 bishops for collaboration (the actual number dismissed was 7) (Halls 1995, 369; Novick
1968, 131; Poulat 1986, 139). The government removed the credentials
of the papal nuncio, Monsignor Valeri, who was replaced by the future
John XXIII, Cardinal Roncalli (Novick 1968, 131; Halls 1995, 376). If
the MRP had been trying to cultivate the Church's favor, it was now in
an awkward spot. One of its leaders, François de Menthon, was justice
minister for the interim government handling the purges. The Vatican
was reluctant to act, arguing that none of its own could have committed
a crime against France. The French hierarchy likewise refused to discipline
its members. Despite this provocation, the French Church supported the
MRP in the 1945 and 1946 elections. Why the initial display of tolerance,
given a genuine motivation to exit?

The answer lies in the relative importance of the two issues, amnesty
and state subsidies to private schools. The former merely affected a few
older population of Church leaders, and in 1944–46, the Church could
still expect that the MRP would defend it on the state subsidies issue.
That second issue affected the Church's ability to reproduce itself in future
generations. The relationship, however, began to change—as the Church
became better informed about the MRP's priorities, and the MRP had
new social issues to consider, many of which put it on a collision course
with the Church.

In 1947, the MRP gave the Church another reason for questioning its
link with the party. The MRP pressed the Vatican to have the French
Church reduce its demand of state support for private schools in order to
facilitate the MRP's alliance with the Socialists.[16] The hierarchy, through
the ACA, however, issued a formal statement asking for state subsidies.[17]
Then, in 1948, the MRP opposed the Church on another key policy area:
amnesty for Vichy collaborators. The MRP, regretting it would be in opposition to the hierarchy, held firm in rejecting generous amnesty laws.[18]

These two issues were important to the Church; they were not, however, the only ones involved in the Church's assessment of its relationship
with the MRP. In the view of the Church, by the 1951 legislative elections
the MRP had still not rectified its position on a number of sensitive issues.
Although the party consulted frequently with the hierarchy and the Vati-

---

[16] APP, MRP box 278.247-1, prefect report, Jan. 8, 1947.
[17] APP, MRP box 278.247–1, Nov. 26, 1947.
[18] APP, MRP box 278.247–1, Mar. 11, 1948.

can on the school issue (Lecourt 1978), it had only reluctantly supported a bill restoring subsidies to private schools. In addition, many members of the MRP were quite openly critical of the Catholic Church.[19] The result was that, as a Paris police informant reported, "in a meeting of the French Cardinals and Bishops recently held in Paris, rather severe criticisms were lodged against the party."[20] Voice, though being used by the Church, was not having the desired effect. Without giving the Church anything concrete in return, the party was supporting programs and policies too divergent from the Church's interests.

Consider the following: the MRP's position on some sensitive issues led to its slowly developing the reputation of being "soft on Communism." In the view of the hierarchy, the MRP too often supported a variety of progressive economic and social policies while not effectively opposing proposals put forth by the Communist Party. This led to serious doubts among the hierarchy concerning the party's future reliability as a partner with which it might expect to gain political influence and support for Church goals. Furthermore, when the Church hierarchy wanted the MRP to support a change in electoral laws that would have disadvantaged the Communist and Gaullist parties, the MRP refused. Some observers concluded that the MRP would, "for the sake of itself gaining a few seats, send 150 Communists to the National Assembly."[21]

Moreover, although the MRP deliberately decided to ally itself with the Socialists in order to limit the political power of the PCF (Communists), this association produced several efforts to squelch controversial religious issues before they could emerge. The Church was not even offered the opportunity to take a position or express its opinion on them; this led to even greater distrust of the MRP by the hierarchy.

Further: the unwillingness of the MRP to procure side-payments and other benefits for its group supporters led to doubts about its level of commitment to, in this case, the Church. The only side-payment that the MRP offered the Church was in 1951, when it sponsored a law providing a trivial level of state subsidies to private schools. Worse, its support for the proposal was more restrained than that of it rivals, the Gaullists and the Conservatives.

As indicated, it can be argued that the relevance and importance of these issues/problems were not equal; for example, the Church did not immediately consider exit as a result of the amnesty issue, probably because it affected only a replaceable, small population of Church officials. On the other hand, state subsidies to schools affected the Church's ability to re-

---

[19] APP, MRP box 278.247-2, prefect report, Mar. 2, 1951.
[20] APP, MRP box 278.247-2, prefect report, May 29, 1951.
[21] APP, MRP box 278.247-2, Jan. 31, 1951.

produce itself in future generations. As the Church hierarchy stated, state subsidies were "the question which, at this hour, retains the attention of the clergy and the faithful."[22]

The Decision: Exit

The Church's response was to exit. The MRP had failed the Church on a nonnegotiable policy issue: school subsidies. Voice had not accomplished its desired goal and policy outputs were the litmus test for continuing the association. Reorienting the clergy and ancillary organizations accustomed to supporting the MRP through three elections in two years (1945 and 1946) should have been a concern, but the policy discrepancy discounted them. Other sunk costs were relatively low, as the Church had not set up (as in Italy) explicit campaign committees on the MRP's behalf, nor had it become financially linked with the party. Further, support of the MRP had not yielded side-payments in the form of creative schemes for Church financing, or access of Action Catholique leaders to jobs in public and para-public agencies.

The result of the Church's disaffection with the MRP was that by 1951, both nationally and in most departments, the Church was instructing Catholics to vote for "Christian" candidates rather than MRP ones. In areas where the local MRP refused to compromise with the Church's preferences, the Church did not assist MRP candidates. For example, in "Catholic" Aveyron (south-central France), a local newspaper noted that the MRP "is considered by many religious persons to be likely to compromise the liberties which are dear to them, in wanting to maintain at any price a position on the left which does not correspond to the spirit of the larger part of its voters."[23] The MRP's pursuit of progressive economic and social policies and its alliances with the Socialists led it "to neglect the problem of subsidized schools" (Prieur 1956, 106). This strategy disturbed the Aveyron hierarchy sufficiently that it began withholding electoral support from the MRP. However, given the decentralized nature of the Church, there were still areas where Church-MRP relations were good enough that the clergy continued to support MRP candidates (Warner 1994, chap. 8).

As indicated earlier, the Church in Italy could not find an alternative to the DC; it therefore exercised "voice" and remained an ally and confederate of the DC for many years thereafter, at some cost to itself and the DC. What was the situation in France? Was there a suitable substitute for the

---

[22] *SRP,* June 10, 1945, 331.
[23] *Rouergue Républicain,* Nov. 6, 1946, 3/659.

MRP? Was the reason the Church stopped its support for the MRP the existence of another party that was more likely to accede to and support Church preferences?

A new, initially large party did form in 1947: General Charles de Gaulle's Rassemblement du Peuple Français (RPF). But, was it a suitable substitute for the MRP? To the extent that the party supported state subsidies for Catholic schools, it was. Yet de Gaulle was hostile to the hierarchy due to its complicity with Vichy (Charlot 1983, 253–54; Halls 1995, 368–69), and was utterly unwilling to let the Church exercise any influence over RPF policies, and not noticeably sympathetic to other Church priorities. De Gaulle disdained the divisiveness implicit in party representation of corporate groups (and parliamentary democracy), and in 1953 disbanded his own, internally divided party. For its part, the Church had not steered Catholics toward the RPF.

Beyond the RPF was a congeries of small conservative parties, tentatively and temporarily united under one party label. While some of them were strong supporters of Church goals, they were decentralized and their potential level of influence uncertain.[24] With unknown returns and high "capital" requirements due to the presence of internal factions and decentralized structures, these parties constituted a potentially risky and costly investment for the Church. Thus, when the Church had reason to reevaluate its links with the MRP, the French political spectrum did not offer a suitable substitute.

There is, then, a major question here: if there was no reasonable alternative to the MRP as a party sympathetic to Church policy preferences and goals, why did the Church choose exit over voice in the French case, and voice over exit in the Italian one?

One might argue that the Church broke the link because the MRP was unwilling or unable to accomplish *any* of the goals the two agreed upon. For instance, in 1948, when the MRP still had about 25% of the seats in the National Assembly, the MRP opposed the nationalization of Catholic schools belonging to a mining concern, but was unable to block the move.[25] It may be, in other words, that the Church became disillusioned with the MRP's inability to influence national parliamentary and local council decisions. Party size, however, does not appear to have been an important issue. First, two and three years earlier, when it had the choice between supporting the PRL (a small, poorly organized conservative party) and the MRP, the Church chose the MRP, even though it had not been able to achieve all the Church's policy goals. In 1948, the MRP's

---

[24] In 1946, "Conservatives" won 7.5% of the parliamentary vote; in 1951, 9.3%; and in 1956, 13.8% (Warner 1994, 276a). See also Dupeux 1957, 32–37.

[25] APP, MRP box 278.247, May 18, 1948.

parliamentary strength was the same as in 1946. Second, after the Communists were ejected from the government, and de Gaulle created his opposition party (the RPF), the MRP was an important member of the "Third Force" governing coalition, and still influential in the success and failure of legislation and governments (Williams 1964).

If party policy capability was not the issue, perhaps Church structure was. How did the lack of a central authority affect the Church's evaluations of exit versus voice? Due to the decentralized structure of the French Church, Assembly of Cardinals and Archbishops statements of support were, perforce, of the lowest common denominator. The hierarchy's assessments were complicated: each diocese had to anticipate the likelihood that other dioceses would continue to support the MRP, yet no one diocese would want to take the lead in doing so, for fear of going down with a lost cause. If the ACA were able to signal the diocesan hierarchies that a majority position was developing, the calculations of the individual dioceses would be easier. Such informational signals went to the dioceses in the form of the Archdiocese of Paris's weekly bulletins, and ACA meetings, but the latter were infrequent. Dioceses had to rely on their self-constructed networks and on national news if they wanted to track party behavior elsewhere. For local issues, the dioceses could keep tabs on the MRP through the prefect, but his willingness to dispense information varied with his political sympathies. Yet information access was not the key to the Church's exit decision: what mattered to the Church in the early years, state subsidies to Catholic schools and anti-Communism, were issues on which the local MRP's stance was easy to follow. The Church stopped endorsing the MRP when it concluded that the party was an unreliable and ineffective ally, and when it specifically refused to endorse and work for Church-desired public policy goals. The Church had wanted an ally in government, one that would press for its goals.[26] Since replacements were not available, perhaps partly because the MRP was not a substantial enough ally, the Church pursued other means of influence.

CONCLUSION

The policy effort and output of a party matter to an interest group. Both Churches evaluated their respective party allies on that basis and, when the party was found wanting, considered exit. The cases indicate that exit is more likely when the group's involvement has been relatively limited. It may also be that decentralized churches are less effective at mobilizing support for any cause, due to the lack of clear leadership; the "default"

---

[26] APP, MRP box 278.247-2, no. 622, Aug. 20, 1951.

position is thus defection. Yet, in Italy, even if the DC *had* failed the Church on core policies, the Church would have found it difficult to retaliate by exiting: in its efforts to eliminate smaller pro-clerical parties to strengthen the DC for the 1948 election, the Church inadvertently ensured that there would be no suitable substitute immediately available. Creating one would have taken time, perhaps allowing the Left to gain control of the parliament and cabinet in the interim.

Party permeability was also a factor: the DC was willing to let itself be penetrated by external allies. The MRP, in contrast, went so far as to pressure sympathetic clergy not to take an obvious role in the party. Permeability created barriers to exit: being extensively intertwined with the DC and the Italian state apparatus made exit exceedingly difficult.

While those differences help explain why the Italian Church did not disavow the DC, they do not explain why that Church was only partially successful in using voice to sanction party behavior. The Italian Church's connections with the DC were such that the Church could not easily control everything that the DC did with the Church's investment of resources. First, having removed the threat of exit, having placed clerics and ancillary organization activists into the DC, the Church found that its agents' allegiance and vested interests shifted toward the DC. Second, the Church's massive support in the 1948 electoral campaign, and the DC's resultant majority in the parliament, gave the DC control of the Italian state, something the MRP was never able to accomplish. The DC was able to begin setting up its patronage system and was able to occasionally distance itself from, and thereby reduce its dependence on, the Church. Thus, many of the Church's protestations would fall on deaf ears.[27] On the other hand, some control was made possible by the Church's extensive presence *inside* the DC, its influence over devout Catholics, and the structure of the Italian electoral system (which allowed the use of preference votes, enabling the Church to target individual candidates within the DC—a technique that it occasionally used).

The French Church's decentralized structure meant that it was difficult for the Church to be fully informed about the MRP's behavior and inten-

---

[27] While the Vatican's maintaining the alliance with the DC was partly due to sunk costs and side-payments, it may also have been due to a perpetual lack of complete information. Given the unending stream of coalition governments, the Church could never be sure of the DC's true policy preferences. After the 1953 legislative elections, when the DC needed partners to form majority coalitions, one could ask if the DC were allying with secular parties because it was not genuinely Catholic, or because it had no other choice. The French Church asked the same questions of the MRP, since that party, also, was always in coalition governments, and the MRP also claimed it had no choice. In the absence of high sunk costs and side-payments, the French Church made the conservative decision—to quit supporting the MRP.

tions; therefore, sanctioning was sporadic and dependent on local communication. While one diocese may have had no reason to quit supporting a party, the party's behavior elsewhere may have indeed warranted exit. The national party could take advantage of discrepancies between dioceses.[28] The fact that the Church had invested less in the MRP meant that when it transgressed the limits of the Church's tolerance, the Church's resources could easily be withdrawn or redeployed. The Church's main leverage against the MRP's misuse of the Church's investment in it was its influence over the votes of devout Catholics (since in France it could not target individual candidates on a party list, as in Italy). The Church's decentralized structure meant, however, that the Church could not threaten the MRP with a full-scale nationwide withdrawal of support.

In the end, both Churches relied on many of the same factors in their calculus of voice/exit; what mattered was the variation in the ability and commitment of the parties to accomplishing Church goals as well as the value of the resources that the Church(es) had invested in accomplishing them, though clearly the more intertwined and the more extensive relations between an interest group and a political party are, and the longer relations continue, the more difficult it is to sever the link and embark on a search for new allies.

---

[28] An additional complication is that the local diocese, if it is benefiting from its relations with a party, has no incentive to care about how other dioceses are affected by the party. Despite their Christian ideology, French dioceses did not evince symptoms of group solidarity and sacrifice.

CHAPTER 7

Getting Out the Vote: Mobilization Techniques

Catholic Action is not a political association,
and neither can nor should practice politics,
strictly speaking . . . [but] when the house
is burning, one neither can nor should think
of anything but putting out the fire.

(Diocese president of Volterra, December 31, 1948)

ANY ANALYSIS of the relationship between interest groups and political parties needs to look at the types of techniques that are available to enforce member behavior in such organizations, their usefulness in different circumstances, and their appropriateness to the issues or policy concerns of the group. If the group is paying a party for policy services with member votes and logistical activity, how does the group ensure that it can exchange those assets? The primary emphasis of this chapter is on the techniques that the Church developed to persuade or compel lay Catholics to support the Church's political strategies and goals.[1] It is, in a broader sense, an introduction to the techniques available to religious organizations that may or may not be available to other types of interest groups.

The Catholic Church, especially prior to Vatican II (1960s), never saw itself as being just one voluntary organization/interest group among many, all competing for influence and power in a pluralist, democratic political system. On the contrary, the Church viewed membership in its ranks, and obedience to its directives (including explicitly political ones), as obligatory for all Catholics. It did not accept the liberal idea that individuals have the right to choose their belief systems—religious, social, political. It was, in fact, not until Vatican II that the Church began to accept the idea that Catholics, under limited circumstances, could follow their own political inclinations. Nevertheless, the Church has always had problems in making credible commitments about the behavior of its members. Compliance with Church doctrines has never been automatic; even if it

---

[1] The hierarchy and clergy also may stray (e.g., Martin Luther) but are, given their ties to the Church, less likely to do so. Further, they are far fewer in number than the laity; to have leverage over a party, the Church will be concerned with how many Catholics-as-voters it can turn out. The bulk of its attention will thus be on the laity.

were, the Church would still have had to ensure that its members (whatever their orientation) heard and understood its dogma and directives.[2]

These latter problems of obedience and communication are ones with which any interest group must cope. In order to have any meaningful influence on a political party and its policy priorities, especially a party that values and strives for electoral success, an interest group must have a number of characteristics. First, the group must be able to show the party that it is politically (electorally) useful even if not indispensable: it must deliver members who vote correctly. The ability to do so will give the group some leverage over the political party. The group needs a large membership that is amenable and responsive to the leadership's directives on how to vote: it is, after all, not the group that votes, but individual members. Members, however, may have links to other organizations with competing priorities, over which the group's priorities may not take precedence. Thus, having decided to associate with or support a political party, how does an interest group get its members to do likewise?

Second, the group is likely to be asked to give "ideological" support to the party, that is, promote the general goals and programs of the party as part of its other activities. How does an interest group sell a party, which clearly has multiple motives and goals, to members who may not want the entire package of policy goods that the party sells? And if the group's leadership were to decide to switch to another party, or even no party, how would it make sure its members would understand and comply with the change?

The issue goes far beyond the problem of how an organization gets and retains members. That question has often been the focus of literature on interest groups and collective action (Olson 1965; Hardin 1982). There is general agreement that selective and ideological incentives help attract members; selective incentives include discrete benefits (such as discounts on merchandise), while ideological ones include policy goals and solidarity with that cause (such as environmental improvement). On the other hand, one cannot and should not dismiss the evidence that shows that groups attract some members due to the social and emotional benefits that they provide their members; this is certainly likely to be the case with organized religions.[3] The important subsidiary question is this: how does an interest

---

[2] The Church has always faced the possibility that Catholics would develop their own version of the religion. Scholars attribute the emergence of folk or "popular" religions to a complex set of factors including the dearth of priests in a region, the apparent irreligiosity of the priests, prior folk traditions, and lack of fit between the laity's experiences and the hierarchy's dogma (Badone 1990; Carroll 1996; Gill 1998).

[3] The economic view of such behavior is that religion is "a club good that displays positive returns to 'participatory crowding' ": the more people participate intensely, the more each gets out of the interaction (Iannaccone 1992, 272).

group that provides such a variety of social, psychic, economic, and political benefits to its members get them to cooperate with the leadership's political instructions?

In fact, groups have a considerable array of techniques and methods available that, at least in theory, are available to monitor, influence, perhaps even coerce a particular behavior or stance on the part of their political allies. Use of these strategies is bounded by the institutional and political context in which the group operates, its acceptance by society, and its definition of its role in the sociopolitical milieu. One of the purposes of this section is to analyze these options and how they can be exploited.

The interest group must take into account the costs imposed by various strategies: when it is an issue of steering members toward a new political party in a new political system, the information requirements are very high, since members may be unfamiliar, first, with the party and, second, with the political consequences of any association between them. On the other hand, the organizational costs may be rather low, in the sense that the group is not trying to detach its members from an allegiance or association with a previous party (except perhaps those involved with the previous regime).

The interest group's choice of techniques is obviously affected by the costs of the undertaking and by what is possible. Those parameters are shaped by institutional structures and links with the state, historical burdens, and the agency of leaders. This was clearly seen in the Italian Church, which engaged in greater mobilization than its French counterpart. The structure of the Italian Church, but not the French, facilitated undertaking coordinated capillary mobilization. Since the Vatican was convinced that Communism had to be fought aggressively, and on the political level, it favored mass mobilization techniques.

Providing selective incentives to gain a member's voting obedience is more complicated than merely providing discrete material benefits in order to recruit or retain an individual as a member of the interest group in the first place. To be effective, receipt of the selective incentive must be tied to the individual's voting behavior. But in democracies, the latter, is, allegedly, confidential. Only where that system can be corrupted, or the individual compelled or inclined to admit his or her vote, do such incentives work.[4] Ideological incentives can be created when the interest group plays up a threat, declaring a particular party to be the purveyor of absolute evil, of social, political, or economic collapse. Social incentives can be created when the interest group makes use of peer pressure in ancillary

---

[4] For example, if the Church declares that voting Left is a sin, then the Left-voting devout Catholic is obligated to confess doing so (likewise with abstaining to vote), giving the priest valuable information on that Catholic's political behavior.

organizations or in the group itself, and when it proselytizes, trying to convince each member of the importance and benefits to the group, and thus to the individual, of voting for a particular party. In each of these instances, the group can argue that members' failure to vote correctly will result in loss of the benefits the group provides to them. The effectiveness of that appeal depends on the cost calculus of each voter: what is the value the individual places on those group benefits, and why should that person undertake an action, when he or she might be able to free-ride on the efforts of others? Since voting is a relatively low-cost form of political participation, the individual's incentive to free-ride is less than if he or she were being asked to campaign.

Interest groups confront an important question when it comes to exercising influence over their members: is it more useful to construct a permanent "identity," or is it cheaper to repeatedly persuade, or perhaps even coerce, members to follow instructions? Advocates of the identity argument assume that individuals have to think of themselves as being part of a particular religious or political organization before they will follow its dictates. To react on the basis of identity assumes individuals are not reflective or calculating; the response is built-in, inherent. It is an issue of creating a brand that includes and elicits particular behaviors, here, for instance, a Catholic voting Christian Democratic. This goes beyond building a brand for a product in order to differentiate it from possible substitutes. It means having the brand establish the person's values and filter his or her reactions.

Building a brand identity is a lengthy and costly process; for short-term political goals, such as voting, it is easier to use propaganda, selective incentives, and/or coercion. To deal with coercion first, it is only possible and effective under limited circumstances. If an individual sees the Church not as a "voluntary association," but rather as essential to his or her spiritual existence and social and cultural life, then it becomes considerably easier for the Church to use coercion to produce the behavior it wants.[5] The most obvious and readily available sanctions—the withholding of the sacraments, or excommunication—are only effective if the target is a devout Catholic, and if imposing these sanctions is perceived as socially and religiously legitimate. Coercion may also be feasible if the Church is an essential conduit for access to necessary resources, for example, employment and government dispensations. That is likely to be a function of its creating a symbiotic relationship with a more explicitly political organiza-

---

[5] As some analysts have pointed out, the Church has to be careful not to price itself out of its market. Religious goods have complex demand schedules; some individuals respond to high barriers (asceticism, bizarre rituals, etc.), others to low (casual consumption, few proscribed activities). See Ekelund, Hébert, and Tollison 1992 and Iannaccone 1992.

tion (i.e., the DC in Italy). The general point is important: coercion is dependent upon limiting an individual's alternatives. Thus, interest groups press for monopolies, unions press for closed shops, and religious organizations such as the Catholic Church press for preferred status as state religions.

The evidence from Italy suggests that the effort to create a religio-political brand identity for Catholics and the DC was not effective. While most Catholics did vote DC, it was not because of an inherent connection between being Catholic and being Christian Democratic. Many voters selected the DC without really "identifying" with the party. In fact, if anything they were repulsed by it. Given the chance, they readily abandoned their "party identification."

Because being able to exert control over Catholics was a crucial political asset for the Church, the ability to influence or control Catholic political behavior also depended upon the capacity of the Churches to enmesh Catholics in social organizations in which indoctrination, persuasion, and peer pressure could be brought to bear on the members. The Church's organizational resources and its ability to direct the orientation of the ancillary organizations are important to its ability to retain and exercise influence over parties and policy outcomes.

The Catholic Church is, to some extent, like a vast archipelago, with innumerable organizational affiliates. Some of these affiliates were organized by the laity; only later, having presented the Church with a fait accompli, were they recognized by the Church. Other ancillary organizations were expressly created by the Church. All of these affiliates have been assigned, or have taken up, a political role at one time or another. Several have been active in the sociopolitical life of their particular countries for a long time, and it is those organizations on which I focus here: Catholic Action, farmers' unions, and trade unions.

Like the national Churches, these ancillary organizations have different organizational histories, different outlooks, and different structures across countries. What they have in common is that their national Churches have tried to use them for political ends, and that, at times, they have struggled to gain or retain their autonomy from the Church. Such behavior is not surprising: it is typical of organizational politics. Some have argued that ancillary organizations such as Catholic Action constitute an absolute loss of Church control over the laity (Kalyvas 1996). Instead, Catholic Action could be seen as a relative gain, as some bishops and popes saw it (Vaillancourt 1980, 36, 44–46). In a democratic political system where Catholic Action exists, the Church has greater control over the political involvement and direction of Catholics than it would were there no Catholic Action. In the latter case, Catholics might be tempted to undertake social interaction in secular movements. This points up the fact that organizational costs are relative, partly dependent upon context. As an explicit organization of the Catholic Church, Catholic Action finds itself periodically reined in or redirected by the Church.

At this point, I caution the reader that the techniques each Church developed to control the behavior of its members were not solely directed at increasing the Church's *political* influence. The Churches were also concerned, to varying degrees, about maximizing revenue, membership, and adherence to Catholic orthodoxy, and many in the Church *are* concerned about the well-being of their parishioners. Some of the techniques developed could, however, be put to political purposes. One example is precisely Catholic Action, which initially did not campaign for parties and was only later conscripted into that service.

Catholic Action played different roles in Italy and France after the war, and the obvious question is why. The factors accounting for the differences have to do with their differing structures, including their institutionalized relationship with the Church, their view of their role in the sociopolitical system, and their national Church's view of their appropriate role.

The farmers' unions were important means of collecting farmers within Catholic organizations, often by making them dependent on the organization for continuance of their livelihood. These unions sometimes were founded independent of the hierarchy, though perhaps aided by local clergy. They sometimes competed with Catholic Action organizations for the same potential members and were less likely to do the bidding of the Church. The Catholic trade unions had similar experiences. This was due to the institutional context: the source of the organizations' success, including resources, lay primarily with the state, not the Church (Di Marino 1965; Rossi 1965; S. Berger 1972; Cleary 1989).

The French and Italian trade unions have mistakenly been thought to have been instruments of the Catholic Churches. The Churches could only indirectly affect them, through the clergy who sometimes were affiliated with these organizations. In neither France nor Italy, however, were the occupational unions tractable tools by which the Church could influence politics, or Catholics in general. In France, the linkages between the Church and the organizations were tenuous at best, nonexistent and competitive at worst.

The differences in organizational resources between France and Italy were historical, structural, and ideological. While the French Church may have had fewer devout Catholics to pressure, its main problem was that, burdened by its compromise with the Vichy regime and by French sensitivities to "clericalism," it was more restricted than the Italian Church in its ability to use the sacraments as a sanctioning weapon. In addition, and in contrast to the Italian Church and Vatican, the French Church had only loose connections to Catholic Action. In many areas, the political views of the local priests who ran the Catholic Action sections contrasted markedly with those of the less progressive hierarchy. Further, the Church had fewer resources with which to sponsor Catholic Action's development. Even if the French Church had had a unified political orientation, it would have been, for structural reasons, more difficult for it to impart that to Catholics through social organizations. Finally, the focus of leadership of the French Church was more on "re-Christianizing" France than on dictating and monitoring the political preferences of Catholics.

In this chapter, I first present a statistical assessment of the impact of secondary organizations on party vote, then analyze the techniques the Church used in each country to control the political behavior of its members, and the organizations that were partly involved in that strategy.

ASSESSING THE NUMBERS

The existence of these Catholic ancillary organizations did not transfer into commensurate levels of support for the Christian Democratic parties. Statistical data show that, broadly speaking, the organizations' electoral impact varied by region; archival data show that it also varied by how supportive the organization was of party goals. The following section assesses the statistical data.

In Italy, Church statistics show that Azione Cattolica averaged between 23,000 and 32,000 members per province, or from 4.7 to 6.5% of a province's population (Casella 1990; *Annuario Cattolico* 1954). In France, membership was much lower, on average 2% of a department's population.[6] Yet

---

[6] Good data about Action Catholique do not exist. There are figures for the Catholic youth movement (JAC) from 1945, which are from estimates recorded sometime in the late 1940s by the French priest and scholar Fernand Boulard (Archives Fernand Boulard, report in unmarked box, n.d., n.p). The fact that in 1945 World War II was still going on also weakens the data's reliability. Since I could not get subnational level membership figures for any postwar years (it seems no one ever recorded the numbers), I did an inventory of the number of Action Catholique groups that priests listed for their dioceses in 1954 (Warner 1994, 71a). The latter data are dependent upon what priests in each diocese judged to be a separate subgroup (Guide-Annuaire 1955). Unfortunately, the numbers of reported groups vary randomly against other religious characteristics; they do not correspond to numbers of Action Catholique journal subscribers, nor to mass attendance, nor to the prewar JAC membership, nor to numbers of priests. With Action Catholique journal subscribers, the correlation is .00018, with mass attendance it is .0046, and with priests it is .08. An additional source is a study of the Action Catholique youth movement, and one on Action Catholique as a whole. Both have data on the percentage of the adult and young adult populations reached by Action Catholique's journals in each department (Durupt 1963; Faure 1958). Because one journal might be passed among denizens of the local café, or several neighbors, the figures reflect estimated readership based on subscriptions. From these journal "readership" figures, we can get some measure of how many people were involved in Action Catholique.

for the second parliamentary election in both countries, the relationship between Azione Cattolica's effect on the DC is actually lower than Action Catholique's effect on the MRP (Warner 1998, 563).

While the correlation between Azione Cattolica's presence and the DC's vote appears strong, it weakens considerably when assessing the relationship between Azione Cattolica membership and DC vote by regions—north, center, and south—for the three parliamentary elections (1948, 1953, and 1958).[7] The relationship is statistically strong in the north, noticeable in the center, and nonexistent in the south. Membership figures for the French "Catholic" trade union are not available. Results for the trade unions in Italy and for the French and Italian farmer groups are similarly inconclusive.[8]

ITALY

The Italian Church could not take the political orientation of its followers for granted. To guarantee the DC a victory and ensure that the DC would pay attention to Church demands, the Church had to arrange their obedience. Even if the Church assumed that devout Catholics would vote DC, the distribution of such persons was uneven across Italy. It ranged from between 20 and 30% in most of the center and much of the south, to well over 70 and 80% in parts of the northeast.[9] Given that variance, much of Italy's local and national political offices could have fallen into the Left's control had the Church not actively intervened.

In 1945–46, the lower clergy were not of one mind on what the political strategy of the Church should be. It took a concerted effort from the

[7] Northern regions are Piedmont, Lombardy, Val d'Aosta, the Veneto and Alto Adige; central are Emilia Romagna, Tuscany, Umbria, and Marches; southern are Lazio, Abruzzo, Campagna, Puglia, Basilicata, Calabria, Sicily, Sardegna.

[8] Readers may object that I am falling into the ecological fallacy, assuming that individuals vote as their aggregate grouping does, that it is, indeed, Catholics who are voting for the Catholic party. Presenting the data in this way is actually making a strong case for the argument I am challenging, that is, that sheer numerical strength predicts Catholic voting behavior (or union voting behavior).

[9] Survey data on practicing Catholics comes from a collection gathered and published by Silvano Burgalassi (1968). Burgalassi reprints the surveys for all or parts of about 10% of Italy's dioceses. The years in which the Italian surveys were taken range from 1950 to 1966. For the remaining 198 dioceses, he refers to unlisted studies, estimates the percentage of practicing Catholics in adjacent areas, and prints that information in a set of maps. In imposing a map of Italian provinces over his maps, which lack internal borders, I estimated Catholicism for each province (Burgalassi 1968, 25–61, and figs. 1, 2, 3). For a few, there are no data at all. When part of a province had been surveyed, by virtue of it being in a surveyed diocese, I averaged that percentage with the percentage Burgalassi estimated for the rest of the province.

Vatican down to the diocesan level to compel the clergy to campaign effectively for the DC, and the Church did not entirely succeed. The voting preferences of Catholics and even of the clergy were not 100% anti-Communist, let alone pro-DC. As the director of Azione Cattolica's propaganda unit said, "I found priests and monks sympathetic to Communism, some to Qualunquismo. Among the Catholics who prefer [the retention of] a monarchy, many are oriented toward the Partito Democratico Italiano [a residual fascist, promonarchy party]!" (in Casella 1987, 199).[10] To counter these problems, the Church used coercion and organizational mobilization to supply selective incentives, to provoke ideological agreement, and, ultimately, to get the votes.

Coercion

Coercion was used where the access of individuals to crucial resources (e.g., education, jobs) was severely limited and the Church could influence access, or where beliefs in the necessity of the sacraments were strong. To the devout, the denial of the sacraments, or excommunication, is an unspeakable penalty; denying the sacraments is an easy technique, entailing no cumbersome organizational efforts. Parish priests in northern Italy often refused sacraments to known Communists (Franzinelli 1981, 233), and in the south, "The priest undertook the traditional blessing of the houses, omitting to bless those whose inhabitants were members of the Socialist and Communist parties, unless they renounced their ideas."[11] In 1949, the pope made it official: those who belonged to or associated with the Italian Marxist parties (the PSI and PCI) were excommunicated (Magister 1979, 133–34). A monopoly on the supply of faith to believers and on the supply of rites to members of a particular religion was, and is, a powerful weapon.[12]

---

[10] *Qualunquismo* was the term used to refer to the Uomo Qualunque party's orientation, which was somewhat sympathetic to Fascism and to white-collar bureaucrats. This populist party, which exploited the anomie and exasperation of many, and mostly, southern voters, claimed to represent the "ordinary Italian" (Ginsborg 1990, 99). See chapter 5, note 9.

[11] ACS, MinIntGab, 1947, fondo Attività tra clero e politici, f. 3675 b. 60, Campagna (Potenza), no. 493/VII, July 4, 1947.

[12] The good supplied must be in demand. Ironically, often where the Church has monopolized faith over a long period of time, the devotion of the population to that religion declines. As happens in most monopolies, product quality and service declines, putting off the "customers" (Stark and McCann 1993; Stark and Iannaccone 1994). Further, coercion in the form of holding a job hostage to public acceptance of an ideology might not work where the individual is indifferent or hostile to the ideology. In 1959 in Val d'Aosta, the bishop told candidates who had allied with the Communist Party that they would be denied the sacraments. Only 3 out of 15 affected actually resigned; shortly thereafter, the bishop with-

The Italian Church, which viewed Italian politics as its spiritual battleground, had no scruples about gaining members, and their political cooperation, instrumentally. "The priest suggested to us that the only party was the DC. . . . I became a member because they said to me: 'If you don't become a party member you can't find work.' . . . They convinced me, in short, . . . because they got me a job. . . . I don't know, perhaps it's my own conviction: I think that the party of which I am a member gives me security of employment, that this party gives me life" (Allum 1973, 161). The worker had not converted to Catholicism, he did not have to be convinced that Catholicism was a political issue; the priests had merely convinced him that he had to be a (voting) DC member in order to get a job. In one of the industrial regions of the northern province Brescia, employers and priests colluded on employment: job applicants had to come with "political guarantees," in a letter of recommendation from their priest (Franzinelli 1981, 231; cf. Simoni 1988). Employers were only too willing to cooperate, as DC- and priest-approved workers were less likely to be militant unionists. A PCI militant corroborated this point: "After 1950, [Communist] party activity got less because some factories were opened and in hiring workers discrimination was practised. At the Allocca and Belli Companies [large Neapolitan enterprises] you had to pass through the cardinal, the captain of the *Carabinieri* [police], etc." (Allum 1973, 162). The workers' "debt" to the priest and party did not necessarily develop into loyalty. As another PCI militant declared, "[The worker] says: I've got to live, if I don't become a member they won't let me enter the factory. . . . But once in the factory, they desert the party. You see, for example, in the Belli Company, they all got in through the priests and today they have all become Communists" (Allum 1973, 161–62). Coercion may be expedient but does not assure long-term compliance.[13]

Coercion had its drawbacks for the Church, such as resentment on the part of the denied or hardening of opposition to the clergy and the Church, but because it viewed Catholicism as an obligatory religion, it discounted those costs. Sacraments and jobs should and could be rightfully withheld from those who refused to acknowledge their erroneous ways. The Church was after a monopoly position in the religious market and viewed coercion of the faithful and faithless as a legitimate tool for delivering votes to the party that would guarantee it that monopoly.

---

drew the de facto excommunication (Lengereau 1961, 119–20). In the "red belt" (central Italy), such threats provoked "lacerations of conscience" more than obedience.

[13] Parish population should make a difference: the fewer parishioners to which a priest has to minister, the easier it is for the priest to guard against and punish free-riders—those who received a favor but renege on the obligation that went with it. The priest in a small town in the Italy of 1950 was often the lifeline to opportunities elsewhere.

Bread and Circuses

While the Church promises an intangible, eternal salvation (and its dogma does not include the Calvinist doctrine that divine faith and blessing manifest themselves in material wealth), it still, like any other interest group, sustains its membership by awarding perquisites, such as papal audiences, jobs, bureaucratic favors. Side-payments were feasible for three reasons. First, the Church had extensive financial resources. Second, the Church was linked to a party willing to exploit this mechanism to gain votes. Third, it viewed electoral politics as a battle for the Church's status in Italy and elsewhere and therefore easily rationalized the use of side-payments. A good example comes, again, from Brescia, where the Church worked with the DC to help the latter run an electorally remunerative housing policy, "with the aid of the credit institutions, in particular the Banca San Paolo [a Vatican-funded bank] and of the politics of the local agencies of Brescia."[14] The bank was also active in financing the construction of new churches and insurance cooperatives, as well as other ventures that were either geared toward job creation, or had that as a side effect, thereby expanding the pool of resources the Church and the party could use to obligate or entice individuals to vote for the DC (Bertoldi 1971). Clergy also proselytized for the DC while distributing packets of food and clothing to poor families.[15]

The Church often sponsored free (Catholic) movie shows in small southern towns, leaving some viewers touched that the pope, seemingly with no ulterior motive, sent this type of "relief." "Being a people habituated to consider everything in the light of material interests, they ponder extensively the fact that there is someone who spends money for them without any [ulterior] motive, neither financial nor other. They like him [Pius XII] very much and are disposed to listen to him."[16]

The Church also used religious pageants and the charisma of office to increase the likelihood that it would have willing followers. A side effect, or an intended result, was that the Church could deliver votes to a particular party. Capitalizing on the charisma of the pope, for example, the Church sponsored numerous *peregriantio Mariae* throughout Italy, pilgrimages honoring Mary. The start of the pilgrimages was in the DC's weak spot, the south, in March 1948, one month before the crucial election. Pius XII manipulated the faithful through emphasizing the mythical

[14] The bank was founded in 1888 by Catholic businessmen, including one, Giorgio Montini, who was later a PPI deputy (Bertoldi 1971, 36–45, 212, quote on 174).

[15] ACS, MinIntGab, Incidenti, Mantova, Jan. 4, 1947, no. 75.

[16] AAC, PG, VI f. 35, Calabria, 1947–49, "Relazione sul primo giro del carro-cinema in Calabria," p. 3.

stature of popes: canonizing Pius X (the first one in almost 400 years), beatifying Innocent I, and starting the process for yet others. Pius declared 1950 the Holy Year and proclaimed the doctrine of the Assumption of Mary to 500,000 people gathered in St. Peter's Square (Falconi 1967, 284). He then designated 1954 to be the Anno Mariano, to focus Italians on the pageantry of the Church, contrasting it with the apparent bleakness of the early Cold War years (Riccardi 1985a, 59–61; Allum 1973, 263). By promoting the cult of the Virgin and canonizing and beatifying a number of other Church figures while simultaneously attempting to integrate some local festivals and cult figures into the Church's panoply of ceremonies (Carroll 1996), the Church retained its ostensible control over religious believers. One purpose of these efforts was to demonstrate that the Church was and would continue to be a powerful social actor that could also make credible commitments in the political arena.

Priests used the pulpit and diocesan bulletins to exhort the faithful to vote, and vote DC,[17] and sometimes used the relatively slow process of missionary work, one-on-one persuasion, believing that "if the people were better instructed in religion, they would know how to vote; when they vote differently it is not for lack of electoral propaganda . . . but uniquely from the lack of Christian education." The other problem was lack of esteem for the clergy and for DC politicians who seemed to represent capitalists.[18]

Ancillary Organizations and Their Political Activity

AZIONE CATTOLICA ITALIANA AND THE CIVIC COMMITTEES

The Church used Azione Cattolica Italiana (ACI) to prompt or compel Catholics to do what the Church wanted, and to enable the Church to demonstrate its capacity to influence voters. ACI was an important instrument for exercising leverage. Its capacity to serve several functions was due to its institutional links with the Church, and to the Church's view of its rightful role in society and politics. Some Catholic leaders viewed ACI as an organization that would shore up Catholic unity. Like the Italian hierarchy, ACI viewed its role as directing Catholics to vote for the party that offered the most guarantees for Catholicism.[19] The Vatican had decided that that party was the DC, and since ACI was under the direct control of the hierarchy, it also had to support the DC.

---

[17] ACS, MinIntPS, Pubblica Sicurezza, 1944–46, Mantova, Relazione Mensili, Feb. 4, 1946; ibid., Affari Generali, 1954 b. 16 re. 1953 electoral campaign.

[18] AAC, PG, VI f. 35, Calabria, 1947–49, "Relazione sul primo giro del carro-cinema in Calabria," p. 2.

[19] AAC, PG, Giunta Centrale, M. Ciocetti, meeting of Feb. 16, 1948.

To a number of ACI leaders, however, the DC was not the obvious choice as a political ally.[20] Prior to the explicit directives of ACI's hierarchy, the Azione Cattolica activists in Napoli were leaning toward the Monarchists and those in central provinces toward Uomo Qualunquists (Casella 1992, 169).[21] ACI's mission, broadcast to the entire electorate, was based on the same premise that the hierarchy and clergy were to operate on: "the absolute necessity of . . . the unity of Catholics . . . is the primordial exigency, and it will be most fully realized with unity around the DC."[22] As one bishop responsible for an ACI section noted, "We pray that we can overcome the triple danger: Communism, Protestantism, and masonry."[23]

Nevertheless, there were ACI leaders who argued that "maintaining Catholic unity at all costs inside the DC is not possible; it has to be done in another fashion" (in Magister 1979, 99). The Church eventually went further: it spawned the Civic Committees (CCs), on lines parallel to the structure of ACI. Where ACI still had to be concerned with spiritual matters, the CCs were given an explicit electoral mandate. The CC did door-to-door campaigning, held rallies, and instructed parish priests to give clear directives to their parishioners, telling Catholics that what was at stake "was a way of life and a choice of civilization" (Casella 1992, 154). The CCs had a structure parallel to that of Azione Cattolica; their activists were Catholics, and their goals, their competence, was explicitly electoral: the CCs were to direct Italians to follow the Church's voting instructions. Their political value came in the 1948 campaign, when they were crucial to the DC's gaining the vote share of 48%.

It was not merely numerical presence (in terms of members) that accounted for that contribution. Indeed, while ACI was influential in the north, its impact in the south was uneven: as some ACI activists noted, local groups existed on paper only (Warner 1994, 200a).

ACI's mission in the south became that of convincing voters that they were voting for the party "of God and Christ," not the party associated with priests! The local population had little respect for priests, who were

---

[20] ACS, MinIntPS, fondo K2 Azione Politica del clero, 1946, Piacenza, f. 17. b. 216, Mantova, f. 21 b. 216, Roma, f. 1, b. 216; ACS, MinIntPS, fondo K2 Azione Politica del clero, 1944–1946, Benevento, f. 10, b. 216; ACS, MinIntPS, 1944–1946, fondo Relazioni, Catanzaro, f. 331 b. 18, no. 0195, Apr. 14, 1944, no. 01067, July 5, 1945 (Durand 1991, 541–62).

[21] In southern Italy, some Catholic votes had gone to a secular party of the resistance, the Partito d'Azione. An Azione Cattolica missionary commented, "Unfortunately in the administrative elections, we too were undecided, giving preference to the Partito d'Azione, but you will see that this will not be repeated" (AAC, PG, letter from Sig.na Angelina Rinaldi to Sig.na Teresa Tanco, Jan. 8, 1948).

[22] AAC, PG, Giunta Centrale, Pres. Veronese, minutes of the meeting, Feb. 16, 1948.

[23] AAC, PG, VI f. 39, Calabria, diocese of Miletto, Jan. 20, 1951.

considered swindlers just like other local notables.[24] ACI's intervention helped the DC to eliminate its rivals in 1948, reducing serious competitors to mere nuisances. As shown earlier, where ACI supported the DC, where it had been able to mobilize Catholics, the DC did well. Given ACI's importance to the DC's electoral fortunes, the DC could not ignore ACI requests without penalty (Casella 1992, 192). Rather than abandon the DC when it went against the wishes of Azione Cattolica, ACI increased its efforts to colonize the DC. It shared the Vatican's view that it had to combat the Communist Party head on.[25]

ACI's structure was important to its effectiveness: it was hierarchical and centralized. Its leaders were appointed from the top and controlled by the Church. ACI was run by a national commission of cardinals, the mandate of which was to control ACI's activities "in all the nation and in single dioceses" (in Falconi 1956, 359). With directives to local branches coming from the national level, ACI activities and their political impact reflected national conditions more than local, especially compared to France. A good example comes from the Civic Committees: once the national-level ACI directors agreed to form them, the local ACI units were compelled to go along. The national leadership compiled the propaganda on which all ACI/CC units were to act (Casella 1992, 125). That the decision was made centrally, and that it carried weight, can be seen in the protests from some local clergy and bishops at being compelled to undertake a task they judged of questionable value (Casella 1992, 125, 159). Bishops protested that the CCs were redundant, that ACI could fulfill the same function (Casella 1992, 159–61, 167–68). The Vatican did not agree. The goal was "to involve all Catholic forces in a unified action."[26]

ACI had some concerns that, because of its political activities, the movement would become subservient to a political party, losing its spiritual functions. In the context of alternatives, for ACI the perceived risk of assisting the DC was lower than the risk of Communism. In contrast to France's Action Catholique, ACI thought that Communism should be dealt with in the political plane. For ACI, one of the anticipated benefits was the chance to structure Italian society according to Catholic precepts.

---

[24] AAC, PG, VI f. 35, Calabria, 1947–49, "Relazione sul primo giro del carro-cinema in Calabria," p. 2. On the successful contribution of Azione Cattolica to the DC in the south, see also AAC, PG, VI f. 35, Calabria, letter from Ten. Col. Emilio Froncillo to Ufficio Propaganda e Giunta Azione Cattolica Nazionale, Apr. 20, 1948; and Giulio Andreotti in Casella 1992, 449.

[25] AAC, PG, VI f. 35, Calabria, 1947–49, "Relazione sul primo giro del carro-cinema in Calabria."

[26] AAC, PG, Pres. Veronese, Feb. 18, 1948, to Msr. Alistico Riccò.

It showed no remorse about the Church's relation to the Fascist government, seeing the Church instead as the savior of Italy (Durand 1991, 57).[27]

The question is why ACI, with the Vatican's approval, invested heavily in a political campaign. Political mobilization should have been costly for ACI—politically active members might find a new source of opportunities in the DC. Several factors were, plausibly, motives: if successful, ACI would have access to material resources; and they feared that Communism would undermine the organization's survival. In 1948, the director of ACI demanded "full support of the DC, in order to avoid dangerous dispersion of the vote." The movement couched its actions in terms of the defense of the freedom of religion, and opposition to "Marxist totalitarianism."[28] Size mattered, but so too did ACI's structure and the conviction its leaders shared with the Church that the DC was the party to support.

Organizational structures, though influential in their own right, are malleable. Provided an agent or coalition of agents is sufficiently powerful, structures can be changed. In 1939–40, wanting to remind the laity of whom it served, Pius XII had "clericalized" Azione Cattolica, putting it under the supervision of a Cardinals' Commission for the High Direction of Catholic Action in Italy (Casella 1984a, 38), and substituting ecclesiastics for laical directors (39). With Azione Cattolica firmly under Vatican control, and Pius XII idolized by ACI youth (Magister 1979, 18), the Vatican was assured that Azione Cattolica's politics would be the pope's politics. The Vatican's attitude toward the laity remained the same, as Pius XII confirmed in 1959 to his deputy, Tardini: "I don't want collaborators, I want activists" (Riccardi 1985a, 38; Scoppola 1988, 56).

FARMER AND WORKER UNIONS

Founded in 1945 by DC member Paolo Bonomi (Ginsborg 1990, 171), the National Confederation of Direct Farmers (peasants) (Confederazione Nazionale dei Coltivatori Diretti, commonly referred to as "Coldiretti") was the "Christian" counterweight to the Communist Party's peasant syndicate, Federterra. Since its intention was to protect the interests of the owners of small and medium-sized farms, wage laborers were not allowed in Coldiretti. After the war, the DC-led government established a state

---

[27] In addition to the CCs, ACI had other subsidiary groups, defined in functional terms. Perhaps the most important of these was the workers' group, Associazione Cristiana dei Lavoratori Italiani (ACLI). Founded in 1944, ACLI was intended to provide a social and spiritual outlet for Catholic workers whose economic interests were (until 1948) represented by the single trade union, which had Socialists and Communists in it. Once the trade union split (see below), ACLI's mission had to be redefined.

[28] AAC, PG, "Foglio d'informazione," no. 3 (Feb.–Mar. 1948), p. 3.

agency, known as the Federconsorzi, to distribute agricultural inputs. In 1949, via the Church and the use of fraud and scare tactics, Coldiretti won control of 80% of the provincial Federconsorzi. Thus, Coldiretti had a virtual monopoly on seed, feed, fuel, and access to markets and work. More encompassing and coercive than the French farming syndicates, Coldiretti was a fief unto itself, with considerable leverage inside the DC (Rossi 1965; Ciranna 1958; Rossi-Doria 1963; Cavallaro 1958, 23–39). Using its strength within the DC, it was able to win important benefits, such as pensions, for its membership, further reinforcing its hold over the peasant vote. Coldiretti also claimed to fight for the protection of the Catholic faith (Manoukian 1968, 445, 453). Yet, crucial for the Church's ability to influence it, it was not structurally linked to the Church, nor did it owe its continued existence to Church support. It had its own faction within the DC, which sometimes quarreled with the Church.

Prior to 1948, Italy's industrial laborers had been represented by one trade union, the Confederazione Generale Italiana del Lavoro (CGIL) (Horowitz 1963). Sharp conflicts between the Communist and the Catholic factions of CGIL led the Catholics to break away—a split engineered by a joint effort of the DC and the Vatican. The new organization, the Confederazione Italiana dei Sindicati dei Lavoratori (CISL), shared the DC's and the Vatican's hostility to Communism. CISL depended on the clergy to remind Catholic workers of their duty to adhere to CISL, and to renounce the Communist Party–affiliated CGIL. With the DC as its main sponsor, CISL was an obvious resource for the DC. Theoretically, the two were independent; in practice, CISL was a staunch supporter of the DC's politics, "never questioning the employers' ownership rights and ultimate control" (Ginsborg 1990, 173).

Conclusions on Italy

The Church and its priests took advantage of the sacraments' importance to many Italians and of the limited opportunities many Italians had for jobs, education, and other necessities in the early postwar period. The Church made access to those things contingent upon parishioners' voting as the Church wanted. Nevertheless, there were and are limits on the extent to which any interest group can use coercion to ensure member compliance. In the case of the Church, important and desirable material and spiritual resources had to be in short supply and access to them funneled through the Church. Furthermore, the legitimacy of the Church's behaving in such a way had to be socially acceptable. With major improvements in the Italian economy (especially in the north and center), and a notable decline in the religiosity of Italians in the 1960s, the Church's leverage diminished.[29] The Church supplemented coercion with the creation, and aggressive mobilization, of ancillary organizations. ACI and the CCs were used to mobilize Catholics to vote for the Church's choice. In contrast, the Church had less success in directing the orientations of the agricultural and trade unions because its links to them were looser.

The Church, then, due to its hierarchical structure, its influence over crucial resources and opportunities, its ideological predisposition, and its popular standing, was well situated in the early years of the postwar Italian Republic to behave as a firm delivering a set of assets to a supplier in payment for (anticipated) desired goods.

FRANCE

The situation of the French Church was rather different. Although it had the monopoly on (Catholic) spiritual resources, any attempt to use that monopoly to compel Catholics to vote a particular way would have met with harsh retribution from anticlericals in France. The French Church did not even consider doing so, nor did the MRP want the Church to behave that way. Its ability to act as a conduit to jobs was also limited. Finally, since the French Church was only loosely in control of Action Catholique, its ability to ensure Catholic compliance with its voting preferences was further limited. The techniques the French Church used to influence Catholic political preferences were muted, at least in comparison to those used by the Italian Church. This was not so much because the French Church lacked the institutional resources, but rather because it lacked the *will* to interfere overtly in French politics. The Church had ample capacity, should it have wished, to campaign for a particular political party. This is evident in the first postwar elections, and in some regions of France, where priests worked on behalf of the MRP.

The French hierarchy diagnosed France's problems in spiritual terms; it did not see politics as the key remedy, and it preferred apostolic (pastoral) work as a solution. While recognizable enemies included the Communists, the Masonic movement, and the (secular) Radical Party, the solution was not conceived in strictly electoral or legislative terms. Rather, it involved hierarchically directed missionary work: spontaneous and unsupervised action by lay Catholics and lower clergy were not welcome. Its techniques

---

[29] Monopolies can have significant long-term costs for the organization that initially benefits from them: pricing and service delivery become inefficient, for there is little or no incentive to respond to consumer interests. Should a better alternative ever become available, it will quickly gain market share (Hirschman 1970; Gill 1998; Stark and Iannaccone 1994). This is the irony of having a religious monopoly.

were relatively low in cost with low visibility. For example, priests showed up at local festivals where politicians also gathered. Endorsements could often be made by mere proximity. The French Church's techniques were a reflection of the role it had defined for itself in politics, and the role that others had defined for it; institutional resources only slightly affected efforts.

The hierarchy's ability to gain compliance of its clergy and laity depended primarily upon its spiritual authority, which varied across France. Given its exclusion from the governing parties, it lacked the wide range of selective incentives available to its Italian counterpart for inducing recalcitrant Catholics to adhere to the Church's line. Its lesser ability to guarantee Catholic cooperation also weakened its ability to threaten political parties. When the clergy campaigned for a political party, they did so primarily via their messages at mass. They seldom used coercion: the withholding of sacraments from Communist or Socialist Party card holders or sympathizers was rare, nor was it a common practice to link a job or favor to a particular vote.[30] The clergy just did not think such actions proper, and they were in an environment that, for the most part, conclusively rejected such behavior. Many clergy, moreover, were convinced of the need to not reject Communism directly, but to associate with those who had accepted the ideology, in order to better understand it.

Where the clergy had a strong influence, parties were more likely to compete for their support; this varied by party across regions. In northwest France, the MRP did seek clerical support; in similarly Catholic south central France, the same party did not.[31] In Brittany, for instance, it appears as though the hierarchy sought to compel alliances for the 1951 election.[32] Catholic voters were pressed by the Church to vote for the candidates who would best protect Catholic interests. Given that the Gaullist party in Brittany was also pro-clerical, the local hierarchy's message, which did not name one party, was somewhat ambiguous.[33] In some rural municipalities, "the local clergy, fearing to spread confusion, even commented on the

---

[30] The historical record is not clear on whether it was even possible for clergy to do so. They sometimes were relied upon for character references.

[31] Archives Ernst Pezet, box no. 4, Pezet journal notes, Sept. 13, 1945; Institut Charles de Gaulle, A-RPF, BP2–56a, Morbihan, note from Gaullist (RPF) delegate, Apr. 18, 1951.

[32] The bishop of Vannes demanded that priests read at all masses in the weeks prior to the election a statement outlining the critical nature of the election and explaining that Catholics should think beyond personal interest in the vote, and instead consider which candidate list would support the Church's interests; in sum, "vote, vote Christian, and vote usefully" (bishop of Vannes, Eugène Joseph Marie, "lettre pastorale," *Semaine Religieuse du Diocèse de Vannes,* June 9, 1951).

[33] At the national level, see Charles de Gaulle's affirmation of his Catholicism in his rebuttal to an article in *L'osservatore romano* (the Vatican's paper), of May 26, 1951, by Mr. Ales-

[bishop's] letter and, very clearly, recommended to vote for the Union [list], which included the MRP."[34] Given the variance across France in the bishops' views, and the variation in clergy views (often different from the bishop's), the Church as a unit could never deliver Catholics en bloc to one party.

Where the Church had authority and was the traditional focus of social and political life, the clergy could exercise more direction over Catholic political behavior and thus influence a party's fate. In south central France, when the MRP was favored by the clergy, it did well.[35] When it fell out of clerical favor, its electoral fortunes tumbled. For instance, in Aveyron, the MRP was significantly aided by priests in organizing and campaigning for the party.[36] Commenting on the victory of the Républicains Indépendants in the 1949 Aveyron cantonal elections, the prefect noted that the "clear slide to the right seen in this department was due in part to the very strict instructions given by the clergy."[37] In fact, it was the bishop who "pushed Catholics toward the Indépendants at the MRP's expense."[38] In later years, the Independent/Peasant list again benefited from the support of the clergy, "who had earnestly fought against abstentionism in the very Catholic rural populations, without actively supporting the MRP, whose social program is a motif of fear for some."[39]

An example of clerical influence comes from the fate of Charles de Gaulle's Rassemblement du Peuple Français (RPF) in Aveyron. The RPF had no locally based candidates of note, so a Parisian bureaucrat was brought in.[40] Since the Aveyron Church was hostile to the RPF, the candidate had no significant local backing.[41] The effect was dramatic: the RPF

---

sandrini (in de Gaulle 1970, 447). On the Church, AN, FI CIII dr. 1301, Morbihan, rapport du préfet, July 10, 1951.

[34] The Gaullist party, out of favor with the Church, ran on a separate list. AN, FI CIII dr. 1301, Morbihan, rapport du préfet, July 10, 1951.

[35] AN, FI CII dr. 143, Aveyron, Nov. 12, 1946; Mendras 1953, 57.

[36] *Le Pays*, Sept. 26, 1945; Institut Charles de Gaulle, A-RPF, BP2–12D, Aveyron, Mar. 1, 1948; AN, FI CII dr. 275, Aveyron, Mar. 28, 1949.

[37] AN, FI CII dr. 143, Aveyron, rapport sur les élections cantonales du Mars 1949 [Mar. 1949], s.d.

[38] ADA, fonds Ramadier dr. 52J 19, 1949, letter of Mar. 21, 1949. The Independents won 29.8%, the MRP 18.8%, the PCF, 12.8%, the RGR (Radicals and UDSR), 23.2%, the RPF, 7.8% and the SFIO, 7.8% (AN, FI CII dr. 143, Aveyron, rapport sur les élections cantonales du Mars 1949, s.d.).

[39] AN, FI CII dr. 143, Aveyron, rapport sur les élections législatives du 17 Juin 1951 [n.d., July 1951?].

[40] *Rouergue Républicain*, May 18, 1951; also ADA, fonds Ramadier, dr. 52J15, 1947; Institut Charles de Gaulle, A-RPF, BP2–12d, Aveyron, July 27, 1947.

[41] The prefect implied that the hierarchy apparently suspected the candidate's "Catholic" sincerity (AN, FI CII dr. 143, Aveyron, rapport du préfet, Dec. 15, 1950 and Mar. 13, 1951).

hardly made a dent in Aveyronnais elections.[42] Where the Church was an accepted, major social institution, its influence could be decisive.

Persuasion and Pastoral Work

Much of the French Church's postwar effort to influence Catholics and, perhaps indirectly, political parties was channeled into mechanisms that relied on the persuasive power of living by example: clergy sought to immerse themselves in the temporal lives of their parishioners. The worker-priest movement in France was indicative of the Church's concerns and emblematic of its way of approaching the problem of a de-Christianized society. Just as the Church was decentralized, the "movement" was composed of numerous organizations. One, the Mission de Paris, was established in 1940 by the abbé Godin (Bosworth 1962, 91). Another was set up under Cardinal Suhard in 1943, when priests surreptitiously accompanied forced-labor camp workers to Germany. Priests became factory workers, lived and ate with the workers, even joined "their" union—the Communist-affiliated Confédération Générale du Travail. As a French Jesuit sent to Dachau (a concentration camp) in the early 1940s declared, "How much would the priest gain to be able to realize concretely through personal experience the conditions of life of those he seeks to evangelize!" (Ravitch 1990, 143). In 1954, a priest commented, "That which was valid yesterday absolutely no longer is in the new circumstances" (in Falconi 1960, 300). The war changed many priests' perceptions of useful strategies; they decided to focus less on Action Catholique and more on the workers directly.

In short, the French Church faced up to and penetrated the worker milieu in an effort to understand why the workers thought and behaved as they did.[43] The movement prompted a collective evaluation of the societal role of the French Church. Because under the leadership of Cardinals Suhard and Feltin the French Church defined its role in evangelical terms, it could foster the worker-priest movement as a way to reach and perhaps "re-Christianize" workers. The movement thrived for over a decade, until 1954. Then, to end challenges to Church orthodoxy, Pius XII condemned the movement, restricted priests to three hours a week in the factory, required them to live in religious communities, and ordered them to enter

---

[42] The SFIO section observed that the bishop also intervened against the SFIO, the Radicals, and the PCF (ADA, fonds Ramadier, dr. 52J19, Mar. 22, 1949).

[43] In an ironic recognition of historical materialism, the Church feared that its worker-priests, if they associated with workers in the factories too long, would espouse the political and economic goals of the Communists. When priests joined the Communist-affiliated union, the hierarchy became alarmed.

factories as priests, not workers (Dansette 1957, 225–300; Ravitch 1990, 141–48).[44] The movement was completely eliminated in 1959 by the Roman Curia, though the French Church preferred to allow their activities to continue (Bosworth 1962, 93). The movement represented, to the Vatican, a rebirth of Gallicanism and "a French manner of confronting problems," which conflicted with the Vatican's "grand plan" "to romanize Catholicism, whether French or [elsewhere in] the world" (Poulat 1985, 297).

The clergy also rejected earlier conceptions of pastoral work in the rural areas, one even referring to the prewar model as the "totalitarian parish" (in Pierrard 1986, 326). In contrast to their Italian counterparts, French clergy were not inclined to create and enforce a distinct Catholic subculture; rather, they sought to integrate Catholics into the larger community.

Ancillary Organizations and Their Political Activity

ACTION CATHOLIQUE FRANÇAISE

The Church did not hesitate to create ancillary organizations even in the absence of secular state threats to the Church's status. Missionary work, not the cost of setting up the necessary organizations, nor the potential loss of control over Catholics, was the concern. The adult section of the Catholic Workers movement (Action Catholique Ouvrière, or ACO), intended to minister to the proletariat, was the creation of the Assembly of Cardinals and Archbishops (ACA) (Bosworth 1962, 65; Dansette 1957, 379).[45]

The Church had, in Action Catholique organizations, weak tools by which to affect Catholics' religious, social, and political behavior. Recall that Action Catholique organizations were officially mandated by the Church to carry out apostolic work. The tools were weak not due to the lesser size of Action Catholique, but to its institutional structure, and the divergent views of its leaders. France's Action Catholique had the same debate as its Italian counterpart about whether it could be active in politics and gave similar justifications for allowable intervention. The extent of intervention, however, was less encompassing than in Italy. The Church's control over its ancillary organizations was exercised partly through insti-

---

[44] The contrast with the Italian worker-priest movement is revealing. The Italian movement was weak, and the priests entered the factories as priests, not as workers. They did not share the experience of the workers and sought only to harangue them back to Catholicism (Gariglio 1986).

[45] The hierarchy stated that the ACO "teaches Christians the key duty that they bear as citizens, to engage in the thankless task" of making the world a better, more Christian place (Dansette 1957, 380).

tutional links, and the links between the French Church and AC were loose.

As with the general structure of the French Church, Action Catholique was decentralized. Federations were organized at the diocese level and supervised by the local bishop, who gave each group a "mandate" and could suspend any AC group's activities. Obviously, this gave the bishop "control over the 'tendencies' " of AC groups (Bosworth 1962, 75). There was a national secretariat, and the ACA could overrule a local federation, but for the most part, each bishop regulated his own diocesan associations. This decentralization meant that Action Catholique's political behavior reflected the local context more than the national—local variations were not tempered by a standardized program from the hierarchy. Even had the Catholic hierarchy, in the voice of the ACA, wanted to steer AC toward a particular party, it would have had difficulty doing so. This lack of a centralized structure made it harder for the Church and AC to threaten the MRP, had they so desired, with the consequences of their withdrawal of support, since any such withdrawal would vary according to local preferences and priorities. What vote contribution Action Catholique made to a party depended upon local decisions. The hierarchy had little leverage with which to compel the ancillary organizations to vote for a particular party.

AC was willing to see its members become politically active, if through other organizations. The preference for not using AC institutions for political mobilization was due to concerns about both conserving AC's resources and retaining its emphasis on a spiritual role.

> In counseling some of its [members] to engage themselves in political formations conforming to Christian principles, Action Catholique will remain nonetheless in its own form. And it is precisely in the extent to which Action Catholique can launch its activists in all directions and in all services foreign to itself, that it can most efficiently attain its goal—in relieving itself as much as possible of concerns of a material nature that tend to weigh down its action.[46]

French Catholic Action would alter the political world by sending its leaders into it, but not by campaigning for political parties. Believing that its mere presence in French society would convince others of its "moral effectiveness" and hence bring about conversions, AC did not emphasize religious rallies or high-pressure proselytizing (Bosworth 1962, 99). Contributing to the lack of coordinating capacity were conflicts within AC over its orientation (as an intellectual and spiritual training organization, or as a missionary organization) (Dansette 1957, 391). These manifested

---

[46] *CCR,* Jan.–Feb. 1945, 19.

themselves across regions, and across specific AC subgroups (Bosworth 1962, 107).

The lack of cohesion in Action Catholique organizations is evinced by AC's record during the Vichy years. Initially reluctant participants in Vichy youth parades, some AC members eventually became active in the Resistance. Others were staunch supporters of Vichy (Duquesne 1966, 69–71). Action Catholique provided some Resistance martyrs, and some Jeunesse Ouvrière Chrétienne activists joined deportees in Germany, setting up cells and federations in 400 German cities (McMillan 1996, 58–59). Eventually Action Catholique reevaluated its stance on Vichy, questioning the social and economic status quo and concluding Vichy would have to be dispensed with (Dansette 1957, 396).

For the AC members active in the Resistance, the experience seems to have encouraged them to undertake political action. By launching political entrepreneurs, AC challenged the Church's control over Catholics (Dansette 1957, 375) who, partly from their experience, partly to justify organizational autonomy, developed a program somewhat at odds with the Church. Yet AC did so indirectly, suggesting that its members, at the outset of the Fourth Republic, be active in Christian political parties, in other words, in the MRP. The organization itself would not become entangled, but the endorsement of the MRP was undeniable, and the assistance to the MRP was significant, at least in 1946.

The change came later, as AC activists, disillusioned with the MRP's policies, pulled back. When, in the late 1940s, it began looking as though Action Catholique might veer toward the MRP's rather more leftist tendencies, the Church intervened, making it clear that explicit political action was out of the question, and that the organization was to remain obedient to the hierarchy.[47] Some Action Catholique sections then called on their members to avoid participation in political parties.[48] Catholic Action threatened the Church's control over the representation and definition of Catholicism only so long as the Church permitted it to.

AC's rural organization, Jeunesse Agricole Chrétienne (JAC), was another tool of the Church that sought to "render France to Jesus Christ" (Lambert 1985, 222, 119–26). Had the Church been a centralized organization determined to support one party, JAC could have increased the Church's leverage over such a party. JAC was vibrant, and its members were willing to be active in local politics (Dansette 1957, 389). The organization, led primarily by laity and only loosely responsible to the clergy, largely dictated its own goals. Initially, although very active in rural life,

[47] Assemblée des Cardinaux et Archevêques statement, printed in *SRP*, Jan. 1, 1947, 276.
[48] Archives de la Fédération de la Seine, MRP, July 1954 "Questionnaire," responses of various sections.

the JAC avoided partisan activity. Its intention was to bring rural farming youth back to Catholicism, and to help them in practical aspects of their work (Durupt 1963, 1:199; D'Haene 1954, 95; Epagneul 1976). Given its connections with the peasants, JAC had the capacity to be an influential political force. It was the activists, and not the hierarchy, who discovered that one means of effecting change was to penetrate local politics and, later, national farming organizations (Cleary 1989).[49]

FARMER AND WORKER UNIONS

In France, as in Italy, there was a large network of influential peasant organizations and rural cooperatives. The dominant organization was the Fédération Nationale des Syndicats d'Exploitants Agricoles (FNSEA). Led by an amalgam of conservative farmers, nobles, and priests, France's first major agrarian union was an alliance against Socialists, Communists, and "radical republicans" in general.[50] By offering educational courses and organizing social groups, as well as insurance, credit, and market cooperatives, FNSEA mobilized peasants, agrarian laborers, tenant farmers, and large landowners into a potentially powerful political organization. Some of the local branches were organized by conservative Catholics, others by socially progressive Catholics (those in the Action Catholique de Jeunesse Française).[51] The Catholic Church had no formal authority over FNSEA.

Given its Catholic and anti-Communist orientation, the FNSEA would seem to have been a ready mate for a French Christian Democratic party. By 1956, a progressive Catholic, René Blondelle, was running the organization, and Action Catholique's agrarian group, JAC, animated some of the department federations. However, because the MRP had pushed for a

[49] The MRP, in its turn, with its presence in conservative governments, and its tepid support of family farmers and state subsidies to private schools, had not made itself appealing to the JAC—an organization whose sympathies could have been significant in the process of establishing the party and winning votes.

[50] In 1922, the president of the organization declared that his movement "is anything but revolutionary, it is reformist and creative . . . the very antithesis of socialism, which stimulates the very lowest of passions and appetites. . . . it represents the paragon of good sense, careful reflection, and positive action" (M. Delalande, Union Centrale des Syndicats Agricoles, XI Congrès National [1922], in Cleary 1989, 63).

[51] Agrarian unions were dissolved by the Vichy government, which created the Corporation Paysanne. France's government-in-exile dissolved that in 1944 and replaced it with a Socialist/Communist-oriented Confédération Générale de l'Agriculture. This leftist CGA then created what turned out to be its nemesis: an influential conservative, Catholic farming organization, the FNSEA (Cleary 1989, 104–8; S. Berger 1972). It was intended to be the CGA's representative union at the local level. Yet the FNSEA leaders (partly by adroit maneuvering, partly by the peasant preference for the familiar), mostly came from Vichy and prewar conservative agrarian unions. Rural laborers, those not owning any *élément de l'exploitation,* such as a cow or plot of land, could not join the FNSEA (Tavernier 1969, 64).

rationalization of family farming, relations between the FNSEA and MRP were unfriendly (Warner 1998, 571–72).

The Confédération Française des Travailleurs Chrétiens (CFTC), organized at the turn of the twentieth century to compete with the Socialist unions, was also not part of the Church's institutional structure. While useful to the extent that the CFTC kept workers from joining the Socialist- and Communist-oriented unions, it was not a tool to which the Church had direct access.[52] The CFTC reached the same conclusion about the MRP that Action Catholique had: the party was not a strong advocate of worker interests. As one worker advocate noted, "A Christian trade unionist, above all if he belongs to the militant wing of the CFTC, would think it an insult to be confused with a member of the MRP."[53]

CONCLUSION

The instruments the Catholic Churches used to influence the political views of its followers ranged from persuasion to coercion, from individual interaction to collective mobilization. The techniques used depended on the Church's ideological and institutional links with its ancillary organizations, on its view of its role in society, and on its control over individuals' access to key resources.

The analysis has used a simple cost/benefit logic first, assuming that a Church picks the least costly route. But the key is to identify what relative weighting any Church, with varying priorities, gives to costs. Some scholars argue that the "mobilization strategy" cost each Church its control over the laity. I contend that the laity were not lost to the Church, and in the Church's view, the opportunity costs of not mobilizing the lay ancillary organizations were higher, if measured against a fear of Communism and the lack of legal protections and subsidies for the Church. When political circumstances were such that the Church signed concordats with governments, it incurred costs, too: a concordat acknowledges that temporal rulers have the power to deny the Catholic Church its demands. Through Catholic Action, the Church had the potential to exert considerable political influence on a Catholic political party—the latter might then become dependent upon Catholic Action's campaign support.

---

[52] The Church did urge workers to join the CFTC, rather than the rival unions. The hierarchy "emphatically" exhorted Catholics "to organize themselves more and more numerously into the Christian Union: the teachings of the sovereign pontiffs have made this a duty. . . . For its part, the Assembly of Cardinals and Archbishops assures the CFTC of its full confidence" (*SRP,* Apr. 3, 1948, 355). See also speech at the parish assembly meeting, Jan. 25, 1948, reported in *SRP,* Mar. 6, 1948, 229.

[53] Étienne Borne in *Recherches,* Jan.–Feb. 1955, 27.

It has become a commonplace for scholars to refer to the "Catholic subculture" in Italy, of which the DC was just one part (Prandi 1968; Manoukian 1968; Ginsborg 1990). This chapter has shown that that culture was deliberately constructed and had to be reinforced frequently, and that its status as a "culture" is not clear. Catholic values provided no clear road map on how to vote—the hierarchical aspect of Catholicism would have dictated obedience to Church directives; the egalitarian aspect would have dictated voting Communist. Coercion and selective incentives played large roles in mobilizing Catholics to follow Church political directives; the Catholic "identity" seems to have been of secondary importance. The Church in many parts of Italy effectively made voting DC a part of in-group behavior. Being surrounded by Catholics in all aspects of one's public (and private) life raises the costs to an individual of engaging in non-Catholic (nongroup) behavior.

The Italian Church had, under Mussolini, established itself as the controller of its ancillary organization, Azione Cattolica, which had a centralized, hierarchical structure. The structure was not just parallel to that of the Church; it was responsible to the Vatican hierarchy. That structure enabled the Church to control the organization and facilitated coordinated political action. This made it easier for the Church to direct Catholics' political behavior, especially once it sent Azione Cattolica and the Civic Committees into the political arena. The Church did not use ACI just because it existed—the instrument did not determine its use, or whether it would be used. Rather, the Church used it for political purposes because the hierarchy had a militaristic view of postwar Italian society, as a battle between good (Catholicism) and evil (Communism).

Since the Italian Church had, either directly or through institutional links, control over resources desired or needed by much of the population (sacraments and an institutionalized belief system, jobs, government dispensations), it was able to use coercion to compel Catholic compliance with the Church's electoral preferences. Being able to do so increased the Church's credibility with the DC, which enhanced its ability to punish the party for noncompliance. The corollary to that was that, ceteris paribus, were the Church to lose its position as distributor of desired resources, its ability to influence the politics of Catholics, and to influence the DC, would fall.

That organizational linkages and structures matter to an interest group's actions is clear in the French case as well. The Catholic ancillary organization, Action Catholique, had a comparatively decentralized structure, making coordinated action across France difficult—had that even been the goal of the organization. Action Catholique was also more removed from the control of the Catholic hierarchy, both institutionally and ideologically. Having contributed some of its members to the Resistance and to the MRP, Action Catholique organizations in many dioceses were more progressive than the Catholic Church.

The French Church, even if it had had a Catholic Action organization similarly structured and extensive, probably would not have utilized it in the manner the Italian Church did. Doing so would have triggered a severe anticlerical reaction; many French, including practicing Catholics, would have argued that the Church had greatly overstepped its boundaries (which is partly why the Church did not have an AC organization on the scale of the Italian one). The Church was also limited by the historical burden of its incorporation into the Vichy regime and the postwar repudiation of Vichy. In addition, the absence of a militaristic attitude enabled the Church to consider empathetic proselytizing tactics such as the worker-priest movement. That movement tried to understand the experiences of a set of individuals, rather than trying to compel those persons to fit the Procrustean bed of orthodox Catholicism.

The French Church of the 1950s was a bit more willing than the Italian to adjust itself to changed circumstances, and it defined its possibilities, scope for action, and goals more modestly and moderately. That stance meant, in turn, that the French Church was not inclined to, and did not, try to create new ancillary organizations aimed at campaigning for a political party. Since the French Church did not control the conduits to highly desirable resources (save in limited areas), it could not use similar forms of coercion to influence French Catholics.

What does this say about interest groups and their ability to turn out correct-thinking and correct-voting voters? When an interest group wishes to have political influence, one of its key concerns is being able to control its own membership. It must do so in order to show potential political party allies that it can deliver that which it promises—namely votes and activists. The techniques it uses vary according to its resources, institutional structures, goals, and the normative framework of the society in which it operates—the latter determining the limits of acceptable action. The group's problem is the same as that of a firm that has located a supplier for a desired product, and that, to purchase the product, must pay in some fungible currency or directly invest resources in the supplier. The firm must be sure it has that currency and those resources on hand to deliver. The group's currency is not just its financial assets, but the votes of its members, and its resources are its ancillary organizations and its own "employees," who can provide infrastructural and logistical support to a party. Politics might require a slight departure from the economic metaphor: in politics, a party can affect the ability of an interest group to deliver its members and may have an interest in doing so. It can, if in government, try to enact legislation to increase or restrict the group's ability to use its funds without its members' approval; it can grant the group a representational monopoly. The group's leverage over a party depends on its ability to deliver and withdraw members (from the party's electorate and its organization) and material resources, and on whether the party wants its support in the first place.

The next chapter takes up the question of when a *party* is likely to want an interest group's support.

CHAPTER 8

Christian Democratic Parties and
Their Search for Allies

A PREFECT in southern Italy commented in 1946, "On the occasion of the elections, one could observe in almost all the little villages that, as was expected, family feuds and ambitions that have been perpetuating themselves for decades were masquerading behind the parties in competition."[1] As one might anticipate in light of the prefect's comments, local party links to interest groups in southern Italy were overtly instrumental. In general, however, there are four schools of thought on why a political party cooperates and links with interest groups. First, doing so is their function: parties serve as links between citizens and governments. Thus, when citizens are organized into an interest group, it is natural that parties should provide the same linkage service to them. The parties merely aggregate expressed interests. (Parties, however, sometimes deliberately fail to be transmission belts.) Second and similarly, a party can be the emanation of an interest group that represents a demographic category, such as industrial workers, Catholics, or peasants. The larger the category's voting population, the larger the party. Even taking into account the discriminatory power of electoral systems (Grofman and Lijphart 1986), however, this view fails to account for the nonemergence of parties representing some demographic categories, and for the ability of some parties to combine categories. Third, an interest group is a significant electoral and organizational resource for a party, and since parties need to succeed both electorally and in office, they actively seek out interest groups. But parties discriminate, even when a group's size and resources make it an enticing organization. Fourth, the link can be the unintended consequence of the strategic interaction of political entrepreneurs. Neither the interest group nor the party wanted to be linked, but previous choices produce the link as a side effect. This might explain some cases, but in others, parties and interest groups actively seek each other out. This chapter will attempt to answer some relevant questions in this regard: first, why does the party link with any interest group? Second, how does it choose among interest groups? Third, how does it control the group with which it has linked?

---

[1] ACS, Prefettura di Catanzaro, Relazione Mensili, Apr. 1, 1946, p. 2.

I suggest that parties view interest groups strategically, assessing the latter's resources and ability to contribute to the parties' electoral and policy goals. But that assessment is affected by ideological factors: are the interest group's ideological goals complementary to those of the party? Can the party stand to be seen in public with the group? In terms of the market analogy, the issue is not just one of a product's price, quality, and availability, but of whether the buyer is "irrationally" sensitive to the producer firm's reputation or image.

STANDARD EXPLANATIONS OF PARTY STRATEGIES TOWARD INTEREST GROUPS

One standard explanation of party–interest group links, the "party as an electoral tool" literature, starts with the assumption that a political party is, first and foremost, an office-seeker (Aldrich 1995; Downs 1957) created by office-seeking politicians. A party seeks as allies those interest groups that seem likely to contribute substantially to the party's electoral and office-seeking goals.

When a party does not do this, scholars turn to the party's internal structure (Kitschelt 1994, 207–53; Koelble 1992a). It is possible that a party forgoes interest group support because it is internally divided due to its organizational structure and/or multiple factions. National leaders are not able to enforce adherence to agreements with key external allies. Strategy and policy will be the result of the uncoordinated behavior of the party federations and activists at all levels, acting upon their own ideals and interests. Local party leaders undertake self-interested behavior. Such a scenario reduces the incentive for secondary organizations to come to agreement with party representatives.

While the internal structure factor is an important variable, it is not able to explain the particular cases examined here. Both the MRP and the DC began as confederal as opposed to centralized, oligarchical structures. Both were structurally "weak" at the outset (Gaeta and Luzzatto 1981; Chassériaud 1965, 37–100; Irving 1973, 91–105; Letamendia 1975, 208–66) yet responded differently to similar environmental conditions.

Neither the "transmission belt" nor the "political arm" school can explain why the Christian Democratic party in France failed to serve those functions for French Catholics and the Church. To get around the failure of these arguments to predict the behavior of Christian Democracy in France, scholars cite the severity of the Church-state conflict in France (a severity that in other countries they would expect to yield just such a party) (Hazareesingh 1994). They also point out that the MRP did well in "Catholic strongholds" (Irving 1973; Williams 1964). Yet, they cannot explain why there were so many Catholic strongholds in France where the MRP did *not* do well.[2] The "party as office-seeker" school also cannot explain the MRP's failure to seek the Church as an ally. Though the Church could not match its Italian counterpart in resources, it was still an important organization with an institutional presence in most, if not all, of France. For the MRP, it would have been rational to solicit the Church's support for campaign purposes alone. Finally, though particular characteristics of the parties may have been unintended by various elites, the postwar Christian Democratic parties and their interest group relations were not the contingent outcomes of competing elites' strategies.

To account for why the DC pursued the Catholic Church as an ally, and the MRP did not, the focus must shift to a comparison of the Church's resources, the party's view of the Church's role in establishing the new political system, and the party's ideology and programmatic goals. While one cannot specify exactly to what extent, also important are the respective parties' leadership, their prior institutional connections to the Church, and the Church's current reputation among the electorate the parties wanted to target. The DC had the advantage of being able to repudiate the previous regime without repudiating Catholicism: the Fascists were neither Christian nor democratic. In contrast, the MRP could not disavow the Vichy regime without also implicitly criticizing the Catholic Church, which had allied itself with Vichy.

A MARKET ANALYSIS OF THE KEY QUESTIONS

To answer the questions raised at the beginning of this chapter, we return to the market analogy. Consider the party as the buyer (of political support) and the interest group as the seller. If the interest group did not create the party, then the party links with an interest group because, first, it needs external support,[3] and, second, it estimates that the electoral and organizational support the group can provide outweighs any drawbacks in terms of policy compromises or conflicts, internal organizational inde-

---

[2] Over half of the twenty departments with particularly high percentages of practicing Catholics did not strongly support the MRP. In 1951, the MRP's average vote was 11%, with a standard deviation of 8%. Levels of practicing Catholics averaged 24%, with a standard deviation of 14%. There were 20 departments in which Catholicism was more than 38%; in only 9 of those was the MRP's vote at least 19%.

[3] If the party has other means to attain office (e.g., patronage, independent financing), then it is less likely to need an interest group's support. See Panebianco 1982 and Shefter 1977 for factors potentially affecting a party's demand curve for interest group support. In most instances, a party in a democratic system finds it needs some level of support from external organizations in order to compete successfully in the electoral market.

pendence, or restricted government coalition possibilities. The party's choice of which interest group(s) to have as an ally (allies) is limited by the range of groups available.[4] Given a set of groups, the party assesses the size of the group's membership, the likelihood that the group can deliver its membership during elections, and the organizational resources the group can provide the party. It also assesses the price the group charges for those services: what policies does the group want the party to try to implement, what oversight and directive positions is it demanding (i.e., positions of control inside the party)? Since the party is likely to need or want the support of more than one interest group, the party also assesses the effect that allying with one interest group will have on its ability to attract others. Will an alliance with one group repel others that the party had wanted as allies? If so, is there any way the party can hide its alliances? Does the interest group support the norms and values that the party wants to perpetuate in society, if only to sustain its electoral base?

Party scholars may object that the party's goals and self-image are, of course, affected by internal party politics, by battles over leadership control. Also significant for who gets to define the party's goals and image is the internal struggle over which part of the party, the party in office or the party bureaucracy, is to provide the leadership. In some parties, interest group alliances may be primarily a function of that internal power struggle. A faction might ally with a group, despite the fact that doing so could be costly to the party as a whole, for the benefits that accrue to the group's efforts to unseat the current leadership, or to fend off a challenge. I focus on the *leadership's* definition of the party's goals for two reasons. First, party leaders want to retain control over the party. Second, to prevent being outflanked by new internal coalitions or undermined by significant desertions, they must be attentive to minority views in their party. Rather than explaining how the current party leadership attained its power, I focus on its assessment of potential allies and efforts to get them. Where internal factions affect interest group relations, I discuss them.

As Anthony Gill's work (1998) points out, a Christian Democratic party that aims to govern might find the Church an attractive ally because the Catholic Church usually produces and distributes status quo (often called "conservative") values and norms (the exceptions are the motivation for Gill's work). If a Christian Democratic party is trying to compete against a radical Right or Marxist Left, then granting the Church many of its

---

[4] In addition, the party might also create its own ancillary groups. Whether it does depends on its resources (the MRP tried but often failed for lack of means), and on the savings from vertically integrating this "function" (in organizational resources, policy control, transaction costs). Since my focus is on party interaction with "external" interest groups, I do not analyze this aspect of party behavior, except as it affects the party's decision about external groups.

preferences, enlisting the Church in a joint struggle, may redound to the party's benefit. A quiescent, Catholic population is more likely to vote Christian Democratic than radical Right or Left and is less likely to challenge a newly established political order that has been approved by the Church.

Once a party decides it wants a particular interest group, it attracts it through various incentives (policy promises, ideological stance, promises of material resources). Beyond those incentives, however, the party has to reduce the group's risk that the *party* will fail to perform as promised.[5] The group and party face the familiar problem of malfeasance, and one solution is for the party to post a bond of sorts, possibly by committing specific assets to the relationship (cf. Becker and Stigler 1974; Wimmer and Garen 1997, 544). The amount of the bond or assets depends on the relative bargaining power of each organization. The greater the group's demand for a party ally, and the fewer alternative parties it has, the lower the "bond" that the party must post. The party knows the group's choices are limited, and that it will place a high value even on partial fulfillment of the contract. Conversely, the greater the party's demand for the group's support, and the more alternatives the group has to choose from, the higher the bond the party must post. The group can be more selective and thus require the party to provide a better guarantee against malfeasance. Trust and familiarity may lower the level of bond or specific assets necessary to reassure the group that the party will deliver.

Parties are limited in the types of "bonds" or specific assets they can offer. To create a specific asset, the party might make itself dependent upon group support, e.g., by not developing its own infrastructure. Another is to allow the group to direct the party's development. Hinich and Munger (1994) argue that ideology serves as a third type of bond, committing the party to adopt particular policies, or at least reassuring the group that the policies will not stray beyond the boundaries of the ideology. To the extent that consistency is important to a party's electoral success, it *is* a specific asset—unusable in other market exchanges. Yet for an opportunistic party, ideology is a somewhat weak constraint. A fourth type of specific asset might be the individuals themselves. Because the DC could "offer the sight" of 50 parliamentary representatives praying at mass,[6] and a rival pro-Church party could not, the Vatican had greater confidence in the DC's likelihood of carrying out its promises. If the party is already the governing

---

[5] If the party gets the group's support, the party may create conditions or exploit conditions that enable it to free-ride on the group, putting the group's support to work for the party's other ventures. The party may be able to use the position it gained in government, as a result of the group's initial support, to diversify its portfolio of suppliers, to seek other means of reelection and political dominance.

[6] Pius XII, *La Settimana del clero,* Nov. 30, 1947.

party in office, it could try to stake its existence on the outcome of a vote on a group-supported issue.[7]

Parties are office-seekers and so seek external allies when they need electoral and other forms of political support. They are not indiscriminate: they weigh the consequences of their alliances against the party's goals and its self-image. I expect a party to solicit the Church and to allow it more influence in its internal affairs when the leadership highly values the Church's support and shares some of the Church's goals (cf. Keshavarzian and Gill 1997). The DC's goal of dominating the Italian state, its definition of itself as the political repository of Catholic values and friend of the Church, and as the party taking responsibility for the Church's conversion to democracy, made the Church an important, indeed essential, ally. The MRP's goal of upholding the Fourth Republic, its image of itself as a law-abiding yet revolutionary party, as a progressive party inspired by Christian principles but open to all, made the Church, tainted by Vichy, a less than attractive ally. The MRP's office-seeking interests did not overcome its view of itself as progressive and ecumenical party.

What is striking in the contrast between the Italian DC and the French MRP is that the DC committed some assets to the party-group link, while the MRP by and large did not. The latter's unwillingness to do so stemmed from its view of its role in the new political system, and from the lower priority it attached to having the Church as an ally.

THE DC AND ITS SEARCH FOR ALLIES

> Our adversaries accuse us of being influenced by
> priests. Because Christian Democracy is, above
> all, Christian, it would be absurd if it disregarded
> its pastors, and, on the other hand, the priest can-
> not disinterest himself in his spiritual children.[8]
> *(DC, 1946)*

There were three main reasons that the DC sought the Church as a political ally. First, though not a sufficient condition, the DC wanted to dominate Italian politics,[9] it faced rival parties, and Church had vast resources. Second, the DC leadership viewed the Church's support of democracy as

---

[7] Iteration is also critical here. If the party wants to keep getting reelected to office, it needs to establish a reputation for fulfilling promises.

[8] Giuseppe Sala, editorial in *Il Popolo* (DC newspaper), May 16, 1946.

[9] In the aftermath of World War II, the DC announced that it would be nothing less than "the guarantor of Italian civilization and Christianity" (General Report, Congresso Nazionale, Apr. 24–28, 1946, reported in *I Congressi Nazionali della DC*, 27–28).

essential to democracy's survival. Third, the DC leadership saw the Church as a legitimate ally.

Why Choose the Church as an Ally?

CHURCH RESOURCES

It is not hard to understand the Church's appeal to a party if one looks at its organizational resources, which far surpassed those of the DC's main competitor (the Communist Party). The Church had an extensive organizational network that had the potential to distribute the DC's electoral message and add to the organizational infrastructure of the party (see chap. 7).

ESSENTIAL TO DEMOCRACY

The DC placed great weight on the Church's potential to undermine democracy. With hindsight, democracy in Italy looks to have been inevitable: the fall of Fascism, the Church's limited acknowledgment of democracy's acceptability, the support of the United States; yet at the time, the DC leadership was preoccupied with finding a strategy that would allow democracy to prevail. As an Azione Cattolica leader and friend of De Gasperi noted in June 1944, if "one thinks of the actual structure of the parties, of the still scarce political education and knowledge [of the population], the lack of parliamentary control [of the interim government]," the possibility of a coup d'etat was not far-fetched (in De Gasperi 1974, 1:346). De Gasperi expressed his worries as late as 1952: "All our argumentation in favor of a democratic regime does not succeed in persuading [the Vatican], because it [now] believes that democracy is too weak to resist the extreme [Left]" (in Scoppola 1988, 160).

To prevent the Church from turning against democracy, and to block the PCI, the DC's leadership tried to bring together within it all strands of Catholicism.[10] To do this, the DC had to make itself the party that encompassed all Catholics and convince Catholic political entrepreneurs

[10] Perhaps because it was of the prewar PPI generation, the DC's leadership was particularly sensitive to the dangers for a Christian Democratic party, and for democracy, of the Church's attraction to authoritarian solutions to its perceived problems. De Gasperi and others argued that the PPI's mistake had been to try to effect all reforms at once, thus alienating powerful interests. Azione Cattolica participant and close friend of De Gasperi, Stefano Jacini (1886–1952) commented in 1944, "The sole error [of the PPI] was to have presented such reforms too soon to a country unprepared and exhausted from the labor of war, and to have wanted to bring them about all together, as a kind of frontal attack" (in De Gasperi 1974, 1:273; cf. 342).

to invest their efforts in the DC, not in a rival venture. De Gasperi sensed that only a party with the full support of the Church could control the government, or the "conquest of the state" (Magister 1979, 41; Durand 1991, 638). If the Catholic Left were to form its own party, De Gasperi and other centrists feared the Catholic Right would follow suit. In such a situation, the Church would ally with the Right and perhaps lead to a return to Fascism, or precipitate a civil war leading to a Communist take-over (Scoppola 1988, 128–29).

It was not strictly the context that led De Gasperi to envision such sce-narios and to develop strategies for them. Other factions of the DC, facing the same situation, proposed different courses of action. For example, one left-wing faction, Politica d'Oggi, argued that no government was possible without the continued support of the Left, particularly of the Nenni So-cialists (PSI). Democracy could not coexist with the monarchy, for the latter, failing to protect the former, had collaborated with Mussolini. The other, more important left-wing factions, those of Catholic Action's Gio-vanni Gronchi (Politica Sociale) and of Giuseppe Dossetti (Iniziativa Democratica), made similar arguments. Among other grievances, they cited the party's strident anti-Communism, its collaboration with the small center and right parties, and its limited support for various reforms.[11] In contrast, the unorganized current on the right, the Vespisti, argued that Italy could not exist without the monarchy, or with the Left. The centrists, having won the party's leadership, were able to set the DC's agenda and to establish the dominant paradigm by which circumstances would be judged and strategies formulated, and to which rival factions would have to react.[12]

IDEOLOGICALLY ACCEPTABLE

The DC could justify the Church as an ally because of its ideology and the Church's standing in postwar Italy. The party viewed itself as essentially Catholic. Declaring its link to the Church, De Gasperi stated at a speech in Rome in 1946 that "our party is an organization of believers who, on the politico-economic plane want to bring about true democratic politics

[11] Politica d'Oggi disbanded in 1946 (Chassériaud 1965, 273–74). Dossetti's group sometimes went by the name of its newspaper, *Cronache Sociale*. On Gronchi and Dossetti, see Chassériaud 1965, 275–91; Pombeni 1979; Scoppola 1988, 149–50. On the DC's other factions, see Pridham 1988; Zuckerman 1979.

[12] The role of intraparty conflict and coalition building, and an explanation of how it was that the centrists in Italy and the leftists in France won their respective internal party battles for leadership, are important subjects that call for a separate monograph. The point here is that who leads matters, and that party strategies are not reducible to internal party structures that might give the leadership more or less power (Warner 1998).

and a profound, just, social transformation; but in entering the party, the activist does not change belief, he does not cut the umbilical cord that unites him with his spiritual Mother" (in Durand 1991, 630). In 1944, the DC declared that political action was to be "the projection of religious life into the political field,"[13] with laws based on "the traditional Catholic spirit of the Italian people" (in Falconi 1956, 61; cf. De Gasperi 1946, 203–4.). The party emphasized a "catchall" position with Catholicism as the binding agent.[14] The context of Fascism's demise also facilitated the alliance between the Church and party: the Vatican gained in prestige as the monarchy and army ended in ignominy and disgrace (Webster 1960, 172). Had the Church been an integral part of Fascism's program, the DC might have had trouble selling a link to it to the voters, many of whom genuinely wanted reforms (Ginsborg 1990; see above, chap. 3).

It might be argued that, given the Church's determination to have a party ally and to dominate the postwar sociopolitical landscape, the DC had no choice but to have the Church as an ally. If the Church wanted the DC as an ally, then the DC would comply. To be chosen by the Church, however, the party did have to solicit it, deliberately portraying itself as the Church's best possible ally. Yet the party had reservations about the consequences of allying with the Church, about whether to cater to its interests in all respects, and one faction seemed willing to forgo the Church entirely. Those misgivings manifested themselves in future relations with the Church.

Making and Maintaining the Contract

To win the Church's support, the party leadership tried to meet the Church's key policy demands. It reassured the Church by publicly showing the party's solidarity with it. Doing so was a mild form of posting a bond by building the party's image as an organization linked to the Church. DC politicians early on participated in numerous public ceremonies with the Church and its ancillary organizations (e.g., in January 1947, the DC actively worked with Catholic Action on public demonstrations to show support for the pope [Durand 1991, 638]).

To maintain, even in the face of some disagreements, the Church's support, the DC did not threaten the Church's core values. Further, it offered lucrative incentives for the Church, and the Church had few alternatives. The same assets that reassured the Church that the DC would deliver also guaranteed that the opportunity costs to the Church of exit would be

---

[13] *Il Popolo*, Feb. 27, 1944, 1.
[14] At DC Congresso Nazionale, Apr. 24–28, 1946 (Danè 1959, 23).

high. The DC then reduced its dependency on the Church by using the governing position (market share and profits) the Church had helped it attain to diversify its own portfolio of assets.

Some of the DC's actions were consciously wrought tactics; others, one can argue, came about largely because the DC elite were predisposed to them. Unlike the PPI leaders, who had built the organization by themselves, the DC founders "had grown up under the supervision and protection of the bishops and the Holy See" (Webster 1960, 172). Of 207 deputies in the Constituent Assembly, 122 had been members, if not leaders, of Azione Cattolica. They had been "formed by the clergy" (Durand 1991, 622). Many in the DC's leadership had come from one of two branches of Azione Cattolica, the Federazione Universitaria Cattolica Italiana and the Movimento Lauriati di Azione Cattolica.[15] With these movements under the Vatican's control during the Fascist period, this group was imbued with a sense of the Church's mission, and innately inclined to give high priority to the Church's preferences.

Tensions and Investment Diversification

De Gasperi wanted to prevent the party from becoming the handmaiden of the Church (Magister 1979, 100–101). Throughout his tenure, he rejected both the idea that the party should have a rigorous, clerical program (Magri 1954, 2:50; Scoppola 1988), and the idea that the party was a derivative of the Church. Instead, he stressed that parties are "formations of battle on political terrain, and it is precisely on the political terrain that they must find the rationales of their particular solidarity" (De Gasperi 1946, 203; cf. Falconi 1956, 61). The DC was not merely an extension of the Church or any other social organization. Acknowledging that the principles of the pope should be the ideological base of the party, he added that "this [base] will actually be realized only if it is framed by the environmental conditions in which we live" (De Gasperi 1946, 22). The DC evinced a willingness to use the tools of the state to maintain alliances and repress peasant and worker protests that, in its view, threatened to drive the Church and others on the right toward the neo-Fascists and Monarchists (De Gasperi 1974, 1:204).

The DC, like the MRP, risked losing Church support through its actions in the Constituent Assembly (1946–47) and in its governing coalition strategies. The DC did not support fully the Church's bid to have divorce

---

[15] Among them were the most powerful men in postwar Italy: Giulio Andreotti, Aldo Moro, Giovanni Leone, Emilio Colombo, Mario Scelba, Paolo Taviani, and Guido Gonella. Many others filled the ministries (Moro 1979, 20–22).

outlawed by the constitution or to keep the monarchy.[16] As a result, the Church and its organizational affiliates retaliated with criticism and talk of alternative parties. In the northern province of Brescia in 1946 and 1947, some priests were openly helping Uomo Qualunque organize. They viewed as "suspicious" the "ambiguous surrendering of the DC to too many [Communist-led] initiatives of a demagogic nature."[17] Some priests noted that it was hard to convince their congregations to support the DC when the party appeared less than Catholic. If the DC had merely followed Church dictates, the party's electoral success would have been more consistent with the geographic distribution of the Church's organizational strength.[18] While in government with secular parties, the DC stressed the missionary aspect of these coalitions: they would be a means of converting some secular politicians and voters.[19]

When the Church complained of the DC's performance, the DC could respond in several ways: (1) appeasing the Church with policy or more material benefits, (2) diversifying its sources of support to reduce the Church's importance, and therefore its complaints to minor nuisances, (3) blaming circumstances for the DC's behavior, or, (4) breaking the relationship. One would expect the party to choose the route least costly to it. Since costs depend not just on objective factors but on the lens through which those factors are viewed, the DC leadership found the first option unacceptable—it would render the party "too clerical." The DC sometimes tried to accomplish the second, and most often the third—blaming its policy and other decisions on the situations it was in. The party was too heavily invested in the relationship to break it—the costs of forgoing Church support would have been enormous.

When, between July 1946 and May 1947, the DC was in a tripartite coalition with the Socialists (PSI) and Communists (PCI), De Gasperi

[16] In abstaining from the vote, DC members effectively blocked the Church's wishes: the vote was 194–191 against the unconstitutionality of divorce (Scoppola 1988, 241–43, 201–52, passim).

[17] ACS, MinIntGab, fondo Situazioni Politica ed economica della regione, Lombardia, f. 2493.42, Comando Generale dell'Arma dei Carabinieri, no. 200/I, Feb. 22, 1947, p. 4.

[18] ACS, MinIntPS, fondo Relazioni Mensili, Reggio Calabria, C2I, 1946, f. 441, b. 33, rapporto no. 5641, Dec. 1, 1946; ACS, MinIntGab, 1944–66, fondo Partiti Politici–Democrazia Cristiana, Reggio Calabria, f. 165-P-66, b. 34bis, anonymous letter, "Per l'on. Amintore Fanfani," Apr. 19, 1958, p. 3.

[19] See De Gasperi to Pope Pius XII, Feb. 10, 1949, in Malgeri 1987, 485–87. The politics of Italian Socialism is complicated. Saragat's PSDI emphasized its own anti-Communism when it chose to split from Nenni's PSI in 1947. Other splinter parties satisfied with neither also emerged (Benzoni and Tedesco 1968). Also ACS, MinIntGab, 1953–56, fondo Democrazia Cristiana, "Relazione sulla Situazione Politica, Sindacale, economica, dello spirito dell'ordine pubblico e della pubblica sicurezza durante il meso di Marzo 1956," no. 6998/2, Apr. 26, 1956.

stressed that the coalition was essential in order to not jeopardize the inclusion of the Lateran Pacts in the new constitution (Casella 1992, 10; Magister 1979, 81–82). With the Italian hierarchy, that was a persuasive argument. De Gasperi was also concerned about the peace treaty—were the PCI absent from government, the USSR might press for "a very hard treaty for Italy" (Durand 1991, 636). (In contrast, the MRP had not made a similar argument with regard to protecting state subsidies to private schools in France—its rationale for staying in government was to protect the Republic, not that it could do more for the Church by remaining in office.)

In early 1947, the Church was expressing "disillusionment" with the DC, "because it did not see in that party a sufficient barrier against the overflow of Communism and anticlericalism." The DC responded by giving the Church what it wanted: expulsion of the Communist Party from the government. This episode reassured the Church that the DC was serious about fighting the Communist Party. The result for the DC was to gain the benefits of the Church's endorsement and extensive organizational resources such as door-to-door campaigning, leaflet distribution, rallies, and meeting space (usually churches and parish halls). These resources were crucial in persuading voters to support the DC in 1948.[20]

Despite the Communist Party's conciliatory stance in the early postwar years, the DC demonized the PCI,[21] and framed politics as a battle between good and evil (Warner 1994, chaps. 5, 10–11). Along with preventing the Church from supporting the creation of a new, right-wing Catholic party (Scoppola 1988, 152–53), the strategy reminded Catholics that Communism was a threat to their religion.[22]

[20] On the DC's coalition rationale, see DC memorandum, dated 1944 (in Scoppola 1988, 260–62); and DC leader Palma, Jan. 10, 1947, at meeting of Azione Cattolica's national directorate (the Presidenza generale) (in Scoppola 1988, 245; cf. Casella 1992, 73–74; Ginsborg 1990, 111–12). In France, on May 5, 1947, it was a Socialist prime minister who dismissed the Communists from the government. The MRP remained in the government (Rioux 1987, 125–26).

[21] The PCI's history in the early years of the Republic was complex. The party's activists were stridently anticlerical, while its leader, Palmiro Togliatti, sought an easing of tensions. De Gasperi, among others, at times feared Togliatti's stance was only tactical (Scoppola 1988, 295–99; Bocca 1973; Sbarberi 1980). The DC painted the PCI and PSI as "the enemies of religion and the subversives of society" (ACS, Prefettura di Catanzaro, Relazione, Apr. 1, 1946, p. 2).

[22] The PCI had been stressing that Communism and Catholicism were reconcilable—the former dealt with material matters, the latter with spiritual. Azione Cattolica missionaries expressed concern about the confusion among Catholic voters, which varied within and across regions, even in "Catholic" northern Italy. See AAC, PG, VI, Visite nel Mezzogiorno d'Italia, Oct. 5–15, 1947, Sig. Rossati, n.d.; AAC, PG, VI f. 18, fondo Visite alle diocesi, 1947, misc. files, including Reggio Calabria, Nov. 19, 1947; AAC, PG, VI f. 35, Calabria, 1947–49, "Relazione sul primo giro del carro-cinema in Calabria"; reports from Piedmont

After the 1948 election, the DC formed a government with the splinter Socialists (PSDI), the Liberals (PLI), and the Republicans (PRI). How could the DC ally with secular parties, including a Socialist one, without the Church turning on it? Hadn't the MRP done the same thing, and wasn't this the very same battle the MRP faced, and lost? Couldn't the Church have turned toward the Monarchists?

In this dispute, the DC blamed circumstances and stressed its basic compatibility with the Church. The Vatican was irritated and worried; De Gasperi stated privately that he feared "the worst, that is, that they [the Vatican] are thinking about an initiative for a new party. . . . Every one of our real or presumed insufficiencies will be a pretext."[23] To counter the problem, DC leaders took the almost costless route of blaming circumstances: "Faith is not enough. . . . a Catholic party can attain an absolute majority in some exceptional situations, but not maintain it when in a contest with the rise of the socialists [and] Communists" (De Gasperi 1974, 1:265). De Gasperi told Pope Pius XII that the DC faced two choices: either cultivate only the Catholics, but be too weak to defend "the supreme reasons of the spirit and of civilization," or create a broader alliance around the Catholics that could resist "the still extremely strong enemy organization [the Communists]" (in Malgeri 1987, 485–87). Party leaders were concerned to reassure the Church that the DC would keep up its end of the bargain. The DC was arguing that it had no choice but to ally with the non-Communist secular parties of the center-left.

Second, the DC stressed its basic agreement with the Church's policy goals. The DC increased its investments in anti-Communist rhetoric, again, a low-cost strategy with potential high payoff, given the Church's concern with Communism.[24] In 1949 De Gasperi told the pope that his strategy was to respect Azione Cattolica, but that there was a distinction between the political party and groups that had a social-spiritual role. He reminded the Church that following a strictly clerical line in politics scared powerful individuals and institutions and risked uniting them "in the common denominator of anticlericalism. . . . Unfortunately, many banks, economic institutes, publishing houses, large industries, land owners are in the hands of men who, at bottom, are only anticlerical from fear" (in Magister 1979, 131). He underscored the importance of the

---

in Casella 1992, 265–88. In 1953, in the Communist Party stronghold of Bologna, bishops warned their constituents that "they [the Communists] try to make us believe that Catholic faith and Catholic life can coexist with *atheist* Marxism" (in Kertzer 1980, 109, his translation).

[23] Letter, Alcide De Gasperi to Mario Scelba, minister of the interior, June 9, 1950 (De Gasperi 1974, 1:209–10).

[24] Alcide De Gasperi, "Discorso a Valloro [in Valesia]," July 2, 1950 (in Magri 1954, 2:21).

Church and the party collaborating "for the progress of the Christian civilization," as he told Pius XII (De Gasperi 1974, 1:108, Feb. 10, 1949).

DC leaders knew that, with some policies and in some circumstances, they could occasionally go against the Church. The land reform process had put a damper on peasant Communism. They had made the DC into the conduit for (mostly) American aid and, through the DC-controlled Ministry of the Interior, could and usually did thwart not only the activities of the Left but of Monarchists, neo-Fascists, and potential splinter parties.[25] As long as the Communist Party was a viable, large organization, to what other party could the Church turn? It was Amintore Fanfani, De Gasperi's successor as prime minister and party secretary, who sought new institutional mechanisms for reducing the DC's dependence on the Church. Patronage had a number of effects on the DC (Warner 1994, 399–416; 1998). While in some cases it was a means of reinforcing the Church's material interest in supporting the DC, it reduced the party's dependency on the Church—once the DC had control of the Italian government.

Patronage took a variety of forms. One of the more common, and effective, is illustrated by an event in the southern province of Catanzaro. The local 12-kilometer road that led from Papanice to Crotone had been completely impassable in periods of bad weather, and only mildly better in good weather. The communal administration of Crotone, which was Communist-led, was responsible for improving it, and indeed, some work had been done, but the funds were either insufficient or spent unwisely or embezzled, for the road soon approached its original condition, with, as a Communist party activist reported, "the rain doing the rest." When the communal council proposed to begin again, it tried to elicit the interest of the DC-led provincial government. The latter, "not having an interest in cleansing the sins of a Communist-majority municipal council," refused. In 1957, the council then requested a loan from the southern development agency, Cassa per il Mezzogiorno.

In the meantime, the local PCI's main activist and council member, Pantaleone Paglia, was being overtaken in authority and activity by a younger man. While the two were on good terms, it appears that Paglia was not enjoying his own demotion in standing. Arguing that one must sacrifice for the good of the community, Paglia organized the collective resignation from the PCI of himself and 70 peasants. The road had found its hero. Work would begin on the road, at the province's expense, once the PCI members had become DC members. On the day of conversion, the prefect's inspector arrived with the DC's provincial secretary. The lat-

[25] ACS, MinIntGab, 1950–52, fondo Affari Generali, b. 17468, f. 285, rapporto del prefetto di Como, no. 6834.2.Z, Nov. 20, 1950.

ter "addressed the peasants, who, with Paglia at the front, turned in their [PCI] membership cards to the [DC secretary], asking him for the road in exchange" (Cervigni 1955, 84–86). Once in positions controlling the disbursement of government resources, DC politicians did not always need the Church to bring them voters.

Building on what the Church's electoral aid in 1948 had attained for it—a governing majority—the DC began to use its position not to transform Italy into a more economically and socially just country, but to ensure its electoral success and organizational longevity. When it became the dominant party in 1948, the DC made sure that DC membership was important to one's employment prospects (Allum 1973, 161, 167). A DC secretary explained, "The hirings [in the Belli Company] are made by agreement between the DC Secretary and the Employment Officer, one of our men. In a request for 80 workers he slips in 60 DC members and the others are eliminated by the factory management on the basis of information supplied by the [local police]" (in Allum 1973, 167). While often this arrangement was complemented by the aid of a priest, it could run without one.

The contrast with the MRP's behavior toward the French Church shows that it is necessary to go beyond mere size of an interest group's resources to understand why a party might pursue it as an ally. In contrast to the DC, the MRP did not see the Church as a necessary pillar of the Fourth Republic, as something to which the MRP had to adjust its own principles in order to ensure that the Church would remain inside the democratic tent. The Church was chastened by the demise of Vichy, and the MRP was perhaps a little too sure that it could carry the Republic without the aid of the Church. Ideology and interest group reputation can take the interest group off the market.

THE MRP AND ITS SEARCH FOR ALLIES

> We battle, but on our program. The Movement
> [MRP] is not going to define itself by opportunis-
> tic positions, but by courageous positions.
> *MRP, 1951*[26]

The MRP, in striking contrast to the DC, did not try to buy the Church's support. Church resources were not the issue. The key to the MRP's decision was the fact that the party saw the Church as more of a hindrance to

---

[26] MRP deputy Leo Hamon, at Commission Exécutive meeting, Apr. 5, 1951, AN, A-MRP, 350/AP/49.

democracy than as essential to establishing it, and that appealing to the Church would have required the MRP to alter its program and take on an ideological orientation it had rejected during the Resistance.

Why Not Choose the Church?

CHURCH RESOURCES

The reader might suggest that the MRP eschewed Church support because the Church could not have been a significant electoral or organizational resource. The evidence does not bear this hypothesis out. While the French Church's resources were never as extensive as those of the Italian, it was, especially in Catholic regions, a significant social institution, the political preferences of which were closely followed by many Catholics. Forgoing the Church cost the MRP much of the Catholic vote. The 1951 parliamentary election was a debacle for the MRP. It lost over half its 1946 votes, falling to 11%. The party noted that the big winner was the "classic Right." Indeed, the biggest chunk of the Catholic electorate was on the right: Catholicism was a better predictor of total right-wing voting than of explicitly confessional party voting. A 1952 survey and electoral returns from 1951 showed that most Catholics voted for the MRP, the Independents, Peasants, and Gaullists, not for the left parties (Williams 1964, 109 n. 18, 155 n. 26). Prefect observations confirm this. In heavily Catholic areas (over 38% practicing), the MRP's average dropped 20% from 1946; in less Catholic areas (average or less), the decline, 11%, was not quite as dramatic.[27] Readers familiar with French politics might protest that it was de Gaulle's party that took the MRP's vote. That appears to have been the case in *some* departments. However, in much of Catholic south central France, the Gaullists had virtually no presence; it was the conservatives, preferred by the local clergy and hierarchy, who took the MRP's votes (Warner 1998, 567). Instead of concluding that their campaign and government participation strategies were erroneous for vote winning, the MRP worker section commented that the result "proves that the French lack education and political judgment."[28]

---

[27] The MRP's electoral situation was probably not helped by the argument of influential Catholic intellectuals, who announced that it was acceptable, even necessary, for Catholics to vote for the Left (Charlot 1957, 135–38).

[28] The section report added, "Our role is to undertake a political education of the masses" (AN, A-MRP, 350/AP/65, 3MRP1 dr. 17, Equipes Ouvrières Pres. Jean Sachet, Dec. 2, 1951, pp. 2, 11). Just as a business might misread the sources of its success, attributing profits to product quality when profits might be due to advertising or consumers' lack of alternatives, so too might a political party. Where the party views its electoral success as a mandate to pursue a program, the real reason might have been that voters thought it the

One factor that could have rendered the Church less than attractive was the fact that it was decentralized, making it harder for the MRP to trust that the Church could deliver its membership, and complicating transactions with the party—adding multiple points on which the party had to get agreement. While these factors can be important in party–interest group linkages, in the MRP's case they appear not to have been. Party leaders were focused not upon difficulties of coordination but upon whether they even wanted the Church, in any form, as an ally. To that, the answer was largely negative. Only if the Church's interests did not interfere with the MRP's top priorities was the MRP willing to entertain its support.

ESSENTIAL TO DEMOCRACY?

Another factor that worked against the party–interest group link was that allying with the Church would have meant the MRP was linked with an institution that, in the eyes of the electorate the MRP sought to attract, was tainted. Not only had the Church collaborated with a regime that sent Frenchmen to forced-labor camps in Germany, it had largely ignored the plight of the working class in early twentieth-century France. The MRP wanted to reach the working and other lower classes and feared that linking with the Church would prevent it from doing so. MRP leaders frequently denied that they were the party of the Church. As one said in 1944, "It has never been anyone's intention to create in France a confessional democratic movement" (in Sa'adah 1987, 48).

What the MRP wanted was not so much the Church's direct support as its neutrality. The MRP hoped it could mollify the Church not by changing MRP policy but by having the Church change *its* priorities. Yet because the Church felt compelled to speak on issues of concern to it, and to criticize the MRP's stance on amnesty and on school subsidies, the Church became a de facto opponent of the MRP. For the French hierarchy, school subsidies constituted "the question that, at this hour, retains the attention of the clergy and faithful."[29]

Chronology is important to the understanding of the party–interest group interaction. Recall that the Church endorsed the MRP for the 1945 and 1946 elections, that it also criticized the proposed constitutions for not guaranteeing freedom of education, let alone restoring state subsidies

---

lesser of various evils. The party that mistakenly attributes its success to its program may then cut back on that which made it successful: advertising from an interest group ("we no longer need them"), or on blocking competitors in the electoral arena ("we're so good we'll outsell them anyway").

[29] *SRP,* June 10, 1945, 331.

to private schools. The MRP supported the guarantee and the subsidy but was outnumbered by the anticlerical center and Left. The MRP was one of the Church's antagonists on the issue of amnesty for collaborators, and the party was quick to abandon Church priorities for other party goals.

MRP IDEOLOGY

We are a Movement, not an
electoral machine.
(MRP)

The MRP founders came out of World War II determined to carry on the spirit of the Resistance and to infuse France with a new politics. They refused to be a "normal" vote-seeking party. MRP leaders held that their goal was to "construct economic democracy without destroying political democracy."[30] Georges Bidault, who had served as president of the National Resistance Council, French prime minister, and MRP president, said, "We came because we refuse to have torn away from some their faith and from others their bread."[31] The MRP was trying to bridge the Church-state crevasse, and to reconcile Catholicism with the proletariat. The party rejected both Marxist collectivism and capitalist individualism. Something of a left-wing Moral Majority, the MRP touted the family,[32] high moral values, honest government, and worker interests. In the party's prevailing view of itself, "Our electoral corps is on the left. That marks the seat of our Movement."[33]

The MRP had a quasi-religious spirit. As one party founder stated, "For me, the MRP is not a party, it is a social future for which we act as the apostles."[34] In the early 1950s, one MRP founder reflected, "When the French Resistance spoke of the Fourth Republic, it thought of a Fourth Republic more republican than the Third. Yes, it was the common will of

[30] AN, A-MRP, 350/AP/1, 1MRP2 dr. 2, statement in Commission Exécutive file, Mar. 22, 1949, no author, p. 5; see also Letamendia 1975, 50–73.

[31] APP, MRP box 278.247-3, Georges Bidault at meeting of 15th section of the Fédération de la Seine, June 2, 1955. Bidault was MRP president from 1949 to 1952, prime minister from June to Dec. 1946, and Oct. 1949 to July 1950, minister of foreign affairs from Sept. 1944 to July 1948, and Jan. 1953 to June 1954. He later supported the French Algerian extremists and was exiled to Brazil.

[32] Campaign propaganda at the national and local level proclaimed proudly that the candidates were all "pères de familles nombreux" [fathers of large families]; editorials in support of the MRP would note, for instance, that six MRP candidates between them accounted for 47 children (Joseph Leclerc, "Dimanche je voterai: Pour qui?" in *La Manche Libre*, June 17, 1951, 1).

[33] AN, A-MRP, 350/AP/49, 2MRP2 dr. 20, Commission Exécutive, June 21, 1951.

[34] Jean-Raymond Laurent, deputy of Manche [Normandy], Archives du Paris, ARL, D.51 Z117 (n.d.) 1945.

the Resistance and it was us who in particular had the mission to realize it" (Gay 1951, 32, 31). Another stated, "You know well you are integrally and definitely MRP only from the moment when the MRP costs you much time, hardship, cares, worries, bitterness, and deceptions."[35] Party membership was to be a form of martyrdom. If the French did not share that spirit, or the Resistance principles, the French would have to be convinced of them.[36]

The MRP spirit did not include any concessions to Catholic integralism, or to a notion that the party was responsible for securing the rehabilitation of the French Church. It was the MRP's self-image that prevented it from placing a high value on the benefits of getting the Church's support. The MRP's conflict with the Church over Vichy amnesty is indicative of this. Most party leaders and activists had participated extensively in the Resistance and thus were opposed to amnesty for those compromised with the Vichy regime and for those parliamentarians who had voted to cede the French government to Marshal Pétain in 1940. The Church opposed neither proposition. In 1948, the hierarchy (the Assembly of Cardinals and Archbishops) told the MRP leaders that the Church would be "very unhappy" with the harsh amnesty law. A police informant noted that the MRP feared it would find itself in opposition to the hierarchy, "which until now had given it [the MRP] all its support."[37] However, fully cognizant of the consequences, the MRP did not desist. Party principles prevailed. A few months before the 1951 election, in a sermon at Notre Dame de Paris, Cardinal Feltin spoke favorably of amnesty for Pétain. Many in the MRP were quite critical of the Catholic Church because of this position.[38] Moreover, even those within the MRP who were sympathetic to such a move did not think it a judicious moment: with the election approaching, it was not a good time to offend the core constituency.

Part and parcel of being a party of the Resistance was being the party that would bring a "true Republic" to the French.[39] Because of that, the

---

[35] AN, A-MRP, 350/AP/91, 6MRP3 dr. 1 1952, Réunion des Secretaires et Presidents Fédéraux, Sept. 27–28, 1952, comment of Pierre-Henri Teitgen, minutes, p. 5.

[36] In a bulletin of instructions for campaigning in rural areas, the MRP's Bernard Broussard stated that the party's duty was "to rise above . . class antagonisms and to gather the French in the community of a fraternal ideal." *Comment lancer le M.R.P. dans les campagnes* (Paris: Equipes Rurales du M.R.P., 1946), p. 1.

[37] APP, MRP box 278.247-1, Mar. 11, 1948. The Assemblée de Cardinaux et Archevêques excluded bishops (Dansette 1965, 73–75).

[38] APP, MRP box 278.247-2, prefect report, Mar. 2, 1951.

[39] At the National Congress of May 1951, Andre Colin reminded the MRP that in 1945 what characterized the MRP was "not only its magnificent program of rejuvenated democracy, of total social justice and fraternity. It is also that belief that animates us all, that politics itself also raises up the moral [sense], that politics also brings up the distinction between good and evil, of justice and injustice, of truth and falseness, of honor and dishonor" (AN,

MRP insisted on remaining in the various governments, virtually no matter with which parties it would be allied, or with which policies it would be associated. National MRP leaders feared that in the MRP's absence, other parties would bury the republican ideal—with socialism, capitalism, or authoritarianism.[40] MRP president Georges Bidault asserted that "we must carry out our program. . . . Any coalition is a measure of wisdom that brings with it great difficulties. We find ourselves before the peril of a collapse."[41] If the MRP went its own way, the coalition would disintegrate, leaving France to the Gaullist and Communist blocs.[42] The overriding concern was upholding the French republic. "If the MRP is not firm, the Republic will soon be in question." From there, the party reasoned, it could go on "to work on not losing souls (workers who will go to the Communists) and to continue our policy of family and housing subsidies."[43] Just after the 1951 election, the MRP National Committee "viewed it as normal that the next [governing] majority goes from the SFIO to the Peasant parties and Independents."[44] Because the party was in all 19 governing coalitions between 1946 and 1956 (except one month),[45] it is small wonder that the MRP was described by contemporaries as having "the soul of an opponent and the body of a joiner" (in Williams 1964, 112).[46]

In allying with the Socialist Party in governing coalitions to support progressive policies, the MRP could not simultaneously be an outspoken advocate of clerical issues (Duquesne 1966, 433–35; Letamendia 1975, 296–99). Although it was an MRP deputy, Charles Barangé, who in 1951 successfully proposed a law to restore school subsidies, the MRP did not give him or the law its full backing. As already indicated, the MRP let the Gaullists and Conservatives run away with the issue. MRP policy forwent

---

A-MRP, 350/AP/1, speech, "Pour la République, Pour la Famille, Pour le Progrès, Pour la Paix," Congrès National, May 3–6, 1951; reprinted in *Les Cahiers de Formation Politique* no. 8, May 1951).

[40] Georges Bidault, AN, A-MRP, 350/AP/49, 2MRP2 dr. 20, Commission Exécutive, June 21, 1951.

[41] AN, A-MRP 350/AP/49, Commission Exécutive, President Bidault, Apr. 5, 1951.

[42] Here, as in Italy, there was some concern about loss of American aid (APP, MRP box 278.247-1, prefect observations, Nov. 16, 1946). The MRP refused to give the Ministry of the National Economy to the Communists for that reason.

[43] AN, A-MRP, 350/AP/49, 2MRP2 dr. 20, Commission Exécutive, M. Reille-Soult, June 14, 1951.

[44] APP, MRP box 278.247-2, prefect of police report, June 22, 1951.

[45] Calculated from Dogan and Campbell 1957, table 2, 317.

[46] Party leaders and activists were themselves aware of the problems that the MRP's coalition behavior created for its image. Georges Queste, *Les Problèms du Mouvement*, report presented to the Congrès Fédéral de Clichy [of the Fédération de la Seine] du M.R.P., Oct. 27–28, 1951, uncategorized archives of l'Amicales du M.R.P., Paris.

the opportunity to put a barrier to organization and voter exit in place. By contrast, in Italy, the Church kept organizations in line. In France, because of the MRP's less than firm stance for *l'enseignement libre*, the Church would not do it the same favor.[47]

It was not the case that the Church hesitated to be involved in politics. Various Catholic organizations actually denounced the MRP. This was an important opposition, doing considerable damage to the MRP's later campaign efforts. It was only after its electoral defeat of 1951, after the national organization had spent six years ignoring or offending Catholic organizations on the right and left, that the MRP leaders began to talk seriously about the need to work with Catholic ancillary organizations. But because of the MRP's earlier inaction, such organizations had decided to remain independent of politics or were quietly lending support to other parties.[48]

The MRP did not let the Church's disapproval influence its policies, it did not try to appease the Church through apologetic explanations, and it did not offer the Church any financial or patronage benefits. Nor did it suggest that its policies and goals in other areas might warrant the Church's continued support despite its disapproval of one or two MRP policy positions.

The source of the divergence in views lies in the MRP's ideology. It claimed to be a party of the Republic, which meant, in practice, to endorse the view that the state makes its citizens, and it does so through education. There lies the rub: education of citizens in a republic is a secular matter. French voters, and, significantly, the French Church, did not agree that the MRP could both support state subsidies to Catholic schools and be a "republican" (secular) party.

CONCLUSION

How politicians plan to build their organization, attract voters and allies, and manipulate given conditions affects the nature of the resulting party. What kind of party the leaders want to build, their goals, the policies and allies they are prepared to deal with, all will influence the "how to." Both DC and MRP leaders had relatively clear views of what role they wanted their parties to play in postwar politics and of how to market their parties, and those views affected the strategic choices they made about interest group alliances.

[47] APP, MRP box 278.247-1, police report, Nov. 22, 1947.
[48] AN, A-MRP, 350/AP/91, Commission Exécutive, n.d., 1952.

Not merely because of the context, but because of how they interpreted past events, particularly the factors that had contributed to rise of Fascism, the DC leadership emphasized both the necessity of an alliance with the Catholic Church, and a need to broaden the appeal of the party. The DC leadership was less idealistic than the MRP leadership, more willing to make compromises between ideals and electoral maneuvering in order to win office.

In its own view, the MRP was the "party of the Resistance" and the Republic, drawing upon New Testament teachings to bring to life its social Catholic interpretation of *liberté, egalité, fraternité*. These ideals strongly influenced the strategies the party used to develop itself. But, because the MRP did not define itself as a predominantly Catholic party, it forwent the crucial support that the Catholic Church and other Catholic organizations could have offered. The issue was not one of insufficient resources on the part of the Church: in the French context, the Church had an enviable organizational presence in most regions. Rather, the MRP saw the Church as neither essential to the survival of the Republic nor desirable as an ally, given the demands the Church would have made on MRP policy goals.

Through the DC we have seen that tensions are inherent in the party–interest group relation and that there are various strategies a party can use to minimize their impact. When the Italian Church exercised voice, or threatened to exit, the DC leadership sought to blame the source of the Church's complaint on circumstances and stressed their fundamental policy compatibility. These appeasement strategies had a greater effect than their "face value" might suggest. When an interest group has limited exit options (see chap. 6), a party pays a lower price for its malfeasance.

Parties are often seen as tools by the politicians who create and run them (Aldrich 1995). Parties, in turn, see interest groups in much the same way. A party's links to an interest group, while not entirely under a party's control, must be deliberately constructed. Leaders assess costs and benefits of alliances in terms of resources and the sustainability of matches in light of the party's ideological or programmatic orientation. They react to what they might have to "pay" the group for its support.[49]

---

[49] For cases in new democratic systems, an additional factor is the party's assessment of the group's capacity to undermine the system, and whether, by promising certain policies, the party can persuade the group not to do so.

CHAPTER 9

Comparative Perspectives: Germany

As CHRISTIAN DEMOCRATIC UNION activist Paul Bausch found out, in the months immediately following Germany's unconditional surrender, many in the German Catholic Church had serious misgivings about forming an interconfessional "Christian Democratic" political party:

> I presented to the meeting the view that we had to make a totally new start and that we should be guided by the Word of God. . . . Then I attempted to elucidate the aims and principles of our new party. . . . Afterwards I entered into conversation with the priests. They told me I should not really have spoken about matters that came within their competence. They said they were astonished, as a layman should simply not concern himself with theological questions.[1]

Some, thinking that the Church's conduct during the Weimar Republic and under the Nazis was above reproach, simply did not see interfaith conflict as having contributed to the rise of the Third Reich. Yet within a year, most German clergy and Church hierarchies were urging Catholics to vote for a new interconfessional party—this CDU. What accounts for the startling change of view?

The previous chapters have suggested a number of factors that need to be taken into account in analyzing the political activities of the Roman Catholic Church. As an active participant, or, as I have argued, interest group, in the national as well as regional politics of France and Italy over many centuries, national Catholic Churches had little domestic competition from other religions for members, resources, and government privileges.[2] Germany offers an interesting and relevant instance of Catholic political action where important differences characterized the situation of the Church and led to different calculations of the alternatives.

The Protestant Reformation and the failure of the Counter Reformation to eliminate the Lutherans meant that the Church in Germany had to engage in political action to avoid becoming marginalized, both socially and politically. After the unification of Germany in 1871 and prior to the

---

[1] Paul Bausch, quoted in Pridham 1977, 42.

[2] There were minor instances when this was not the case, e.g., the Huguenots in France (though the victims did not find them "minor").

Third Reich, the Church did so in part by aligning itself with an almost exclusively Catholic political party, the Zentrum (Center Party). The relative political ineffectiveness of the party during the Weimar Republic and the experience of Nazism seemed to bring into question that strategy. It also narrowed the Church's political choices: after the war, most Catholic politicians and some clerics preferred to construct an interconfessional party—not the choice one might expect in a "duopoly" situation. What this chapter shows is that while the German Church faced different conditions, the considerations it applied to its choice of strategies were those by now familiar to the reader: policy stance of parties, available resources, and the ideological predilections of its leadership.

This chapter addresses the question of how the Church's strategies are altered when it is not the only major religion in a country. How does having a substantial religious competitor change its search for a political party ally? In what ways did the history of German Catholicism affect its decision making? One might expect an interest group that is not dominant, but rather faces competition from other groups representing similar interests, to select and invest in a political party that it would not have to share with another interest group. This is more likely when the electoral system is conducive to the representation of multiple parties; arguably, the German system was (see below). The German hierarchy did single out one party, yet it singled out the one in which it would have a lesser voice—a mixed Catholic-Protestant party, the CDU. Why did it not go with the overwhelmingly Catholic party, the Zentrum?

To deal with those questions, this chapter raises others: Did politicians have something of value that the German Catholic Church needed? Could they deliver something that the Church needed? What did the Church think it needed in the "zero hour," as 1945 was referred to? What was the asking price for what the Church wanted? Who was selling it? What factors remained relevant to Church decision making after the experience of Weimar and the Third Reich?

HISTORICAL TRAJECTORY

With the end of the Holy Roman Empire, the Protestant Reformation and then the Thirty Years War, the Catholic Church and its adherents became a minority in much of what is, and was thought of as, Germany (that is, within today's borders, and not including the territories of Austria; see M. Mitchell 1999, 2). Moreover, Rome, and not the German hierarchy (in contrast to the Gallican French), dictated Church policy. Due to changing political arrangements (i.e., Napoleon's conquest, the Congress of Vienna, the Revolution of 1848, and the process of German unification) many Catholics were brought under the jurisdiction of Protestant states (Spotts 1973, 22).[3] After Germany was unified in 1871, the Church ran headlong into a battle over the control of education in the new empire; that battle ultimately turned into "a battle over the independence of the Church and its teachings" (Spotts 1973, 24). Known as the *Kulturkampf,* promulgated by Chancellor Otto von Bismarck, it involved legislation that applied strict controls to Catholic schools, banished the Jesuits and some other religious orders, and refused to honor church weddings that were not preceded by a civil ceremony, among many other restrictions. The Church was joined in defensive efforts by the Zentrum. Founded by Catholics concerned to defend their social and political position and priorities in Germany, it had, like other European Christian Democratic parties of the time, a difficult relationship with "its" national Church.[4]

Between 1803 and 1944, despite considerable economic and political change and population movements within Germany, the distribution and percentage of German Catholics remained essentially the same as elaborated in the political and religious agreements of the seventeenth century (e.g., the Peace of Westphalia), with the Protestants overwhelmingly concentrated in the cities and Catholics in the rural areas.[5] This fact helped create the "ghetto" (or "tower") mentality among German Catholics—a defensive attitude toward the political system that did not begin to change until after World War II.

When the Wilhelmine Empire (1871–1918) was defeated in World War I and replaced by the Weimar Republic, the Church was granted, through the assistance of the Zentrum, state acceptance of confessional schools and other legal privileges. Both Lutheran and Catholic Churches were granted "full control over their internal affairs" (Lönne 1996, 161). Yet while the party of Catholics could accept democracy, the Church was reluctant to

---

[3] The division of Germany after World War II only compounded that problem for the Church. Those Catholics in the largely Protestant East were now not merely the minority in a Protestant state, but under a Communist government.

[4] On the Zentrum, see Evans 1981; Cary 1996; Fogarty 1957, 304–6; Kalyvas 1996, 203–15; Lönne 1996, 157–61.

[5] In 1822, a religious census showed the population of "Germany" (without Alsace) to have been 63% Protestant and 35% Catholic. Despite a massive population increase between that time and World War II, the relative percentages of the two religious communities remained little changed for all of Germany. On the other hand, there was a significant change in the relative percentages in the new West Germany. As a result of the division, the breakdown in the West was around 51% Protestant and 45% Catholic. Catholics still tended to be overrepresented in communities with populations of up to 10,000; as the size of the municipality grows, the percentage of Catholics decreases. Catholics dominate the field of agriculture, mining, and construction but are barely visible in commerce, transportation, banking, or administration. Protestants are, on the whole, far better educated, and more visible in all levels of education, up to and including the universities (H. Maier 1983, 162–63).

do so.[6] In denying the Weimar Republic its endorsement, it gave millions of German Catholics reason to question the Republic. It seemed to see in the Nazis' emphasis on family, social stratification, and the fatherland a political order that more closely matched its conception of temporal government.

Like the French and Italian Churches, the German Catholic Church came out of World War II with reputational baggage. Like the Italian Church and the Fascists, the German Church had never been officially incorporated into the Nazi regime, but it did not emerge triumphant or unsullied. On the one hand, the Church generally rejected National Socialism, and some of its clergy had earlier even prohibited members of the Nazi Party (NSDAP) from taking the sacraments. It frequently criticized the party's racial ideas, social policies, and, of course, the NSDAP's decision to establish nondenominational schooling. On the other hand, it encouraged the Zentrum to vote for the infamous Enabling Act that gave Hitler's government dictatorial powers, and readily turned over Church birth records to the Nazis, facilitating the latter's efforts to identify and exterminate Jews. The Catholic hierarchy in general did not acknowledge any role in the events leading to the establishment of the Third Reich, though a few in the hierarchy regretted the Church's institutional ineffectiveness in denouncing the Nazis' genocidal policies and atrocities.[7]

It was like the Italian Church in that it had been ideologically and institutionally distanced from the Nazi regime: the Church was not a pillar of Nazi policy or the latter's base of legitimacy, as it was for Vichy; it always remained clearly distinct from the regime (Harrigan 1963). Vatican and German Church policies were directed at maintaining the institution in the face of occasional (some assert, frequent) Nazi attacks on Church prerogatives and practices. Also like the Italian, the German Catholic Church

---

[6] There is much scholarly debate over the Zentrum's role in the Weimar Republic and the rise of the Third Reich. On the one hand, some scholars argue that though the Zentrum cannot be equated with political Catholicism in Weimar, it "turned political Catholicism into a major force" and played a major role in the political system generally through its participation in one-half the cabinets that governed Germany up to 1933, thus "representing an extremely important force for political integration" of Catholics (Lönne 1996, 161–62). On the other hand, Evans argues that the Zentrum "retreated into a narrow clericalism of the type which the party had consistently repudiated throughout its previous history.... This change in policy only led to further decline and disintegration [and eventually] the Center capitulated to National Socialism in a distinctly unheroic manner" (1981, xi). After the war, the party "was not merely dormant, but dead; it could perhaps be recreated but not revived [and many] were not at all certain of the desirability of restoring [it]" (397).

[7] On the Church's view of its social and political role in the interwar period, see Evans 1981; Lönne 1996; and Gotto 1983; on its hierarchy and their role, see Kraiker 1972; and Bark and Gress 1989, 145–48. The most famous critique along these lines came from Rolf Hochhuth, in his drama *Der Stellvertreter* (The Deputy) (Hamburg: Rowohlt Verlag, 1963).

was one of the very few institutions that survived the unconditional surrender in 1945 with its basic structural and organizational characteristics
intact. The upper levels of the hierarchy survived the Nazi period and the
war years, providing a measure of leadership continuity. This, however,
had its negative side when it came to effectuating compromises with other
social elements after the war. The Church's main loss was that the Nazis
had stripped it of its many ancillary organizations, reducing the organizational network upon which it could rely after the war.

While one cannot ignore the actions of the Allies when studying postwar German history, their contradictory views of the Church had little
effect on it. Neither the Americans nor the British were particularly supportive of the Church; furthermore, the Americans and the French were
not sympathetic to the lack of a clear separation of Church and state that
characterized the German experience. Nevertheless, none of the three
Western Allies placed any significant restrictions on the operations of the
Church and its personnel, and indeed often accepted the priests and bishops as temporary interpreters and representatives of the interests of the
German people (Forster 1981, 214). In the first few months of the Occupation, the Catholic and Lutheran Churches were among the only institutions permitted organizational meetings (Hürten 1986, 243). The Allies
also provided a very significant amount of survival assistance to the population in the miserable aftermath of the summer of 1945 (Gatz 1981,
344-45).

CHURCH INTERESTS, IDENTITY, AND ROLE DEFINITION

During the Third Reich, the Church retained most of its position through
the *Reichskonkordat*, the 1933 treaty between the Vatican and the Nazis,
which, like the Italian one, kept some ideological and institutional distance between it and the Nazis. Unlike the Vichy regime, the Nazi regime
did not want or need to make the Church one of its pillars; indeed, it
dissolved all Catholic lay organizations, leaving the Church alone intact.
The Church, as a result, saw itself as having been wronged by the Third
Reich and deserving of better treatment from the next regime.

Its leadership emerged essentially intact (Zapf 1965, 103) and, in contrast to the French Church, did not face calls for its removal on charges
of collaboration. In fact, both the Catholic and Protestant hierarchies had
some outspoken critics of the Nazis in their ranks (among the Catholics,
Michael von Faulhaber and Josef Frings, and among the Protestants Martin Niemoeller and Gustav Heinemann) who achieved prominence precisely because of their "clean record" during the Nazi era. One result was
that the Church came out of the war and Third Reich with little change

of attitude and few compunctions against undertaking political action. Many elements of the Catholic Church saw no need to reevaluate the Church's ideology or actions; indeed, they almost immediately began to intervene in German politics, willfully obstructing the Allies' denazification efforts. For many, the main lesson of the Nazi experience was only that laws protecting the Church and its social position had to be enforced by the state, sympathetic political parties, and voters.

This behavior is, in part, attributable to the Church's understanding of Communism (or, as it was frequently called, "Bolshevism"), Fascism, and liberalism. Fascism and Communism were both understood in Catholic writings as a reaction to liberalism. The equating of the two stems from the Catholic idea that both have their basis in a materialist worldview, the only difference being that Fascism included concepts about race, rejected equality of persons, and saw social hierarchies as natural. Even Konrad Adenauer, future CDU leader, seems to have viewed Fascism as only a variation of Marxism (Kraiker 1972, 20). A Fascist regime was preferable since it at least eliminated the workers' movements, thus reducing the likelihood of the Bolsheviks taking over, and it recognized social hierarchies and corporate groups. With liberalism dangerously linked to Protestantism and having given rise to Marxism and Fascism, many Catholics, including Church leaders, saw the necessity of creating a Christian society to defend against the possibility of Communism's taking over, especially because of the presence of the USSR in the "Eastern Zone." Democracy, on the other hand, was also suspect since the Church equated it with the "equalization" of everybody, and therefore the progenitor of Communism. Liberalism, "individualism," Communism, "collectivism" were decried as anathema and blamed for the excesses of the Weimar Republic as well as for the Third Reich (Kraiker 1972).

The Church created a myth of itself as the "implacable foe" of the Nazi regime, rejected the idea that it bore any guilt for the Nazi period, and dismissed the idea of a collective German guilt, in a short statement regretting that some Germans, "even in our own ranks," had become accessories to the crimes of the regime. A prominent cardinal stated, "We German Catholics were not National Socialists" (in Spotts 1973, 89–90). The Church perceived itself to have been the most important opponent of the Nazis, citing its condemnation of National Socialist ideas in 1931, while not mentioning its statement in 1933 telling Catholics that the new regime was legally theirs to obey (Kraiker 1972, 26). Closing the book on the Third Reich, the Church argued that the attribution of guilt was to be left to God. As an organization, it did not appear chastened by its behavior during the Nazi regime and was prepared to press for the return to it of a privileged social and political position.

Like all organizations that are engaged in politics, the Church had contradictory stances about the level and legitimacy of its political involvement (less so on the goals). On the one hand, the Church voiced a determination and saw an opportunity to foster a more Catholic-oriented society, and was willing to use politics to do so. It became active in the development of new political parties (Schmidt 1983, 493–94) and in the resolution of the confessional schools question. Like the Italian Church, it explicitly stated that even democracy and the rule of law did not give Catholics "enough guarantees," and that because of this, Catholics had to band together and present themselves as an organized bloc. Further, the Church had no qualms about trying to eliminate political undesirables, such as the "various Catholic splinter parties that grew up following the war," especially the Zentrum and the Bavarian party (Spotts 1973, 152). On the other hand, with few exceptions, the Church also kept its clergy from actually running for office (but see below).[8]

Like the Italian Church, the German Catholic Church was determined to have the concordat remain valid, and this time be honored. The *Reichskonkordat* was neither a complete victory for the Nazis nor for the Church. For example, although bishops had to be German, trained in Germany, and have a minimum of theological training, the government could object to the appointment of a specific bishop on political grounds and require he take an oath of loyalty to the state (Spotts 1973, 191). The state provided for the education of the clergy, by funding and running the theological faculties, and got to appoint the faculty. What the Church got in return was a guarantee of confessional schools "everywhere in Germany" (Spotts 1973, 209), and it was determined that the new Federal Republic honor that guarantee.

The Church turned its attention to the reconstruction of the physical and moral structure of Germany, viewing that moral structure in particularly narrow terms: it was to proceed along strictly Catholic lines, as dictated by the Church (Fehrenbach 1997). Looking at the extent of physical and moral destruction throughout Germany, and the Russian presence on the Elbe, the Church thought the population particularly vulnerable to Communism. Along with chastising the Allies for their allegedly harsh policies, the Church sought to ensure that people had "Christian" political options. Defining its security and survival in narrow social and doctrinal terms, many of the postwar leaders of the Church condemned progressive elements, including the refounded Social Democratic Party, as treasonous threats.[9]

---

[8] The Vatican saw actual membership by its hierarchy as a violation of Article 32 of the concordat (H. Maier 1983, 494).

[9] See esp. Kraiker 1972. The author is very critical of the Church (the work is subtitled "An Ideological Critique"). The book is, nevertheless, invaluable as a source of information and material that demonstrates clearly how the Church reinterpreted its past and glossed over its failures, and the ideological bases of its views on Marxism, social democracy, liberalism, and fascism.

The Church's institutional resources also influenced its actions. Where prior to the Third Reich it had had an extensive and dense network of Catholic organizations (the *Kirchliche Handbuch* listed 246), afterward it had only one;[10] in other words, it did not have the resources to create or significantly influence the type of Catholic political organizations that developed after the war. In contrast to the Italian Church, it could not mobilize tens of thousands of activists all trained to push the same program on voters and parties. Further, it could hardly coerce or materially entice Catholics to vote for the party it preferred: given the thorough physical destruction from the war, the Church could not conceive of withholding basic needs from a devastated population. If the Church was going to sustain its flock, it had to concentrate on providing them food, clothing, and shelter, regardless of how they voted.

Since the Nazi regime had violated the terms of the concordat, the postwar Church demanded not just legal guarantees of its protection, but (like the Italian), political ones as well. In addition, it faced a substantial number of political activists (mainly on the Left) who were reluctant to see the Church extensively involved in public activities, such as schools and hospitals (Forster 1981, 214). It thus was going to be in need of political (party) allies.

SELECTING AN ALLY

The Catholic Church chose to support only one political party and chose the one that included Protestants. Given that a solely Catholic party was reorganizing, there are two questions: why did the Church choose to rely on only one party, and why did it elect to enter into a situation wherein there would be contests between several orientations—including with members of the Evangelical (Lutheran) Church for influence over party policy? It would make sense to support one party if the Church feared that another party would not cooperate on key policy votes, that two separate parties competing for the Catholic vote might do worse than one, that Catholics (including clergy) would feel free to vote for *any* party claiming to be "Christian," or because negotiating with several parties is costly in terms of organizational time and resources. While such a multiplicity of motivations may be unsatisfactory to the social scientist, the historical record indicates that the Church was prompted by all but the first of those concerns.

---

[10] One Catholic public association survived the Nazi era: the Deutscher Caritas Verband; its function has always been (and remains) to operate charitable institutions (e.g. hospitals). See Bark and Gress 1989, 148.

First, a summary description of the relevant political parties—the Zentrum and the CDU. The fact that, by 1945, the Zentrum had been in existence for about 75 years led some of its Weimar leaders to argue that it should be revived. There were, however, some pronounced differences among its surviving leaders: some wanted to create a "centrist" party that was not tied to a specific religious "confession"; some argued for an expressly biconfessional party, while yet others were hesitant to start a new party for fear that it might wind up dominated by "reactionaries who had no place else to turn" (Cary 1996, 153–56). One result was that the efforts to create any primarily Catholic political organization lagged behind the efforts of Catholic and Protestant leaders who had decided that an alternative to the old party system and its confessional affiliations was necessary.

Those former Zentrum leaders who preferred to create an interconfessional party, and who discovered substantial support for the idea, began to organize (in Berlin) immediately after such efforts were permitted (June 1945) (Kaack 1971, 157–59). Emphasizing their concern with the creation of a democratic political system and with the introduction of Christian values into politics to avoid scenarios like the Nazi period, and fearing that the reaction to the Nazi era might lead to a system dominated by the Left (the Social Democrats and Communists), the new organization took the name Christian Democratic Union—the latter word recognizing that the new organization was biconfessional as well as developing at the grassroots level throughout (West) Germany (Pütz 1971, 36–40).

Its leadership, which at the outset included some rather progressive and "leftist" oriented individuals with their roots in the Weimar period, soon devolved into the hands of Konrad Adenauer, former mayor of Cologne (and again briefly after the war) and future chancellor of Germany, who argued that the CDU was essential because "the German system had always contained parties that 'purposefully fought Christianity' " (in Cary 1996, 183). Reasoning that the problem of Weimar and the Third Reich had been the aggressiveness of the non-Christian parties, the CDU was not shy about calling itself a "Christian" party.[11]

The CDU's Bavarian counterpart was organized soon after the Berlin section. While the former chair of the Bavarian version of the Zentrum (the Bavarian People's Party) favored reviving it, most of the remaining Catholic politicians in this Catholic and agricultural state preferred to found an interconfessional party (Cary 1996, 158–60; Evans 1981, 401; Wieck 1953). The Christian Social Union (CSU), however, retained and

---

[11] There is a considerable literature on the early CDU. See especially Schwering 1952; Wieck 1953; Gurland 1980; Pütz 1971; Kaack 1971; Cary 1996, among many others. On cooperation between Catholics and Protestants in the founding and development of the CDU, see also M. Mitchell 1999.

still retains a separate organizational apparatus and operates in coalition with CDU governments.[12] Rather like the DC in Italy, but perhaps even more so, the CDU emerged as a confederation of distinct local and regional CDU sections. It did not even formally organize itself as a *national* party until after the first federal (Bundestag) elections, and its national party headquarters did not open until 1952 (Scarrow 1996, 64). Its extra-parliamentary group has been far less powerful than the parliamentary group, and, partly due to the powers the *Länder* possess in the upper house, the state-level party sections and personalities are strong.[13] The CDU at first exhibited an unusually broad range of Christian, democratic, and even socialist and nationalist policy tendencies, but as Konrad Adenauer asserted his leadership the party downplayed its confessional side, quashed the left-wing progressives, stressed pragmatic politics, and moved toward the political center-right (Heidenheimer 1960; Pridham 1977; Kaack 1971; Pütz 1971).

If anything, it was the Zentrum that demonstrated that it would be the staunchest defender of the Church's interests in core policy areas, such as confessional schools and recognition in the constitution of the *Reichskonkordat*. Certainly it was more sure of where its interests and priorities lay: with Catholics, rather than with Protestants *and* Catholics. Yet at the time that the Church was looking for allies, the party was having serious internal disputes about its orientation. One faction insisted that political parties should not be the embodiment or representative of an entire socioeconomic and cultural milieu, a Weltanschauung. In its view, "As long as parties persisted in reducing political discourse to posturing about philosophical first principles, neither a multiparty nor a two-party system could be stable" (Cary 1996, 214). The Zentrum should not defend Catholic interests because they were Catholic interests, but because defense of those interests fell under various legitimate political rights. In contrast, another faction argued that the party should "hold unmistakably fast" to "the Catholic *Weltanschauung*" (in Cary 1996, 219) and that the religious affairs of Catholics were also the political affairs of the party. While it is plausible that these disputes discouraged the Church from supporting it, the CDU's Catholic blocs were having similar disputes (Cary 1996, 194–202; Pridham 1977, 61).

Some in the Church feared that the whole would be less than the sum of its parts were Catholics to try to establish several political parties. Cardinal Frings of Cologne declared that "it was deeply painful to him to see how

---

[12] For the sake of simplicity and unless otherwise noted, I will use *CDU* to refer to the combined CDU-CSU.

[13] On the CDU's structure, see Gurland 1980; Panebianco 1982, 216–29; Pridham 1977, 81–89; Scarrow 1996, 64–70; on personalities, see Pütz 1971, 171–73.

the energies of the Christian-Catholic camp could not be fully realized because the two groups [supporters of CDU or of Zentrum] could conduct a discussion together up to a certain point but then parted ways because the one was in the CDU and the other in the Zentrum," and each party was trying to establish, and was asserting, ideological and policy differences (in Spotts 1973, 153).

It is also possible that the characteristics of the electoral system were a factor in the calculus of deciding on whether and how to support a single party. The system was (and remains) a hybrid of proportional representation and single-member majority districts. Beginning with the 1953 parliamentary elections, a 5% threshold in the proportional national vote was also applied.[14] Any Catholic votes that went to a party that did not make that threshold, or win in any single-member districts, were wasted as far as the Church was concerned. The bishop of Trier wrote to his clergy in 1948, "When such important matters as divine right, natural rights, human rights, and human worth are at stake, the complete unity of a party invariably supporting these rights is more important than an aberrant private opinion. To work for this unity is one of the highest political objectives of the priest" (in Spotts 1973, 153).

Church officials did not mention as a reason for supporting only one party the organizational costs of maintaining negotiations and watching over several Catholic parties. It may have been an issue, but given the organizational energy the Church was willing to invest in one party, while getting less than it wanted in return, it appears that the Church was less concerned about organizational costs than about ensuring a minimum of pro-Catholic policy.

The question remains, though, why the CDU? One could argue, as members of the Zentrum did, that a party such as the CDU that crossed confessional lines could hardly be an adequate defender of Catholic interests (Cary 1996, 190). At most, it would defend some watered-down version of "Christian" interests. The cardinal archbishop of Cologne, Josef Frings, had stated flatly, "The work of reconstruction should be done by Catholics and Protestants in alliance but each acting separately" (in Spotts 1973, 151). The Church had concerns that Catholic-Protestant partisan intermingling would have the effect of diluting the Catholic faith.[15] Further, many lower clergy and rural Catholic voters were already supporting the revived Zentrum and would have to be compelled by the hierarchy, at some costs in organizational effort and even trust, to switch to the CDU

---

[14] Since 1956, if a party wins in at least three of the single-member district races, it then is entitled to have its overall percentage converted proportionally into seats in the Bundestag.

[15] On the important role of Frings and his relationship with Adenauer at the beginning of the CDU, see Morsey 1983.

(M. Mitchell 1999, 16; Schmidt 1987, 149, 288–98). By supporting an interconfessional party at the expense of a Catholic one, the Church seemed to compromise its ability to promote Catholic interests. Another strike against the CDU was its newness. Some clergy feared that since the CDU would face old established parties such as the SPD and KPD, it would not be able to compete with their organizational and programmatic strength (Gurland 1980, 17–24).[16] It is also possible to argue that, with the demographic change brought about by the division of Germany into East and West, and the increase in the relative percentage of Catholics in the new West Germany, there was less reason to continue in the old "tower" mentality, and less reason to fear Protestant domination of public institutions (Evans 1981, 398–99).

Why Choose the CDU?

While its later steadfast support of the CDU implies an initial decisiveness, the Church hierarchy was not of one mind on its choice of party. Some bishops first broached the idea of reestablishing the Zentrum (Gurland 1980, 472); others quickly argued that the Church's fundamental interest was protection against Communism, and that protection could be provided only by a broad-based Christian party (Spotts 1973, 299). This "concession" to the Protestant Church and politicians was, of course, only possible when Protestants indicated an interest in compromising, too.[17] "Instead of a controlling voice in a medium-sized party, German Catholics had gained an important voice in a large party" (J. Whyte 1981, 92). The decision of the Church and many Catholic politicians not to support the Zentrum is typically credited to the Zentrum's vote for Hitler's Enabling Act, "and the absence of any significant resistance activity" by Zentrum politicians or members (Lönne 1996, 177; Evans 1981). It often is also claimed that Catholics (though not necessarily the Church) realized the

[16] The Church's choice does not seem to have been influenced by Pope Pius XII. Available studies indicate that Pius was (surprisingly) vague about the Church's partisan choice, and even about whether the Church should resuscitate and be in charge of any Catholic interest groups, including workers' organizations, that might develop after the war (Forster 1981, 216–17). It is remarkable that none of the major German-language works on the development of the CDU go into any detail as to the thinking of the Vatican. There is a reference in Spotts 1973, 293, to Pius agreeing with some German Jesuits who during the war argued that Protestants and Catholics would have to work together in the future. Pius was vocal on the confessional schools issue, and on the *Reichskonkordat* (Martini 1966).

[17] In August 1945, the Protestant Churches at the Treysa Conference supported efforts to erase political conflict between the two faiths. There were, however, important Protestant dissenters. For the Protestant perspective, see Spotts 1973, 119–49, 298–305; Pridham 1977, 38–39; and Bark and Gress 1989, 150–53.

separation of faiths was no longer politically reasonable, or possible, given the Allies' demands that democratic governance be quickly set up (Lönne 1996, 178; Merritt 1995). To some extent, the Zentrum's vote for the Enabling Act created problems for the party's postwar brand image, so the party leadership attempted to overcome the damage by marketing a new name and policy—most of the Zentrum politicians went into the CDU, and a number were active in founding sections throughout Germany (rather like Allegheny Air's changing its name to USAir, then to US Airways after the public relations disasters of plane crashes).

Policy considerations were significant. The Church balked when in the Catholic stronghold of Cologne, one of the early leaders of the CDU proposed a nonconfessional school system with religious instruction. As soon as the party altered that program, the Church was willing to consider the CDU (Forster 1981, 220). The dispute actually delayed the official founding of the Rhineland CDU (Spotts 1973, 299). Not helpful to the Zentrum was its support in 1947 of the Social Democrat and Communist parties' economic policy program (Cary 1996, 189–90). As with the MRP, the Zentrum appeared too willing to collaborate with the Marxist parties. In the Church's eyes, it was the CDU that was positioned on the correct end of the left/right spectrum.

Yet perhaps even more important were the Church's estimate that "Catholics alone would not be able to assure a Catholic or Christian or conservative influence in the new German state" and the fact that the CDU was organizing rapidly while the Zentrum was not (Evans 1981, 397, 406). To increase the size of the Christian bloc, Protestants had to be brought into a joint party with a common program opposing the Social Democrats (Spotts 1973, 307), and many Zentrum leaders were unwilling to have Protestants in their midst. The single-member district portion of the ballot made the idea of joining forces in a coalition after an election untenable: on their own, a Protestant and a Catholic party might each lose in a district to the SPD or other secular parties. Furthermore, Catholic CDU politicians had presented the Church with a fait accompli. For various reasons, they were already soliciting and working in tandem with Protestant politicians to build the new biconfessional party. In the Catholic stronghold of North Rhine-Westphalia, the CDU had active sections in 21 of 39 electoral districts by November 1945 (the same month they officially launched the party there). Two months later they were in all but 3 of those electoral districts, and by April 1946, the CDU had sections in every district and administrative subdivision (Gurland 1980, 37). The April 1947 elections in the *Länder* clearly indicated that the CDU was the stronger party: the CDU won 38% of the vote, the Center Party only 10%, with the SPD at 32%, the liberal party (FDP) at 6% and the Communists (KPD) at 14%. The Allies tipped the scales when they declared that the

Parliamentary Council would have 52 seats, 20 of those going to the CDU, 20 to the SPD, 4 for the FDP, 3 for the KPD, and only 2 for the Zentrum (2 for a northern conservative party, and 1 for another non-Socialist party).

The question of which party to support thus boiled down to the question of what the Church wanted, how quickly it needed it, and whether an already constituted party could serve as an expedient solution. The Church faced an imperfect set of suppliers: it had to choose between one that, if the Church invested heavily in it, might yield returns in a number of years (the Zentrum), and one that, while not producing exactly what the Church wanted, at least had a rough facsimile already on the market in many areas (the CDU). In terms of organizational energy devoted to protecting against a perceived Communist threat, the Church had a greater incentive to support the CDU.

Cardinal Frings explained to Zentrum leader Wilhelm Hamacher,

> Be assured that none of the bishops support the CDU because its program is perceived as basically better or more correct; rather, this has occurred for tactical reasons, to spare the world the spectacle of a political division and of a mutual animosity within German Catholicism. Your party has the disadvantage of getting on board too late; the CDU has already constituted itself in many places. So do everything to come to a union with the CDU or at least to a concrete alliance. (Wieck 1953, 65–66)

Frings highlighted the virtues of going with a party that was already widespread, and of avoiding embarrassing and debilitating divisions. He also indicated the Church's readiness to tell politicians what they should do! Moreover, he himself joined the CDU, though he was persuaded to cancel his membership under criticism from the pope and other Catholic elements (Morsey 1983, 495–96).

Finally, the first regular Bundestag elections, held in 1949, reconfirmed the CDU's dominance vis-à-vis the Zentrum, and its capacity to win enough votes to form a coalition government (table 9.1).

LEVEL OF SUPPORT

Once the Church hierarchy decided to support the CDU, it brought its full weight to bear on the party formation and electoral campaign efforts. Priests were dispatched to coordinate the entry of former Zentrum politicians into the CDU, they harangued Zentrum holdouts (Cary 1996, 189), they told their congregations to vote CDU ("If Christ were alive today, he would certainly be in the CDU"). Moreover, like the Italian Church, the German was rather coercive: it forbade Zentrum members and politi-

TABLE 9.1
German Federal Election Results, 1949–1957, by Party

Party	1949		1953		1957	
	% of Vote	% of Seats	% of Vote	% of Seats	% of Vote	% of Seats
Christian Democrats (CDU)	31.0	34.6	45.2	49.9	50.2	54.3
Social Democrats (SPD)	29.2	32.6	28.8	31.0	31.8	34.0
Liberals (FDP)ᵃ	11.9	12.9	9.5	9.9	7.7	8.2
Communists (KPD)	5.7	3.7	2.2	0.0	—	—
"Old" Christian Democrats (Zentrum)	3.1	2.5	0.8	0.6	—	—

Source: Oberreuter and Mintzel (1992, 380–81).

ᵃ The 1949 and 1953 results are the combined totals of the FDP and the German People's Party (Deutsche Volkspartei, or DVP).

cians from belonging to the Catholic ancillary organizations and did not permit them to present their views at Church gatherings or in the Catholic press. The Church's developing network of ancillary organizations was mobilized on behalf of the CDU, often passing out campaign material making a nod to freedom of conscience but then stating that "every true Catholic's voice of conscience recommends" voting for the party and candidate "which offers really adequate guarantees" for Catholicism (in Spotts 1973, 163; his translation). This pressure not only destroyed the Zentrum but also helped the CDU win enough votes to form the coalition majority government after the first elections, and hold it until 1969.[18]

Because the Catholic Church supported a party that included a substantial Protestant minority, its influence in policy was somewhat diminished; it was compelled to compromise. A Church leader later, in 1965, lamented the apparent consequences of the Church's choice: "We sacrificed to the CDU the chance of a purely Catholic party[;] we sacrificed to it many of our desires in the educational field—for example, the establishment of a Catholic university." He complained that "this mixed marriage" had brought the Church only a pragmatic party headed by the Protestant Ludwig Erhard (in Spotts 1973, 166). An exaggerated claim, no doubt, as even Erhard turned to both Churches on questions of social and especially education policy, yet it indicates the extent to which elements of the Church felt it needed special treatment by a Catholic party.

The German Catholic Church, although not to the degree of the French, had a decentralized structure (in part due to the federal nature of

---

[18] The CDU formed a "grand coalition" government with its chief rival, the SPD, in 1966.

the political system), and the Conference of Bishops had no specific authority over the individual dioceses. Therefore, the decision over which party to support seems to have often been taken on a relatively decentralized basis. Indeed, there is evidence that some priests continued to support the Zentrum, partly for its stance on confessional schools, partly for its being an overwhelmingly Catholic party.

CONSIDERING EXIT?

The party led by Konrad Adenauer put his definition of the national interest and his emphasis upon pragmatic politics ahead of Church priorities (Spotts 1973, 172–73; Heidenheimer 1960; Kaack 1971, 177–78). In fact, Adenauer seemed even less concerned about the Church's interests than did De Gasperi and was sometimes dismissive of its demands. Did the Church not anticipate that the CDU might be led by someone like that? He had already, in the Weimar years, shown that he was a rather liberal Catholic; in the 1949 Parliamentary Council debates about the content of the Basic Law, he gave up the fight for state-financed confessional schools (Spotts 1973, 174). The CDU also compromised with the SPD and FDP; the latter allowed religious instruction to be given in state schools, and, in return, private (parochial) schools were permitted provided they met certain economic and legal criteria.

Private schools were not guaranteed funding. Whereas the Church had wanted the *Reichskonkordat,* which guaranteed such funding, to be an explicit part of the new constitution, the CDU chose not to expend its political resources on the issue. The concordat's provisions were covered in the Basic Law only by virtue of an article (123) upholding all prewar treaties that the Allies did not veto, so long as they did not violate the rest of the Basic Law. When challenged in court, the Basic Law has prevailed over the concordat. The outraged German hierarchy stated they would "under no circumstances" give up their confessional school crusade and enlisted (the only too happy to intervene) Pius XII—to no avail (Spotts 1973, 187–88).

Why did the Church support a party that had abandoned it on a core policy issue? The Church, after all, was facing the same problem that the French Church faced vis-à-vis the MRP. Not only that, but the CDU's leader, Konrad Adenauer, had little interest in Church concerns, thought the hierarchy too demanding, and tried to maintain his distance from them (Spotts 1973, 174–75; Heidenheimer 1960).[19] In fact, the Church had to deal with a Christian Democratic party more interested in establish-

---

[19] Adenauer held these views despite the fact that his son, Paul Adenauer, was a monsignor well connected to the German Church hierarchy.

ing a democratic state with the support of the Social Democrats than in having confessional schools.

When the CDU failed the Church on the schools question in 1949, the Church had to see whether there was a suitable substitute party. The answer was not obvious. Although the Zentrum still existed and held positions more in line with what the hierarchy wanted (Cary 1996, 242), it was, even prior to the 1949 election, extremely small and looked considerably less effective as a political ally.[20] The fact that the Church had been, up to the constitutional assembly debate on confessional schools, steering its clergy and its members toward the CDU had the unintended effect of eliminating potential substitutes and making the Church wholly dependent upon the CDU. It found itself in a situation similar to that of the Italian Church's relations with the DC.

There were mitigating factors. The Church's taxing, property, and social work privileges were reinstated by the Basic Law.[21] Many *Länder* funded confessional schools just as the Church wished.[22] The Church's socioeconomic presence in society was protected by its maintaining hundreds of hospitals, rest homes and hostels, and thousands of kindergartens, with construction and renovation costs paid for by the federal, *Land* (state), and local governments. In addition, the CDU did not fail the Church in another area of concern: anti-Communism (Spotts 1973, 174; Cary 1996, 202–5). Finally, the Church had several institutional mechanisms for representing its views to the CDU, the Catholic Bureau in Bonn being one of them (Hürten 1986, 253–54).

COMPARATIVE CONSIDERATIONS

The Catholic Church in postwar West Germany was subject to countervailing forces. The optimal party for its policy interests was also the weakest of potential allies; the party that appeared large enough to stand a chance at being influential in the new Federal Republic was less interested in catering to the Church's interests. Moreover, once that party consoli-

[20] By 1957, it had no seats in the Bundestag and "was reduced to splinter status even in its home state of North-Rhine Westphalia" (Evans 1981, 402).

[21] The Lutheran and Catholic Churches have long been granted taxing rights over their members. Individuals are registered at birth with one or the other Church and, when they begin paid employment, are taxed at a nontrivial rate (10% in the early postwar years, 7% in the 1990s). To avoid the tax, an individual must officially notify the state that he or she is leaving his/her church. At that point, the person cannot turn to the church for the standard products of marriage, baptism, burial or other services. Due to provisions carried over from the Weimar constitution, the churches could, until 1965, tax corporations as "juridical persons" (Spotts 1973, 183–207).

[22] The Basic Law set minimum standards for Church support; *Länder* were allowed to exceed those provisions.

dated itself in the first federal election, the Church could not credibly threaten the CDU that it would steer Catholics away from the CDU to the Zentrum. The Church itself was convinced that the Communist threat was of too great a magnitude to wait for a small party to grow, even with the Church's support. An additional wrinkle was that Catholic lay leaders probably would not have accepted any directive to support the Zentrum. The Church almost frantically threw itself behind the CDU; to admit it had been wrong would have exacted a high price in its credibility. Like the Italian Church, the German was trapped by its initial choice to purchase political protection and policy goods from just one political party.

Unlike the Italian Church, and more like the French, it found itself with few institutional resources with which to affect the actual construction of the Christian Democratic party. Its reconstituting ancillary organizations may have assisted the CDU at elections, but they do not appear to have been central to its development. Nor is it clear that the ancillary organizations were tightly linked to the Church hierarchy: the largest and most important Catholic organizations reconstituted themselves with their own resources (Hürten 1986, 249), making it harder for the Church to control their political orientation.

Although this survey is not as detailed as the coverage of France and Italy, designed as it is only to provide a check on the applicability of the ideas developed in earlier chapters, it provides abundant evidence that conceiving of the German Catholic Church as an interest group seeking political suppliers in the postwar era is a useful mechanism in understanding its views of how to operate in the new political environment, and particularly its association with the CDU/CSU therein. Moreover, historical experience, the new institutional structure, as well as the influence and priorities of important leaders were important factors in the outcome.

CHAPTER 10

The Political Crossroads of Catholicism in Postwar Europe: Contributions to a Theory of Interest Groups

About this Catholic situation. Not what
people *believe,* that's their business. But
how the organization operates. . . . these
Vatican fellows got such a good thing going
they should spread a little more around.
I mean, they got investments, son.
"Mac" in Robert Ludlum's *The Road to Gandolfo*

THE Catholic Church has been a central political and economic actor in Europe from the very beginning of the nation-state. In the several centuries prior to the democratization of these states, it was seen, not as one political actor among many, but as the principal rival to national governments or monarchs for authority over the people, for power, and for resources. As a religious organization, concerned (allegedly) with salvation, it was often said to have higher and more exacting goals than other political actors. It is a strictly hierarchical organization whose claim to authority came from its being sole interpreter and deliverer of a divine being's doctrine. For these reasons, scholars have had some difficulty in understanding the role of the Church in modern democratic politics. It is a premodern institution that, as many of its prelates would acknowledge, does not seem entirely at home in or amenable to democratic politics. And perhaps for these reasons, analysts have been slow to study it as a political actor in conventional terms. It has been difficult to find categories that could be used to describe and explain its behavior.

This book's central analytical objective has been to find a framework for understanding and explaining the behavior of the Catholic Church in modern democratic polities. The precise field of empirical problems on which I focused to test the conceptual framework is that of politics in the immediate postwar period in Italy, France, and Germany. And here the preeminent decision of the Churches was whether to form explicit alliances with a political party, what resources to devote to that alliance, and whether to exit from the alliance in the face of strains in it.

The Empirical Questions

The empirical questions are why the French Church, which needed far more political help than the Italian to recover lost ground after the war, linked only superficially and briefly with a political party, whereas the Italian Church, emerging triumphant from the war and needing little help, forged strong connections with a party. This book has also sought to explain why the German Catholic Church agreed to support a party that had a significant Protestant component. The strength of linkage varied, with the French Church's being the weakest. In the election in which the French Church did support the MRP, it was mainly by priests and hierarchy reading instructions at mass. Only in some regions did clergy try to do door-to-door work. In Italy, the Church engaged in full-scale mobilization of existing ancillary organizations and went so far as to create one devoted exclusively to campaigning on behalf of the DC. It encouraged priests to organize local party sections and hold meetings in Church buildings; it let priests run for office. It denied the sacraments to those who voted incorrectly or who belonged to the wrong political party. It organized religious festivals and permitted them to be co-opted by DC politicians, or strategically timed them to coincide with elections. Its leaders were in frequent informal contact with DC leaders. Finally, in Germany, the Catholic Church endorsed the CDU but found itself without the resources to significantly direct the CDU's early development.

The political choices of the Catholic Church, or any sizable interest group, are important for several reasons. One reason has to do with politics in its traditional sense, the making of public policy, redistribution, and values; the other with the politics of religion itself. When an interest group supports a party and helps bring it to office, it also brings into office a whole package of orientations, goals, and policies that the party intends to implement, and criteria by which it will act in other issue areas. The Catholic Churches of Italy, France, and Germany were most concerned about religious and educational policy areas, yet in some cases they helped, in other cases they hindered, the coming to power of parties that nationalized industries, established social welfare schema, and sought to construct a united Europe. The political choices of the national Churches were thus consequential for European societies. This had an impact not just within each country, but on Western Europe as a whole, as it was Christian Democratic leaders who were the staunchest advocates of the European Community.

The Churches' actions in postwar Western Europe helped shape party politics for decades. The Churches gave the parties they assisted the means by which to establish themselves in government. The Italian Church was decisive in enabling the DC to win a legislative majority in 1948, and to retain dominance in the 1950s. The French Church's refusal to support the MRP helped fracture the French Right, giving Charles de Gaulle room to enter politics with his ephemeral party in 1947. This meant that French Catholics could, without qualms, distribute their votes across the moderate side of the political spectrum, contributing to the divisiveness, and perhaps ultimately the collapse, of the Fourth Republic (which, some might argue, may have been a positive development). While the Fourth Republic saw the French foreign ministry led by Christian Democrats who facilitated the European project, the Fifth saw Charles de Gaulle put a variety of conditions on it. In Germany, the Church clearly helped the CDU retain its dominance. In all, where the Church remained steadfast in its support of a Christian Democratic party, it also contributed to the stagnation and absence of innovation in politics and political parties. Not until the DC's other key props (anti-Communism and patronage) fell through did Italy get something of a political renewal. The Church remained its ally until the DC's last days. Moreover, the Churches of Italy and Catholic Germany brought to power parties with conservative moral standards that affected all citizens (e.g., family policy).

The Churches' choices about party allies had repercussions for the condition of Catholicism itself in each country. The French Church's withdrawal from direct politics meant it faced the issue of adapting to modernization prior to Vatican II. In not relying on a party to provide artificial support mechanisms, it had to find other means with which to retain the authority to "speak and act" on political and social issues (Vassort 1984, 1:114). The German and Italian Churches may have gotten a false sense of security, or were certainly sluggish, about responding to changes in conditions in which they operated, including the decline in numbers of those who attended religious services. Though constrained by the dictates of Roman Catholicism, French priests even prior to Vatican II were more apt to innovate, and French Catholic Action was more responsive to the urban and rural poor than its Italian or German counterparts.[1]

RELIGION AND RATIONALITY

My argument imputes rationality to a sociocultural institution—a religion—that is generally perceived to be a purveyor of values and morals, and to have a Byzantine bureaucratic structure. Those two factors would

---

[1] As some analysts of religion have been arguing, the decline in Church attendance does not necessarily signal a decline in the "demand" for religion. Rather, it points to a failure on the supply side, with the Catholic Church (or other traditional churches) not providing the

seem to make it unlikely to exhibit rational behavior. Yet for the sake of maintaining its organizational integrity, for survival, and for increased resources (including more members), the Church, operating like everyone else in a world of scarcity, must compete for resources. Being subject to making choices in conditions of scarcity, the organization's leadership weighs costs and benefits. Changes in the competitive environment, in the operating environment, put pressures on the clergy and hierarchy to rationally evaluate their actions. Assuming (and sometimes it is a big assumption) that survival is a priority, they will respond rationally. The Church exhibits the behavior of a firm—trying to gain advantages in a competitive environment, attain a monopoly (inelastic demand for its product), and have regulations written to its benefit and its competitors' detriment.

Because organizations do not engage in a daily assessment of the costs of a chosen strategy (that, too, is a costly undertaking) or have internal politics and structures that enable them to make the collectively "best" decision, the analyst is forced to fall back on the notion of "bounded rationality." The assumption of rationality says nothing about the rationality of the organization's goals or "products," nor does it predict what those goals will be; it merely stresses that, because of limited resources and other constraints, the organization's leaders will try to reach those goals in what *they* perceive to be the most effective way. Nor does rationality necessarily define the criteria of "effective": this is why I devote extensive space to analyzing the Churches' respective histories and the ideologies of their leaderships.

The presumption is that when an organization is subjected to pressures, it will react. In the end, the validity of the microeconomic approach lies in its ability to explain outcomes consistently. For instance, a rival approach might say that the reason the Italian and German Churches supported their countries' Christian Democratic parties was that Christian Democracy is a natural outgrowth of a Catholic Church in a democratic polity, or that Catholics inherently vote for Christian Democratic parties, just as Churches support them. At the very least the French case undermines that argument. The economic approach points out that, in rationally evaluating options, the French Church found the MRP wanting. Alternatively, without a better understanding of the ties that bind an interest group to a party, one might have expected the Italian and German Churches to have reduced or stopped their support of the DC and CDU, respectively.

---

kind of religion people want or will respond to (Iannaccone 1991, 157; Chaves and Cann 1992; Stark 1993, 396; Stark and Iannaccone 1994, 232–34; Gill 1998).

THE ARGUMENT RESTATED

The presence or absence of a close relationship between a political party and the Church should not be seen as an artifact of historical development, more or less given by the kind of historical conditions to which Lipset and Rokkan and others allude. Instead, it should be construed as an alliance between Church and party, and that alliance should be seen as something that is constructed and maintained, or abrogated, by political actors who are operating in a strategic and rational way. In sum, my core contention is that we can explain the presence and character of alliances between the Roman Catholic Church and political parties as an outcome of strategic action, notably on the part of the Church.

Second, at the heart of this approach is the contention that, in democratic polities at least, it is useful to view the Church as an interest group. By this I mean that with regard to the political system (government), the Church seeks certain kinds of policies. It does so because the actions of governments are salient to its capacity to pursue its more general goals: it has a stake in the resource allocation that is at the heart of governance. The reader may object that this view of politics ignores the symbolic, ritualistic, and values sides of politics. Politics is not just about who gets what from whom, but about deciding *why* "who should get what from whom," about what the redistributive system stands for, about its ultimate goals. Expanding the notion of politics to include those considerations does not undermine my argument about the Church acting strategically as an interest group. Interest groups, including the Church, have lobbied governments about ultimate goals and about incorporating their vision of justice into the political system.

The question of political party allies is acute in most Western democratic political systems, in which it is a party or parties that control the executive and legislative branches, and in which individual members of parties have been less important than the party as a whole.[2] Party influence over public policy varies across countries, over time, and perhaps by policy area. Party importance expanded considerably after World War I. Certainly after World War II, Western European political parties were influential in eco-

---

[2] The latter situation may be changing in Europe, where elections have become more focused on the party leader (as potential prime minister or incumbent) than on the party as a whole. Party discipline, that is, the extent to which members of a party vote as demanded by its leaders and program, remains high in Europe. There is some controversy over the existence of party discipline in the United States, and, of course, on the significance of parties themselves. If party discipline is weak, and parties themselves are less important than key political figures, then interest groups will be less inclined to rely on party allies than on particular politicians. On the significance of Christian Democratic parties for public policy, see van Kersbergen 1994; Misra and Hicks 1994; Huber, Ragin, and Stephens 1993.

nomic, welfare, and social policy, and therefore the obvious targets of interest group attention. The Church was initially reluctant to enter into
democratic politics as an interest group. Its leaders, not liking the task of
dealing with the common professional politician, the egalitarian principles
of democracy, nor democracy's giving voice to anticlerical politicians, parties, and trade unions, viewed democratic politics with distaste and distrust. So, in some sense, it is worth noting that the Church had to learn
to be an interest group, had to accustom itself to the role. And accustom
itself it did.

Third, if we see the Church as an interest group, we can see that it faced
a particular type of problem: whether or not to form an alliance with a
political party. The issue becomes what calculations went into this decision
and what the basis for them was. Some dimensions of those calculations
were those any interest group would have to make. Others were more
distinctive because the Church is a particular kind of organization, that
is, a mass membership organization where the allegiance of the membership flows not primarily from the material benefits the organization delivers (nor where the leadership feels compelled to alter its ideology in order
to appeal to a larger constituency) but from the loyalty generated by deep-
seated beliefs (or, in some instances, coercion).

The Church is not altogether unique in this regard. It is arguable that
many trade unions are similar; that is, some members (especially militants)
belong not simply for the material benefits the union delivers but also
because they see the union as the expression of, and a vehicle for, some of
their deep-seated beliefs, endowed, in political and social terms, with a
moral as well as a material mission. Thus, the calculations of the trade
unions, like those of the Churches, on whether to make or break an alliance with a political party will be colored by ideological convictions as
well as by assessments of material and political benefits.

Fourth, the problem then is to model the key factors affecting the calculations the Church made about alliances with political parties. The first of
these issues is why the Church might be tempted to form a strong alliance
with a particular party, rather than shifting its support from party to party
as other interest groups often do. After all, there is a strong argument for
the latter strategy: the threat of exit (to another party) strengthens the
force of voice with the party currently receiving the Church's support.

I propose an answer that draws upon microeconomic theories of the
firm. Outcomes are related to an organization's decisions about costs and
benefits of alternative strategies. For an interest group like the Church to
form a close alliance with one party is analogous to the decision of a firm
to integrate vertically rather than to rely on markets for various kinds of
transactions. This builds upon Oliver Williamson's powerful argument
that, in the economic world, such decisions are driven by asset specificity.

I suggest that we can understand such decisions in the political world in terms of asset specificity as well. The important point is that for the Church to provide support in any major way to a political party (beyond the very limited support that some financial contributions provide) requires its officials, especially its priests, to proselytize among the membership in a concerted way so as to mobilize support for the party. On the one hand, this means that the Church (like some trade unions) is in a position to provide a very significant amount of support to a party and to demand considerable concessions in return. On the other hand, and this is the key point, once mobilized in one direction, this support is not readily diverted in another. Indeed, the more effectively the faithful are mobilized to support one party, the harder it is to later mobilize them against that party and for another. Why? Because the appeal the Church makes in order to achieve this mobilization is not primarily a material one: it is a symbolic or moral or spiritual one. In many cases, it means associating the party with the moral mission of the Church, and its opponents with immorality or worse. Such appeals, if they are to be credible, cannot be made and remade frequently. While not exactly a "once for all time" decision, it is close to such, and there is little doubt that the ability of the Church to mobilize its members again, on the same moral basis, for another party (and especially one that it had earlier rejected) declines with each successive effort at mobilization. One of the main assets of any religion is the trustworthiness of its representatives, and trustworthiness demands consistency (Gill 1998, 52–53; Anderson et al. 1992, 344).

Furthermore, the Church's agents, especially its priests and bishops, develop institutional links with a party and may find their particular position relative to the party (access to party office, meetings, candidate selection) of greater benefit than the cost of trying to establish such a relationship with a different party. Providing incentives to entice priests to shift to another party may be more costly than whatever losses the Church is currently incurring.

Given that the decision of the Church to enter into an alliance with a specific party is parallel to the decision of a firm to enter into a strategic alliance akin to vertical integration, it is a very weighty one, and the analytical question is, what cost/benefit calculations affect the decision to do so?

Benefits

I argue, in a challenge to sociological and cultural views of religion, that the decision will involve an evaluation of the costs and benefits to the Church of the alliance. What are the most important potential benefits?

First and most generally, any policy that promotes the institutional survival and expansion of the Church. This implies preferential treatment for itself in light of rival religions, perhaps with the elimination of opponents, including the elimination of political parties that deny its legitimacy. It will also prefer support for Church-led religious education, seeing this as the best means of guaranteeing itself a future generation of Catholics. It will also resist limits on its ability to act to promote its vision and goals.

Next, the Churches have to consider the character of potential political allies: can the party in question deliver, and *what* is it likely to deliver? Is it possible for the party to secure a significant share of political power so it can implement the Church's preferred policies? Can the Church trust it to do so? What is the prior record of the party politicians? Are they familiar to the Church hierarchy? The less well the hierarchy knows the party leadership, the less likely it is to trust it. In addition, obviously, were the hierarchy to know that the leadership is and has been opposed to or ambivalent about Church policy preferences, it is unlikely to ally with that party.

These factors all had ramifications for West European Church-party interactions. In Italy, the DC appeared to be the largest nonsecular party after the war. Its leadership, in addition, was known to the hierarchy, and known to be largely sympathetic to the Church's top priorities. Its electoral prospects appeared somewhat better than those of other parties that professed to be sympathetic to the Church (e.g., Uomo Qualunque). However, it was not immediately apparent that the party could gain a parliamentary majority, and thereby avoid a Communist- or Socialist-led government. In France, it was clear that the MRP's leadership was less sympathetic to the Church's interests and priorities. Although one can argue that for that reason alone, the French Church had less reason to invest heavily in a strong link to the party, there was an additional reason: given France's history of anticlericalism, the likelihood that the MRP could win a parliamentary majority, obviating the need for a coalition with secular parties, was very small. In Germany, on the other hand, the rapid abandonment of the old Catholic party by postwar politicians left the Church searching for an ally in a fragile, developing system where even the Allies were indicating greater sympathies for parties of the Left than the Right. The CDU seemed the best possible solution.

The Church thus looks for a party that can go some distance in meeting its fundamental desires. Specific histories and leaders fill out the details of preferences: for the Italian Church, preventing the rise of a Communist government, under which the Churches might have been outlawed or at least deprived of key resources, was paramount. Preserving educational and other prerogatives obtained in the Lateran Pacts was another key concern. The French Church, for which Communism was less a political than a religious concern, sought to retain the means to provide confessional schools. The German Church, though concerned about the "Bolshevik" threat, especially for the Eastern Zone, was more concerned about getting guaranteed funding of confessional schools and the explicit recognition of the 1933 concordat in the Basic Law.

Costs

Every benefit incurs some costs, and mitigating these costs relative to the expected benefits is the essence of strategic action. What were the costs to the Church of entering into a political party alliance? The core point is that doing so is not and was not costless. Some might think it so: after all, the Church seems to many to be a massive organization with great mobilizational potential for political purposes. Why should it ever hesitate to throw its support to a party by which it might gain advantages? Here again, I turn to the new economics of organizations for answers. First, the Church is not a unitary actor but an organization composed of many actors and, like a firm, faces the problem of maintaining the good-faith performance of its members, personnel, and those external to it with whom it contracts. In particular, it faces malfeasance problems on several fronts. First, there is the threat that, having reaped the benefits of membership, some of its militants or adherents may stray from the dictates of the organization, like employees who shirk their duties. Entering into an alliance with a party while developing quasi-secular organizations such as Catholic Action for the purposes of political mobilization or social control increases the number of people who may lay claim to speaking authoritatively on behalf of the Church. This dilutes the chain of command and the hierarchical authority of the pope and his immediate subordinates. In an era when various secular pressures represented the principal challenges to the authority of the teachings of the Church, endowing secular officials like party politicians or laymen involved in Catholic ancillary organizations with a measure of authority on behalf of the Church increased the risk that the Church hierarchy would lose control of its doctrine, that is, its trademark and product distribution, or of the faithful, its membership.

Second, the Church runs the risk of malfeasance by the political party. The latter may take the Church's support and convert it into resources that enable the party to stay in government without catering to the Church's wishes. The political party, once in office, may be able to use various techniques, including patronage, to develop its own following and lessen its dependence on the Church or other interest groups. It may not pursue policies the Church wants and yet be able to hide its shirking in a coalition government (in which policy responsibility is hard to attribute).

Costs, or risks, also vary according to whether the Church supports one or several political parties. If the Church supports several parties, it has more options should one of those parties die or fail to deliver on policy. Yet, if the parties know that the Church is spreading its risk, each has less incentive to tailor a policy for the Church and, if cabinet and legislative votes are secret, may be able to blame policy failure on the other parties. Spreading support means the Church will be able to "buy" less policy from each party.

These costs have been set forth in the abstract. I now turn to specifying the kinds of factors that might have made these costs and benefits different across countries. Historical conditions and context specified a significant portion of those costs and benefits, varying with several distinct aspects of the historical position of Catholicism in these countries. First, the past affects the position of the Church vis-à-vis other political and social actors, and the Church's perception of its role in that milieu. In particular, the Church's relationship to the previous regime affects the allies it has available in the new political system, and its general moral authority. Second, the Church's structure affects the way it processes information and its capacity to act. Third, the Church's leadership can influence the timing of its response to conditions, its assessment of the value of any particular course of action. Note that I am speaking of the costs each Church assigned to a particular outcome, not the *likelihood* of that outcome.

First, the costs of losing control of the government to the Communists was highest in Italy because it is there that the headquarters of the Church are located and where restrictions on its operations would be the most damaging to its global enterprise. Thus, it stands to reason that the Church would view the benefits of securing a sympathetic government and the costs of getting a hostile one as greatest compared with France or Germany. In this instance, the Church would be willing to yield on its other policy goals, which could be realized at a later date, to obtain a stable, anti-Communist government.

Second, any calculation about the potential benefits to be secured in the realm of education had to take into account the historical context for such issues in each country. In Italy, the Church had had a strong presence in education for many years, and the benefits it could expect in this realm from a sympathetic government were great. In France, the secularizing impact of the Revolution and the subsequent development of a secular republic meant that the level of control the Church could secure over education, even with the most sympathetic government, was lower. The main objective had to be a less rewarding one, that is, maintaining some right to conduct religious education with some subsidy. In Germany, despite the *Kulturkampf,* the Church had maintained a strong position in education and was eager to regain it after the restrictions imposed by the Nazi regime.

The relation of any interest group to the prior regime is relevant for analyzing group behavior in transitions to democracy. If the Church bet on the wrong horse during Fascism, or did not maintain some institutional and ideological distance from the previous regime, it was likely to be repudiated by a large share of the public and thus look, to interested political parties, like "tainted goods." The reputation it developed at earlier historical moments became a significant factor during the postwar, democratic era. Certainly, with its moral suasion reduced, it would be less effective at mobilizing Catholics, particularly nominal Catholics, to vote for its party ally. It also mattered whether its ancillary organizations were put under its exclusive control, so it had a better chance of directing its sociopolitical activity. Some suggest that the German Church was more willing to support a biconfessional party because of its disgrace under the Nazis. Relying on the renewal of the old Catholic Center Party would have been an awkward reminder of the Church's earlier complicity in providing a legal basis for Nazi rule.

Why Exit?

Organizational linkages create inertia, and so one would think they would seldom be broken. Indeed, in the case of parties and interest groups, they are broken less frequently than the tensions between the two organizations might suggest. Specific assets geared to that relationship are not easily redeployed. Also, in building a link with one party, the interest group helps to destroy, or at least cripple, the alternatives. Thus, although the group may want to exit, there may be no suitable substitute at hand.

Nevertheless, groups sometimes do exit. They are most likely to do so, first, when the political party has failed it on a key issue of concern (as the MRP did with the French Church). This situation could include the party becoming so minor that it is politically irrelevant. Second, they may exit when the political context changes such that it is far more profitable to be independent. Third, they may exit when reputation becomes an issue: association with the party becomes costly to the group's own reputation, hence its ability to retain and attract members. Indeed, reputation was an issue for the Italian Church but was outweighed by the advantages of remaining associated with the DC and by the difficulties of exiting.[3]

---

[3] As the French and Italian cases both show, interest groups need not and do not rely solely on parties for attaining their goals. Clearly, if the aim is to become a successful national or multinational organization, then relying on political parties to alter the terms of competi-

Political Parties

This book has paid some attention to the second half of the interest group–party relationship. In chapter 8, I suggested that parties view interest groups strategically, assessing the groups' resources and ability to contribute to a party's electoral and policy goals. But that assessment is also affected by ideological factors: are the interest group's ideological goals complementary to those of the party? Can the party stand to be publicly associated with the group? In terms of the market analogy, the issue is not just one of a product's price, quality, and availability, but of whether the buyer is "irrationally" sensitive to the firm's reputation or image. One of the reasons the French Church–MRP alliance was shallow and then broken was that the MRP did not, for the most part, want to be known as the party of the Church. The party regarded itself as the party of renewal; it regarded the Church, given its actions during the Vichy regime, as morally compromised. The DC, in contrast, had no such qualms about the Church. Yet neither did it completely hand itself over to the interest group, demonstrating the point that parties and interest groups, though they may seem to be of the same ideological and/or sociological family, have distinct, sometimes conflicting interests. Whether the CDU catered to the German Church seemed to depend more on the preferences of its voters, activists, and leaders than on leverage the Church tried to exert.

While the three cases evaluated here have given some answers to the question of how parties evaluate interest groups, the results encourage testing in other contexts and countries. Further, much remains to be done on the consequences to a party of allying with an interest group. In terms of the economic analysis of politics, how does the party manage its investors? Has the need for some kinds of interest group support declined over time? (Perhaps now that televised advertising is increasingly important, financial contributions matter more than logistical support; nevertheless, endorsements appear to still matter to electoral success). Can the party use a group to help the party further its own policy agenda? What leverage do different types of interest groups give a party over its competitors in society at large, in the legislature, in administrative agencies, and in the cabinet?

A THEORY OF INTEREST GROUPS?

In their work surveying accumulated research on American interest groups, Baumgartner and Leech deplore the lack of cumulative knowledge

---

tion is not enough. Groups can push their issues onto national agendas and compel political parties to address them, they can attempt to directly enlist the population in their cause ("grassroots mobilization"), and they can stage protest rallies and boycotts.

about groups in American politics (1998, xvi, 17–19, 148). Much the same could be said of the study of interest groups elsewhere. My work, however, has attempted to provide a framework to guide further research, and in which to couch earlier case studies and surveys. Without repeating the entire argument here (see chap. 2), I remind the reader that analyzing interest groups as firms in a competitive market (a democratic polity) highlights their tendency to try to alter the rules of competition to their advantage, to weigh strategies according to goal attainment, to invest resources in light of possible returns, and to be constrained by earlier investments. Interest group history, structure (of the interest group and of the political system), and leadership alter the weights put on various strategies and outcomes, not to mention their effect on the goals the group pursues.

While specific words may vary across political systems and groups, categories describing different levels or types of interest group support of parties should be "transportable" to other research projects (cf. Petracca 1992). Among those that the Churches exhibited were membership or grassroots mobilization, public endorsements, financial and logistical support, campaign staff and advice, threats to withdraw support, "buttonholing" of party members, and coercion of voters.

One might ask how internal organizational politics affects group strategies and goals. The analysis here skirted that question by assuming that the leadership of the organization represents the "sum" of the internal politics, and by showing that when leadership changes, there may be some change in goals and strategies. An organization may have fairly independent factions within it that could strike their own deals with another organization. Doing so undercuts the leverage the leadership has over the other organization, since it cannot claim to be the exclusive representative of the membership. It cannot command the price corresponding to exclusive representation, nor can it get the rents from the exchange, save what might filter up indirectly. Furthermore, a faction may use a link to another organization in order to increase its own power and, eventually, use that to challenge the leadership. Social Democratic parties with links to trade unions are vulnerable to these dynamics; so too, it should be said, was the DC (Zuckerman 1979; Warner 1997).

Mainstream political science began its study of interest groups with a pluralist model of politics: open competition between groups for access to political power, with public policy being the vector of these forces (Truman 1951). The current work joins those that have shown, in contrast, that access to political power tends to be dependent on resources and structures. Those groups that have resources and socioeconomic or political positions making them more attractive to key political parties are more likely to gain policy influence. Noting that fact raises the question, in turn, of the impact an interest group–party link, such as that between the Church and the DC or a large trade union and a Social Democratic party, has on the access of other interest groups and citizens to that political party and the policy process. Depending on the extent of support the party already has and on its potential electoral market, the party may "need" only a few group suppliers, so the existing link may make the return to the party from other group links (and their attendant costs) less significant, hence less attractive. There may be first-mover advantages to the group that first links with a party. That group is the first to influence the party's policy priorities, perhaps even the party's structure and internal statutes. The bias thus created may work against other groups trying to find a party ally.

The objective utility of a party to an interest group (and vice versa) can change for a variety of reasons. Parties may become less or more important in the policy process, the interest group's goals may change, the ideological acceptability of the link may change. If the links between an interest group and a party have been long-standing, becoming institutionalized and routine, a change in utility may not produce a corresponding change in the links. The decision to link with a party imposes immediate costs on a group: resources committed to the link cannot be deployed for other uses. It also imposes costs on the group's future opportunities. If the links were established through a significant dedication of assets, the group faces new costs if it wants to redeploy them with a different party. It faces the additional "cost" that through its initial support of a particular party, it may have helped that party eliminate alternatives. In addition, the fact that the groups and parties are competing in a political "market" and not an economic one means that inefficient, suboptimal outcomes (alliances or failed alliances) will be the norm. As Pierson has noted, "Political institutions rarely confront a dense environment of competing institutions that will instantly capitalize on inefficient performance, swooping in to carry off an institution's 'customers' and drive it into bankruptcy" (1997, 25). Giving voice, or complaining, may be the group's least costly option; competing with activists in the party for control of the party's policymaking apparatus may be another, though more costly in resources. The long-term connections between some interest groups and parties may merely be the side effect of the high costs of breaking the alliance, the absence of alternatives, or a lack of sufficient incentives to do so, rather than a true harmony of interest.

Finally, alliances between groups and parties may fail to obtain, or once struck, may persist despite frequent disputes, because in the political market it is very hard to evaluate with any precision just what is being exchanged and whether it really has been delivered (North 1990, 362). Information uncertainties create barriers to action by leading to a reluctance to commit to an alliance, or to break one. Ironically, it is the market analogy that highlights the fact that the political realm, with high barriers to entry and exit, or to contracting and contract termination, is a relatively ineffective "market" for interest group–party interaction.

CATHOLICISM IN THE "POSTINDUSTRIAL" AGE

> Episcopal pronouncements on political questions should contribute to the outlook of the faithful but may not use the Catholics' religious bonds and their confidence in the pastorate for the church's own purposes.[4]

As this quote of German priests indicates, Vatican II appeared to unleash sentiments even in the clergy protesting excessive hierarchical control over Catholics' political preferences and behavior. In Germany in the latter half of the 1960s, the Church lost its battle against reform of the religious schools and religious curriculum; it was repudiated by its own laity and clergy. When an organization loses control of its members and activists, political parties hardly need take note of what it demands. Whereas in the early postwar years the national Churches in Western Europe constituted a powerful set of interest groups, their efforts now appear to be concentrated on regaining control of their internal human and fiscal resources (Della Cava 1993). Finding it increasingly difficult to deliver more than a modest number of Catholic voters to the Christian Democratic parties, the Churches are ill-situated to extract concessions from those, or any other, political parties.

This book has focused on the Churches' behavior in the first 60 years of the twentieth century, and it has argued that the Church's behavior can best be understood in the context of interest group behavior, and that its decision to ally with a political party can be modeled on the theory of the firm. But what of the later years? After Vatican II, when the Church apparently modified its political claims, can one say that the Church still behaves as an interest group in West European politics?

Vatican II was meant to alter the Catholic Church's relation to the temporal world. So named for the convening in Rome of the Second Universal Vatican Council (1962–65), it accepted as one of its key doctrines individual freedom of conscience and, thus, converted the Church into an organization that was noncompulsory for non-Catholics (Casanova 1994, 72). Second, Vatican II recognized the separation of church and state. The Church no longer claimed to have a privileged place in politics or in state authority. It defined the Church as "the People of God," in which everyone belongs to the priesthood of Christ, albeit at different levels of authority. It embedded the change already made by John XXIII in 1958, making

---

[4] Priests in the German diocese of Paderborn (in Spotts 1973, 167).

the Church's divine mission that of action on behalf of "peace and justice" in the world. The Church's purpose is to change the existing world, not just convert people to a particular doctrine.

Vatican II thus changed some the Church's expectations and demands. Many of the Church's previous activities can be seen as efforts to get what it thought it deserved by right, by virtue of being the Roman Catholic Church. Vatican II acknowledged that there might be limits on what it could demand of a political system, of a state. Yet while in some countries the Church may have stopped lobbying politicians to make the Church the official religion of state, Vatican II did not change the Church's desire for the resources to maintain itself and to continue its evangelical work, and for protection from religious competitors. One would expect national Churches to continue to press for subsidies where they could, and for restrictive definitions of religious freedom (Gill 1998, 177–79). Furthermore, the Church under John Paul II has reversed itself on various aspects of Vatican II.

Owing to differences in the histories of different national churches, one might also expect them to internalize Vatican II's messages in different ways. One could even expect variations within the same country. Indeed, the French hierarchy showed a range of views of the Church's role in French political and social life, even though as a whole it had removed itself from direct political action (Vassort 1984). The Italian Church remained, instead, a political actor, pressuring DC politicians on social policy (the divorce and abortion referenda), and pressuring Catholics to continue to vote for the DC in its capacity as the Church's ally. Similarly, the German Church continued to see itself as a major participant in the making of public policy.

I have described an interest group as an organization that grants or withholds some resource that politicians and bureaucrats (those with the capacity to influence public policy outputs) are likely to want (votes, financial assistance, public goodwill, endorsements) in order to get what the group wants. The organization may campaign on its own to get sympathetic politicians into office. I have argued, counter to intuition, that the Church fits the definition of interest group that economists usually use: it is a rent-seeking organization, one that tries to further its interests through preferential government redistribution of revenue or preferential regulation that alters the conditions of competition to the group's favor. While the Church may have idealistic or spiritual goals, as an organization in the temporal world it is subject to the constraints all organizations face: the need for self-perpetuation and for growth, which means financing, staffing, and membership.

The question remains, is it still legitimate to argue that the Church is an interest group? There are numerous reasons to suggest that it still is and will remain so. Suppose, for the sake of argument, that the Church turned its attention and efforts to bringing peace and justice to the world, and that it de-emphasized obtaining privileges and implementation of its moral positions. The problem is that even peace and justice require politicians to undertake (or not) various actions, and require the Church to expend its own organizational resources. The Church will still want favorable government financing and freedom to do as it pleases and will try to impose its own definition of justice and morality.

Although Vatican II altered some aspects of the Church's behavior and policies, it did not alter several of the conditions that give rise to the Church's interest group behavior. Because the Church did not give the laity carte blanche to operate the religion, personnel needs remain high, and as has been pointed out elsewhere (Gill 1998, 180), the Church maintains high barriers to personnel entry. Moreover, it is saddled with a very old infrastructure that is expensive to maintain. The staff problem gives it the incentive to seek protection from lower cost religions (e.g., the Protestant Evangelicals, cf. Gill 1998) and the infrastructure costs give the Church an incentive to lobby governments for state subsidies. Further, the Church has property and other financial investments for which it has the incentive to seek favorable government action. The Church still views Catholic education as an essential means of reproducing the Church. Like other interest groups, the Church has goals and preferences that it believes government action can help it reach. In democratic governments, political parties are still the intercessors for government policies on education and morality.

In addition, the effort of the Catholic Church to mitigate some of what its current leadership views as the detrimental consequences of Vatican II (doctrinal relativism due to freedom of conscience, for one; reduction of papal authority due to the collegial structure of the episcopacy and the Church as "God's people" for another) means it remains an inefficient competitor in the religious market. Since it appears not to want to undertake the radical restructuring that might make it more competitive with other religions (Gill 1998, 179–82), it is likely to want politically wrought protection. Yet, because the Church's capacity to influence Catholics' political behavior has diminished considerably, the Church may not automatically be a significant ally for a political party, and hence may not be able to find powerful party allies.

There are numerous indications that the Church still acts as an interest group in various European countries. Of our three countries, it is in France that one might least expect it. The structure of the Fifth Republic has created many obstacles: the parties in parliament are almost an afterthought, having little effect on legislation, and the bureaucracy is rather resistant to interest group input (F. Wilson 1987; Keeler 1987), and while a number of Catholics are politically active, they do not attend mass regularly, and they tend to vote for the Left (S. Berger 1987). In the framework of the Fifth Republic, the Church has few effective lobbying targets and, given its financial status and dearth of devout parishioners, few assets with which to "pay" a party for its support.

In Germany, despite Vatican II, the Church has vigorously opposed the removal of crucifixes from classrooms; in Italy, it had been a tireless promoter of the DC until that party's demise, and an advocate of Catholic unity in one party after the DC. Its condemnation of organized crime seems only to have come with the DC's demise and the rise of religious competition from Protestant Evangelicals.

The reader might object that with so many possible variations in costs and benefits, in histories, structures, and leadership, it is impossible to verify the significance of any one of them when only a few cases are analyzed. The justification for the small-N, or case study, methodology used here lies in its being able to point to the variety of factors that need to be analyzed, in showing that there is plausibility to the analytical approach used, and in bringing a new tool (microeconomics of the firm) to the study of interest group–party interaction and to the action of the Catholic Church (George and McKeown 1985). Moreover, assessing the role of history, structure, and leadership requires more detailed analysis than a large-N study allows. Such a study, attempting to assess the importance of just several costs, should be possible; it is the task for a different research project. I have controlled for several significant variables: the type of group (hence, very broadly, its goals) and the type of party with which it interacts. Finally, the case study approach enabled me to shed light on the behavior of three powerful national Churches at a significant point in the political history of three important European states.

OTHER RELIGIONS

Adopting the lens of organized religion as an interest group, we observe that when an organized religion perceives that its goals require access to political resources of some sort, its leadership will search for the closest policy match with a political party and will try to use its membership and logistical resources as assets to be exchanged with the party. In extreme cases, one would expect that if no suitable party can be found, the religion may try to create its own party. Whether it does so would be limited by its resources and any internal or external proscriptions against direct political activity. Because organized religions require resources to pursue their goals, they will exhibit rent-seeking behavior. Further, because their ideology seldom is ecumenical in tenor or genuine spirit, they will be at least as aggressive as traditional economic sector interest groups in pursuing their political ends.

The structure of the religious institutions is likely to play a significant role, as will the ideological outlook of the leadership. Take, for example, Islam. Although Sunni Islam has no recognizable institutional "church," nor any supranational "synod" or dominant leadership, even such over-whelmingly Sunni states such as Egypt have religious institutions that are more influential and powerful than other institutions (cf. the role and function of al-Azhar in that country). One could test some of the themes of this book in a Shia state such as Iran, which has an established religious hierarchy and a relatively centralized system of administration and control over the thousands of mosques that exist—indeed its structure looks a bit like that of the Catholic Church. Iran also has a functioning parliament, functioning political parties, and some very clear ideological and policy conflicts among the clerics—from mullahs all the way to the grand ayatollahs. In view of the fact that major political and administrative offices have occasionally been filled with nonclerics since the revolution, how does the religious hierarchy there exercise its influence, especially now that major cities such as Tehran have mayors and other public officials who are no longer slavish to the wishes of the clergy? What leverage does the high clergy have over the various political parties? How does the clergy exercise its influence and power to obtain what it wants in the new circumstances?[5]

Organized religious entities have entered the political arena as rent seekers (demanding perquisites and the use of the state or polity's enforcement mechanisms) from the time of ancient Egypt and Mesopotamia to the present. This book has focused on organized religions in democratic systems, finding that those religions tend to behave as interest groups and can be fruitfully analyzed as such. It has also argued that the content, structure, and history of an organized religion affects its assessment of costs and benefits. There is reason to suspect that those factors affect the actions of organized religions in nondemocratic contexts as well.

In 1798, when an aging Pope Pius VI was being forcibly taken to France by the French army, he asked his captors that he be permitted, instead, to die in Rome. The French reply was, "One can die anywhere" (Hales 1966, 115). The leveling effects of democracy had reached even the papacy, making the politics of religion the politics of interest.

---

[5] Another investigation could be undertaken in the United States, where the religious Right has been trying to commandeer the Republican Party, or at least dominate it to the extent of requiring specific policy commitments from its representatives in exchange for electoral support. Its goal of legislating morality and controlling education is strikingly similar to that of the West European postwar Catholic Churches (and to the "orthodox" religious activists in Iran and Israel).

References

Alberigo, Giuseppe. 1986. "Santa Sede e vescovi nello Stato unitario: Verso un episcopato italiano (1958-1985)." In Giorgio Chittolini and Giovanni Miccoli, eds. *Storia d'Italia*, Torino: Einaudi, Vol. 9. *La Chiesa e il potere dal Medioeva all'eta contemporanea.*

Aldrich, John. 1995. *Why Parties? The Origin and Transformation of Party Politics in America.* Chicago: University of Chicago Press.

Allison, Graham. 1971. *The Essence of Decision: Explaining the Cuban Missile Crisis.* Boston: Little, Brown.

Allum, Percy A. 1973. *Politics and Society in Post-War Naples.* Cambridge: Cambridge University Press.

Anderson, Gary M., Robert B. Ekelund, Jr., Robert F. Hébert, and Robert D. Tollison. 1992. "An Economic Interpretation of the Medieval Crusades." *Journal of European Economic History* 21 (2): 339–63.

Andreotti, Giulio. 1977. A. Gambino, ed. *Intervista su De Gasperi.* Bari: Laterza.

Annuario Cattolico delle diocesi. Turin: Marialli Editore, 1954.

Arnal, Oscar L. 1985. *The Ambivalent Alliance: The Catholic Church and the Action Française, 1899–1939.* Pittsburgh: University of Pittsburgh Press.

———. 1986. *Priests in Working Class Blue: The History of the Worker-Priests (1943–1954).* New York: Paulist Press.

Azéma, Jean-Pierre, and François Bédarida. 1992. *Le Régime de Vichy et les Français.* Paris: Fayard.

Badone, Ellen. 1989. *The Appointed Hour: Death, Worldview, and Social Change in Brittany.* Berkeley and Los Angeles: University of California Press.

———, ed. 1990. *Religious Orthodoxy and Popular Faith in European Society.* Princeton: Princeton University Press.

Baget-Bozzo, Gianni. 1974. *Il partito cristiano al potere: La DC di De Gasperi e di Dossetti, 1945–1954.* 2d ed. 2 vols. Firenze: Vallechi.

Bardi, Luciano, and Leonardo Morlino. 1994. "Italy: Tracing the Roots of the Great Transformation." In Richard Katz and Peter Mair, eds. *How Parties Organize.* London: Sage Publications, 242–78.

Bark, Dennis L., and David R. Gress. 1989. *From Shadow to Substance, 1945–1963.* Vol. 1. Oxford: Basil Blackwell.

Bates, Robert H., Avner Greif, Margaret Levi, Jean-Laurent Rosenthal, and Barry R. Weingast. 1998. *Analytic Narratives.* Princeton: Princeton University Press.

Battelli, Giuseppe. 1986a. "Santa Sede e vescovi nello Stato unitario. Dal secondo Ottocento ai primi anni della Repubblica." In Giorgio Chittolini and Giovanni Miccoli, eds. *Storia d'Italia* Vol. 9. *La Chiesa e il potere politico dal Medioevo all'età contemporanea.* Torino: Einaudi, 809–54.

———. 1986b. "Vescovi, diocesi e città a Bologna dal 1939 al 1958." In Andrea Riccardi, ed. *Le Chiese di Pio XII.* Bari: Laterza, 257–82.

Baumgartner, Frank R., and Beth L. Leech. 1998. *Basic Interests: The Importance of Groups in Politics and in Political Science.* Princeton: Princeton University Press.

Bazin, François. 1981. "Les députés MRP élus les 21 octobre 1945, 2 juin et 10 novembre 1946: Itinéraire politique d'une génération catholique." Vols. 1–2. Thèse du doctorat, Institut d'Études Politiques, Paris.

Becker, Gary S. 1983. "A Theory of Competition among Pressure Groups for Political Influence." *Quarterly Journal of Economics* 48:371–99.

Becker, Gary S., and George J. Stigler. 1974. "Law Enforcement, Malfeasance, and the Compensation of Enforcers." *Journal of Legal Studies* 3:1–17.

Bédarida, Renée. 1992. "La hiérarchie catholique." In Jean-Pierre Azéma et François Bédarida, eds. *Le Régime de Vichy et les Français.* Paris: Fayard, 444–62.

Benzoni, Alberto, and Viva Tedesco. 1968. *Il Movimento Socialista nel Dopoguerra.* Padua: Marsilio Editori.

Berger, Peter. 1967. *The Sacred Canopy.* Garden City, N.Y.: Doubleday.

Berger, Suzanne. 1972. *Peasants against Politics.* Cambridge: Harvard University Press.

———. 1987. "Religious transformation and the future of politics." In Charles S. Maier, ed. *Changing Boundaries of the Political.* Cambridge: Cambridge University Press, 107–49.

———, ed. 1981. *Organizing Interests in Western Europe.* Cambridge: Cambridge University Press.

Berstein, Serge, and Pierre Milza. 1991. *Histoire de la France au XXE Siècle.* Vol. 2: *1930–1945.* Paris: Éditions Complexe.

Bertoldi, Ennio, ed. 1971. *Tempi ed Uomini nella vita della Banca S. Paolo: Contributo per una storia.* Brescia: Centro di Documentazione Cattolica.

Bevilacqua, Piero, and Augusto Placanica, eds. 1985. *La Calabria.* Torino: Einaudi.

Bianchi, G. 1971. "I cattolici." In Leo Valiani, ed. *Azionisti cattolici e comunisti nella Resistenza.* Milano: Angeli, 151–300.

Blackmer, Donald L. M., and Sidney Tarrow, eds. 1975. *Communism in Italy and France.* Princeton: Princeton University Press.

Bobbio, Norberto. 1995. *Ideological Profile of Twentieth Century Italy.* Trans. Lydia G. Cochrane. Cambridge: Harvard University Press.

Bocca, Giorgio. 1973. *Palmiro Togliatti.* Bari: Laterza.

Bogdanor, Vernon. 1990. "Founding Elections and Regime Change." *Electoral Studies* 9 (4): 288–94.

Borzomati, Pietro. 1977. "La Democrazia Cristiana e la società meridionale nell'età degasperiana." In Pietro Borzomati, ed. *La Calabria nell'Età contemporanea (ed altri studi).* Reggio Calabria: Meridionali Riuniti, 107–32.

Bosworth, William. 1962. *Catholicism and Crisis in Modern France.* Princeton: Princeton University Press.

Boulard, Ferdnand. 1946. "Réflexions sur le péril Marxiste." *Cahiers du clergé rural* 82 (Nov.): 36–38.

Boutry, Philippe, and Alain-René Michel. 1992. "La Religion." In Jean-François Sirinelli, ed. *Histoire des droites en France.* Vol. 3. Paris: Gallimard, 647–95.

Bragaglio, G. 1981. "Riflessioni sul blocco politico-sociale a Brescia." In Roberto Chiarini, ed. *Brescia negli anni della Ricostruzione 1945–1949.* Brescia: Micheletti, 149–84.

Breunig, Charles. 1957. "The Condemnation of the Sillon: An Episode in the History of Christian Democracy in France." *Church History* 26 (Sept): 227–44.

Brown, Marvin L., Jr. 1974. "Catholic-Legitimist Militancy in the Early Years of the Third French Republic." *Catholic Historical Review* 60 (July): 233–54.

Buchanan, Tom, and Martin Conway, eds. 1996. *Political Catholicism in Europe, 1918–1965.* Oxford: Oxford University Press.

Burgalassi, Silvio. 1968. *Il Comportamento Religioso degli Italiani.* Firenze: Vallecchi.

Caciagli, Mario. 1977. *Democrazia Cristiana e Potere nel Mezzogiorno: Il sistema democristiano a Catania.* Rimini-Firenze: Guaraldi.

Callot, Émile-François (1978). *Le Mouvement Républicain Populaire: origine, structure, doctrine, programme et action poitique.* Paris: Marcel Rivière et Compagnie.

Campbell, Peter. 1965. *French Electoral Systems and Elections since 1789.* Hamden, Conn.: Archon Books.

Carroll, Michael P. 1996. *Veiled Threats: The Logic of Popular Catholicism in Italy.* Baltimore: Johns Hopkins University Press.

Cary, Noel D. 1996. *The Path to Christian Democracy: German Catholics and the Party System from Windthorst to Adenauer.* Cambridge: Harvard University Press.

Casadio, Stefano. 1982. "Clero e industria a Torino negli anni cinquanta." *Italia contemporanea* 148 (Sept.): 27–40.

Casanova, José. 1994. *Public Religions in the Modern World.* Chicago: University of Chicago Press.

Casella, Mario. 1984a. *L'Azione Cattolica alla Caduta del Fascismo: Attività e progetti per il dopoguerra (1942–'45).* Rome: Edizioni Studium.

———. 1984b. "Per una storia dei rapporti tra azione cattolica e democrazia cristiana nell'età del centrismo (1947–1954)." In G. Rossini, ed. *De Gasperi e l'Età del Centrismo.* Roma: Cinque Lune, 271–93.

———. 1987. *Cattolici e Costituente: Orientamenti e iniziative del cattolicesimo organizzato (1945–1947).* Perugia: Edizioni Scientifiche Italiane.

———. 1990. "Aspetti Quantitativi e Diffusione Territoriale del Cattolicesimo Organizzato nell'Italia del Secondo Dopoguerra (1947–1949)." Special edition of *Itinerari di Ricerca Storica.* Vol. 3. Lecce: Congedo.

———. 1992. *18 Aprile 1948: La mobilitazione delle organizzazioni cattoliche.* Lecce: Congedo.

Castronovo, Valerio, ed. 1976. *L'Italia contemporanea 1945–1975.* Torino: Einaudi.

Cavallaro, Vincenzo. 1958. *Corvi in Poltrona: Documentazione sul costume politico.* Roma: A.R.N.I.A.

Cervigni, Giovanni. 1955. "Le defezioni dal [*sic*] Partito Comunista in Calabria." *Nord e Sud* 2 (6): 65–95.

Chaigneau, V.-L. 1955. *L'Organisation de l'Église catholique en France.* Paris: Éditions SPES.

Charlot, Jean. 1957. "La Presse, les Catholiques, et les Elections." In Maurice Duverger, François Goguel, and Jean Touchard, eds. *Les Élections du 2 janvier 1956*. Paris: Armand Colin, 131–41.

———. 1983. *Le Gaullisme d'opposition, 1946–1958*. Paris: Fayard.

Chassériaud, Jean-Paul. 1965. *Le Parti Démocrate Chrétien en Italie*. Paris: Librairie Armand Colin.

Chaves, Mark, and David E. Cann. 1992. "Regulation, Pluralism, and Religious Market Structure." *Rationality and Society* 4 (3): 272–90.

Chélini, Jean. 1983. *L'Église sous Pius XII: La Tourmente, 1939–1945*. Paris: Fayard.

———. 1989. *L'Église sous Pius XII: L'Après-Guerre, 1945–1958*. Paris: Fayard.

Chisholm, Darlene C. 1993. "Asset Specificity and Long-Term Contracts." *Eastern Economic Journal* 19 (2): 143–55.

Chittolini, Giorgio, and Giovanni Miccoli, eds. 1986. *Storia d'Italia*. Vol. 9. *La Chiesa e il potere politico dal Medioevo all'età contemporanea*. Torino: Einaudi.

Ciranna, Giuseppe. 1958. "Un 'gruppo di pressione': La Confederazione Nazionale Coltivatori Diretti." *Nord e Sud* 5 (38): 9–39.

Clark, Martin. 1984. *Modern Italy, 1871–1982*. New York: Longman.

———. 1996. *Modern Italy, 1871–1995*. London: Longman.

Cleary, Mark Christopher. 1989. *Peasants, Politicians, and Producers*. Cambridge: Cambridge University Press.

Clemens, Elisabeth S. 1997. *The People's Lobby: Organizational Innovation and the Rise of Interest Group Politics in the United States, 1890–1925*. Chicago: University of Chicago Press.

Collier, Ruth Berins, and David Collier. 1979. "Disaggregating Corporatism." *American Political Science Review* 73 (4): 967–86.

Corsini, Paolo, and Gianfranco Porta, eds. 1985. *Aspetti della società bresciana tra le due guerre*. Brescia: Micheletti.

Danè, Carlo, ed. 1959. *I Congressi nazionale della Democrazia cristiana*. Roma: DcSPES–Cinque Lune.

Dansette, Adrien. 1957. *Destin du Catholicisme français: L'Église catholique dans la mêlée politique et sociale*. Paris: Flammarion.

———. 1965. *Histoire Religieuse de la France Contemporaine*. Paris: Flammarion.

Darbon, Michel. 1953. *Le Conflit entre la droite et la gauche dans le catholicisme français, 1830–1953*. Paris: Privat.

De Gasperi, Alcide [Demofilo]. 1944. "Tradizione e 'ideologia' della Democrazia Cristiana." Reprint, ed. Società Editrice Libraria Italiana. Roma: Società Grafico Ro., 9–33.

———. 1946. *Studi ed appelli della lunga vigilia*. Roma: Magi-Spinetti.

———. 1974. Maria Romana De Gasperi, ed. *De Gasperi Scrive*. 2 vols. Brescia: Morcelliana.

De Gasperi, Maria Romana Catti. 1964. *De Gasperi, uomo solo*. Milan: Mondadori.

De Gaulle, Charles. 1970. *Discours et messages*. Vol. 2. Paris: Plon.

Delbreil, Jean-Claude. 1990. *Centrisme et Démocratie-Chrétienne en France: Le Parti Démocrate Populaire des origines au M.R.P. 1919–1944*. Paris: Publications de la Sorbonne.

Della Cava, Ralph. 1993. "Financing the Faith: The Case of Roman Catholicism." *Journal of Church and State* 35 (1): 37–59.

Delzell, Charles F. 1961. *Mussolini's Enemies*. Princeton: Princeton University Press.

Deroo, André. 1955. *L'Épiscopat Français dans la mêlée de son temps, 1930–1954.* Lille: Bonne Presse.

D'Haene, Père Michel. 1954. *La J.A.C. à vingt-cinq ans.* Paris: Collection Semailles.

Di Marino, Gaetano. [1965?]. *La Confederazione di Bonomi nella vita politica Italiana.* Roma: Editrice Cooperative.

Di Nolfo, Ernesto. 1978. *Vaticano e Stati Uniti 1939–1952: Dalle carte di Myron Taylor.* Milano: Angeli.

Dogan, Mattei, and Peter Campbell. 1957. "Le Personnel Ministériel en France et en Grande-Bretagne (1945–1957)." *Revue Française de Science Politique* 7 (2): 313–45.

Domenach, Jean-Marie. 1947. *Celui Qui Croyait au Ciel.* N.p.: ELF.

Downs, Anthony. 1957. *An Economic Theory of Democracy.* New York: Harper.

Dupeux, Georges. 1957. "Les Plates-Forme des Partis." In Maurice Duverger, François Goguel, and Jean Touchard, eds. *Les Élections du 2 janvier 1956.* Paris: Armand Colin, 31–67.

Duquesne, Jacques. 1966. *Les Catholiques Français sous l'Occupation.* Paris: Bernard Grasset.

Durand, Jean-Dominique. 1991. *L'Église Catholique dans la Crise de l'Italie (1943–1948).* Roma: L'École Française de Roma.

———. 1995. *L'Europe de la démocratie chrétienne.* Brussels: Éditions Complexe.

Durkheim, Emile. 1995. *The Elementary Forms of Religious Life.* Trans. Karen E. Fields. New York: Free Press.

Durupt, Marie-Josephe. 1963. *Les Mouvements d'Action Catholique Rurale, facteur d'évolution du milieu rural.* 2 vols. Thèse du Troisième cycle, Fondation Nationale des Sciences Politiques de Paris.

Duverger, Maurice. 1954. *Political Parties: Their Organization and Activity in the Modern State.* Trans. Barbara North and Robert North. London: Methuen.

Duverger, Maurice, François Goguel, and Jean Touchard, eds. 1957. *Les Élections du 2 janvier 1956.* Paris: Armand Colin.

Edinger, Lewis J. 1993. "Pressure Group Politics in West Germany." In Jeremy Richardson, ed. *Pressure Groups.* New York: Oxford University Press, 175–90.

Ehrmann, Henry. 1957. *Organized Business in France.* Princeton: Princeton University Press.

Einaudi, Mario, and François Goguel. 1952. *Christian Democracy in Italy and France.* South Bend, Ind.: University of Notre Dame Press.

Ekelund, Robert B., Jr., Robert F. Hébert, and Robert D. Tollison. 1989. "An Economic Model of the Medieval Church: Usury as a Form of Rent Seeking." *Journal of Law, Economics, and Organization* 5 (2): 305–31.

———. 1996. *Sacred Trust.* Oxford: Oxford University Press.

Eldersveld, Samuel. 1964. *Political Parties: A Behavioral Analysis.* Chicago: Rand-McNally.

Elgie, Robert. 1994. "Christian Democracy in France: The Politics of Electoral Constraint." In David Hanley, ed. *Christian Democracy in Europe*. London: Pinter, 155–67.

Eliade, Mircea, ed. 1987. *Encyclopedia of Religion*. Vol. 12. New York: Macmillan.

Epagneul, Frère Michel-Dominique. 1976. *Semailles en terre de France, 1943–1949*. Paris: Editions S.O.S.

Ertman, Thomas. 1997. *Birth of the Leviathan: Building States and Regimes in Medieval and Early Modern Europe*. Cambridge: Cambridge University Press.

Evans, Ellen Lovell. 1981. *The German Center Party, 1870–1933: A Study in Political Catholicism*. Carbondale: Southern Illinois University Press.

Evans, Peter B., Dietrich Rueschemeyer, and Theda Skocpol, eds. 1985. *Bringing the State Back In*. Cambridge: Cambridge University Press.

Falconi, Carlo. 1955. "Primo tentativo di una statistica dell'organizzazione cattolica." *Nuovi Argomenti* no. 12: 80–110.

———. 1956. *La Chiesa e le organizzazioni cattoliche in Italia (1945–1955)*. Torino: Einaudi.

———. 1960. *La Chiesa e le organizzazioni cattoliche in Europa*. Milan: Edizioni di Comunità.

———. 1967. *The Popes in the Twentieth Century: From Pius X to John XXIII*. Trans. Muriel Grindrod. Boston: Little, Brown.

———. 1970. *The Silence of Pius XII*. Trans. Bernard Wall. Boston: Little, Brown.

Fappani, Antonio. 1974. *Cattolici nella resistenza Bresciana: Andrea Trebeschi-astolfo Lunardi-Emiliano Rinaldini*. Roma: Cinque Lune.

Faure, Marcel. 1958. "Action Catholique en milieu rural." In Jacques Fauvet and Henri Mendras, eds. *Les Paysans et la politique dans la France contemporaine*. Paris: Fondation Nationale des Sciences Politiques, 345–60.

Fehrenbach, Heide. 1997. "The Fight for the 'Christian West': German Film Control, the Churches, and the Reconstruction of Civil Society in the Early Bonn Republic." In Robert G. Moeller, ed. *West Germany under Construction: Politics, Society, and Culture in the Adenauer Era*. Ann Arbor: University of Michigan Press, 321–45.

Ferguson, Thomas. 1995. *Golden Rule: The Investment Theory of Party Competition and the Logic of Money-Driven Political Systems*. Chicago: University of Chicago Press.

Fiorina, Morris P. 1981. *Retrospective Voting in American National Elections*. New Haven: Yale University Press.

Fogarty, Michael P. 1957. *Christian Democracy in Western Europe, 1820–1953*. London: Routledge and Kegan Paul.

Ford, Caroline. 1993. *Creating the Nation in Provincial France: Religion and Political Identity in Brittany*. Princeton: Princeton University Press.

Forster, Karl. 1981. "Der deutsche Katholizismus in der Bundesrepublik Deutschland." In Anton Rauscher, ed. *Der Soziale und Politische Katholizismus*. München: Guenter-Olzog Verlag, 209–64.

Fouilloux, Étienne. 1992. "Le clergé." In Jean-Pierre Azéma et François Bédarida, eds. *Le Régime de Vichy et les Français*. Paris: Fayard, 463–77.

Franzinelli, Gerolamo. 1981. "Valcamonica 1945–1947: I Communisti e il clero." In Roberto Chiarini, ed. *Brescia negli anni della Ricostruzione 1945–1949.* Brescia: Micheletti, 231–42.

Frieden, Jeffry A. 1994. "International Investment and colonial control: A New Interpretation." *International Organization* 48 (4): 559–93.

Gaeta, Maria Ida, and Patrizia Luzzatto. 1981. "L'organizzazione della Democrazia Cristiana." In Carlo Vallauri, ed. *L'arcipelago democratico: Organizzazione e struttura dei partiti negli anni del centrismo (1949–1958).* Vol. 1. Roma: Bulzoni, 37–250.

Galati, Vito Giuseppe. 1968. "Quello che ho visto e quello che spero in Calabria." *Parellelo 38* Oct.–Dec.: 518.

Galli, Giorgio. 1978. *Storia dell Democrazia Cristiana.* Bari: Laterza.

Galli, Giorgio, and Alfonso Prandi. 1970. *Patterns of Political Participation in Italy.* New Haven: Yale University Press.

Gallup, George H. 1976. *Gallup International Public Opinion Polls, France 1939, 1944–1967.* Vol. 1. New York: Random House.

Gambetta, Diego. 1994. *La mafia siciliana: Un'industria della protezione privata.* 2d ed. Torino: Einaudi.

Gariglio, Bartolo. 1986. "Chiesa e società industriale: Il caso di Torino." In Andrea Riccardi, ed. *Le Chiese di Pio XII.* Bari: Laterza, 161–90.

Gatz, Erwin. 1981. "Caritas und Soziale Dienste." In Anton Rauscher, ed. *Der Soziale und Politische Katholizismus.* Vol. 2. München: Olzog Verlag, 312–51.

Gay, Françisque. 1951. *Les Démocrates d'Inspiration Chrétienne a l'épreuve du pouvoir.* Paris: Bloud et Gay.

Geertz, Clifford. 1973. "Religion as a Cultural System." In *The Interpretation of Cultures.* New York: Basis Books, 87–125.

George, Alexander L., and Timothy McKeown. 1985. "Case Studies and Theories of Organizational Decision Making." *Advances in Information Processing in Organizations* 2: 21–58.

Gheza, Franco. 1981. "Movimento Cattolico e Dinamica Sociale a Brescia (1945–1950)." In Roberto Chiarini, ed. *Brescia negli anni della Ricostruzione 1945–1949.* Brescia: Micheletti, 93–145.

Ghini, Celso. 1968. *Le Elezioni in Italia (1946–1968).* Milano: Edizioni del Calendario.

Gill, Anthony. 1998. *Rendering unto Caesar: The Catholic Church and the State in Latin America.* Chicago: University of Chicago Press.

———. 1999. "The Economics of Evangelization." In Paul E. Sigmund, ed. *Evangelization and Religious Freedom in Latin America.* Maryknoll, N.Y.: Orbis Books, pp. 70–84.

Ginsborg, Paul. 1990. *A History of Contemporary Italy: Society and Politics, 1943–1988.* London: Penguin.

Giusti, Ugo. 1922. *Le Correnti Politiche Italiane attraverso due riforme elettorali dal 1909 al 1921.* Firenze: Alfani e Venturi.

Goldthorpe, John H., ed. 1984. *Order and Conflict in Contemporary Capitalism.* Oxford: Clarendon Press.

Gotto, Klaus. 1983. "Zum Selbstverständnis der katholische Kirche im Jahr 1945." In Dieter Albrecht, et al. *Politik und Konfession*. Berlin: Duncker und Humblot, 465–81.

Gough, Austin. 1986. *Paris and Roma: The Gallican Church and the Ultramontane Campaign, 1848–1953*. Oxford: Oxford University Press.

Gourevitch, Peter, et al. 1984. *Unions and Economic Crisis: Britain, West Germany, and Sweden*. London: Allen and Unwin.

Gramsci, Antonio. 1971. *Il Materialismo Storico e la Filosofia di Benedetto Croce*. Roma: Editori Riuniti.

Greenberg, Joseph, and Kenneth A. Shepsle. 1987. "The Effect of Electoral Rewards in Multiparty Competition with Entry." *American Political Science Review* 81 (2): 525–37.

Grofman, Bernard, and Arend Lijphart, eds. 1986. *Electoral Laws and Their Political Consequences*. New York: Agathon Press.

Guasco, Maurilio. 1997. *Storia del Clero in Italia dall'Ottocento a Oggi*. Bari: Laterza.

Guide-Annuaire Catholique de France, 1948–1949. 1952. Paris: Les Presses Continentales.

Guide-Annuaire Catholique de France, 1954–1955. 1955. Paris: Les Presses Continentales.

Gurland, A. R. L. 1980. Ed. Dieter Emig. *Die CDU/CSU: Ursprünge und Entwicklung bis 1953*. Frankfurt am Main: Europäische Verlagsanstalt.

Hales, E. E. Y. 1966. *Revolution and Papacy, 1769–1846*. Notre Dame, Ind.: Notre Dame University Press.

Hall, Peter. 1993. "Pluralism and Pressure Politics in France." In Jeremy J. Richardson, ed. *Pressure Groups*. New York: Oxford University Press, 159–74.

Halls, W. D. 1995. *Politics, Society, and Christianity in Vichy France*. Oxford: Berg.

Hanley, David, ed. 1994. *Christian Democracy in Europe: A Comparative Perspective*. London: Pinter.

Hanson, Eric O. 1987. *The Catholic Church in World Politics*. Princeton: Princeton University Press.

Hardin, Russell. 1982. *Collective Action*. Baltimore: Johns Hopkins University Press.

Harper, John Lamberton. 1986. *America and the Reconstruction of Italy, 1945–1948*. Cambridge: Cambridge University Press.

Harrigan, William M. 1963. "Pius XII's Efforts to Effect a *Détente* in German-Vatican Relations, 1939–1940." *Catholic Historical Review* 49 (2): 173–91.

Hatch, Edwin. 1972. *The Organization of the Early Christian Churches*. New York: Burt Franklin.

Hattam, Victoria C. 1992. "Institutions and Political Change: Working-Class Formation in England and the United States, 1920–1896." In Sven Steinmo, Kathleen Thelen, and Frank Longstreth, eds. *Structuring Politics*. Cambridge: Cambridge University Press, 155–87.

Hazareesingh, Sudhir. 1994. *Political Traditions in Modern France*. New York: Oxford University Press.

Header, Harry. 1983. *Italy in the Age of the Risorgimento, 1790–1870*. New York: Longman.

Heidenheimer, Arnold. 1960. *Adenauer and the CDU: The Rise of the Leader and the Integration of the Party.* The Hague: Martinus Nijhoff.

Helmreich, Ernst Christian. 1979. *The German Churches under Hitler: Background, Struggle, and Epilogue.* Detroit: Wayne State University Press.

Hinich, Melvin J., and Michael C. Munger. 1994. *Ideology and the Theory of Political Choice.* Ann Arbor: University of Michigan Press.

Hirschman, Albert O. 1970. *Exit, Voice, and Loyalty: Responses to Decline in Firms, Organizations, and States.* Cambridge: Harvard University Press.

Hochhuth, Rolf. 1963. *Der Stellvertreter.* Hamburg: Rowohlt Verlag.

Holmes, Derek. 1976. "Pope Pius XII: Impressions of a Pontificate." *Clergy Review* 61: 430–40.

Horowitz, Daniel. 1963. *The Italian Labor Movement.* Cambridge: Harvard University Press.

Howell, Chris. 1997. "Constructing Industrial Relations Institutions." Paper presented to the 93d annual meeting of the American Political Science Association, Washington, D.C., August 28–31.

Huber, Evelyn, Charles Ragin, and John D. Stephens. 1993. "Social Democracy, Christian Democracy, Constitutional Structure, and the Welfare State." *American Journal of Sociology* 99: 711–49.

Hughes, H. Stuart. 1965. *The United States and Italy.* 2d ed. Cambridge: Harvard University Press.

Hürten, Heinz. 1986. *Kurze Geschichte des Deutschen Katholizismus 1800–1960.* Mainz: Matthias-Grünewald-Verlag.

Iannaccone, Laurence R. 1991. "The Consequences of Religious Market Structure: Adam Smith and the Economics of Religion." *Rationality and Society* 3: 156–77.

———. 1992. "Sacrifice and Stigma: Reducing Free-Riding in Cults, Communes, and Other Collectives." *Journal of Political Economy* 100: 271–92.

———. 1994. "Why Strict Churches Are Strong." *American Journal of Sociology* 99: 1180–1211.

———. 1995. "Household Production, Human Capital, and the Economics of Religion." In Mariano Tommasi and Kathryn Ierulli, eds. *The New Economics of Human Behavior.* Cambridge: Cambridge University Press, 172–87.

Ikenberry, John G. 1988. "Conclusion: An Institutional Approach to American Foreign Policy." In John G. Ikenberry, David A. Lake, and Michael Mastaduno, eds. *The State and American Foreign Policy.* Ithaca: Cornell University Press, 219–43.

Irving, R. E. M. 1973. *Christian Democracy in France.* London: Allen and Unwin.

———. 1979. *The Christian Democratic Parties of Western Europe.* London: Allen and Unwin.

Isambert, François-André, and Jean-Paul Terrenoire. 1980. *Atlas de la pratique cultuelle des catholiques in France.* Paris: Fondation Nationale des Sciences Politiques.

Jemolo, A. C. 1960. *Church and State in Italy, 1850–1950.* Trans. David Moore. Oxford: Blackwell.

Jones, Paul M. 1985. *Politics and Rural Society: The Southern Massif Central, c. 1750–1880.* Cambridge: Cambridge University Press.

Kaack, Heino. 1971. *Geschichte und Struktur des Deutschen Parteiensystems.* Opladen: Westdeutscher Verlag.

Kalyvas, Stathis S. 1996. *The Rise of Christian Democracy in Europe.* Ithaca: Cornell University Press.

Katz, Richard S., and Peter Mair. 1995. "Changing Models of Party Organization and Party Democracy: The Emergence of the Cartel Party." *Party Politics* 1 (1): 5–28.

Keeler, John T. S. 1987. *The Politics of Neo-Corporatism in France.* New York: Oxford University Press.

Kertzer, David I. 1980. *Comrades and Christians: Religion and Political Struggles in Communist Italy.* Cambridge: Cambridge University Press.

Keshavarzian, Arang, and Anthony Gill. 1997. "State-Building and Religious Resources: An Institutional Theory of Church-State Relations in Latin America and the Middle East." Paper presented to the 93d annual meeting of the American Political Science Association, Washington, D.C.

Kitschelt, Herbert. 1989. *The Logics of Party Formation: Ecological Politics in Belgium and West Germany.* Ithaca: Cornell University Press.

———. 1994. *The Transformation of European Social Democracy.* Cambridge: Cambridge University Press.

Klein, B., R. G. Crawford, and A. A. Alchian. 1978. "Vertical Integration, Appropriable Rents, and the Competitive Contracting Process." *Journal of Law and Economics* 21 (2): 297–326.

Koelble, Thomas A. 1992a. "Recasting Social Democracy in Europe: A Nested Games Explanation of Strategic Adjustment in Political Parties." *Politics and Society* 20 (1): 51–70.

———. 1992b. "Social Democracy between Structure and Choice." *Comparative Politics* 24 (3): 359–72.

Kraiker, Gerhard. 1972. *Politischer Katholizismus in der BRD: Eine ideologiekritische Analyse.* Stuttgart: W. Kohlhammer Verlag.

Krueger, Anne O. 1972. "The Political Economy of the Rent-Seeking Society." *American Economic Review* 64 (2): 291–303.

Lacouture, Jean. 1985. *De Gaulle.* Vol. 2: *La Politique 1944–1959.* Paris: Seuil.

Lambert, Yves. 1985. *Dieu Change in Bretagne: La religion à Limerzel de 1900 à nos jours.* Paris: Éditions du Cerf.

LaPalombara, Joseph. 1964. *Interest Groups in Italian Politics.* Princeton: Princeton University Press.

Larkin, Maurice J. M. 1964. "The Vatican, French Catholics, and the *Associations Cultuelles.*" *Journal of Modern History* 36 (Sept): 298–317.

———. 1974. *Church and State after the Dreyfus Affair: The Separation Issue in France.* London: Macmillan.

Latreille, André. 1978. *De Gaulle, La Liberation et l'Église catholique.* Paris: Editions du Cerf.

Lawson, Kay, ed. 1980. *Political Parties and Linkage.* New Haven: Yale University Press.

Le Bras, Gabriel. 1945. "La vitalité religieuse de l'Église de France." *Revue d'Histoire de l'Église de France* 31: 277–306.

———. 1955. *Études de Sociologie Religieuse.* Vol. 1: *Sociologie de la pratique religieuse dans les campagnes françaises.* Paris: Presses Universitaires de France.

Lebrun, François, ed. 1980. *Histoire des catholiques en France.* Paris: Privat.

Lecourt, Robert. 1978. *Entre l'Église et l'État: Concordat sans concordat.* Paris: Hachette.

Lee, Mushin, and Howard Rosenthal. 1976. "A Behavioral Model of Coalition Formation: The French Apparentements of 1951." *Journal of Conflict Resolution* 20 (4): 563–88.

Lengereau, Marc. 1961. *La Vallée d'Aoste: Minorité linguistique et Région autonome de la République italienne.* Grenoble: Société des Écrivains Dauphinois.

Letamendia, Pierre. 1975. "Le. M.R.P." Thèse du doctorat, Université de Bordeaux I.

Levi, Margaret. 1988. *Of Rule and Revenue.* Berkeley and Los Angeles: University of California Press.

———. 1997. "A Model, a Method, and a Map: Rational Choice in Comparative and Historical Analysis." In Mark Irving Lichbach and Alan S. Zuckerman, eds. *Comparative Politics: Rationality, Culture, and Structure.* Cambridge: Cambridge University Press, 19–41.

Libecap, Gary D. 1997. "The New Institutional Economics and Economic History." *Journal of Economic History* 57 (3): 718–21.

Lipset, Seymour Martin, and Stein Rokkan. 1967. "Cleavage Structures, Party Systems, and Voter Alignments: An Introduction." In Seymour Martin Lipset and Stein Rokkan, eds. *Party Systems and Voter Alignments: Cross-National Perspectives.* New York: Free Press, 1–64.

Locke, Richard M., and Kathleen Thelen. 1995. "Apples and Oranges Revisited: Contextualized Comparisons and the Study of Comparative Labor Politics." *Politics and Society* 23: 337–67.

Lönne, Karl-Egon. 1996. "Germany." In Tom Buchanan and Martin Conway, eds. *Political Catholicism in Europe, 1918–1965.* Oxford: Clarendon Press, 156–86.

Ludlum, Robert. 1985. *The Road to Gandolfo.* New York: Bantam Books.

Lynch, Edward A. 1993. *Latin America's Christian Democratic Parties: A Political Economy.* Westport, Conn.: Praeger.

Lyttelton, Adrian. 1973. *The Seizure of Power: Fascism in Italy, 1919–1929.* New York: Scribner.

Mack Smith, Denis. 1969. *Italy: A Modern History.* Ann Arbor: University of Michigan Press.

Mady, Jean. 1955. *Sociologie Électorale de l'arrondissement de Fontenay-le-Comte.* Thèse, Paris: Université de Paris, Institut d'Études Politiques.

Magister, Sandro. 1979. *La politica vaticana e l'Italia 1943–1978.* Roma: Riuniti.

Magri, Francesco. 1954. *La Democrazia cristiana in Italia.* 2 vols. Milano: Editrice La Fiaccola.

Maier, Charles S., ed. 1987. *In Search of Stability: Explorations in Historical Political Economy.* New York: Cambridge University Press.

Maier, Hans. 1983. "Zur Soziologie des deutschen Katholizismus 1803–1950." In Dieter Albrecht et al. *Politik und Konfession.* Berlin: Duncker und Humblot, 159–72.

Mainwaring, Scott. 1986. *The Catholic Church and Politics in Brazil, 1916–1985.* Stanford: Stanford University Press.

Malgeri, Francesco. 1977. "Il Popolarismo in Calabria." In *Aspetti e problemi di storia della società Calabrese nell'età contemporanea: Atti del I convegno di studie Reggio Calabria 1–4 novembre 1975.* Ed. Deputazione di Storia patria per la Calabria. Reggio Calabria: Meridionali Riuniti, 309–20.

———. 1985. "La Chiesa di Pio XII fra guerra e dopoguerra." In Andrea Riccardi, ed. *Pio XII.* Bari: Laterza, 93–121.

———, ed. 1987. *Storia della Democrazia Cristiana.* Vol. 2: *De Gasperi e l'età del centrismo, 1948–1954.* Roma: Cinque Lune.

Manoukian, Agopik, ed. 1968. *La Presenza Sociale del PCI e della DC.* Bologna: Il Mulino.

Martin, Victor. 1978. *Les origines du Gallicanisme.* Genève: Mégariotis Reprints.

Martini, Angelo, ed. 1966. *Lettres de Pie XII aux évêques allemands.* Vatican City: Libreria Editrice Vaticana.

Mayeur, Jean Marie. 1986. *Catholicisme social et démocratie chrétienne: Principes romains, experiences françaises.* Paris: Éditions du Cerf.

Mayeur, Jean-Marie, and Madeleine Rebérioux. 1987. *The Third Republic from Its Origins to the Great War, 1871–1914.* Trans. J. R. Foster. Cambridge: Cambridge University Press.

Mayhew, David. 1974. *Congress: The Electoral Connection.* New Haven: Yale University Press.

McBrien, Richard P. 1994. *Catholicism.* San Francisco: Harper.

———. 1995. *Inside Catholicism: Rituals and Symbols Revealed.* San Francisco: Collins.

McChesney, Fred S. 1991. "Rent Extraction and Interest-Group Organization in a Coasean Model of Regulation." *Journal of Legal Studies* 20 (Jan): 73–90.

McMillan, James F. 1996. "France." In Tom Buchanan and Martin Conway, eds. *Political Catholicism in Europe, 1918–1965.* Oxford: Oxford University Press, 34–68.

Meadwell, Hudson. 1991. "The Catholic Church and the Breton Language in the Third Republic." *French History* 5 (3): 325–44.

Mendras, Henri. 1953. *Études de sociologie rurale: Novis & Virgin.* Paris: Armand Colin.

Merritt, Richard L. 1995. *Democracy Imposed: U.S. Occupation Policy and the German Public, 1945–1949.* New Haven: Yale University Press.

Mershon, Carol A. 1996. "The Costs of Coalition: Coalition Theories and Italian Governments." *American Political Science Review* 90: 534–54.

Meynaud, Jean. 1958. *Les Groupes de pression en France.* Paris: Armand Colin.

Meyriat, Jean, ed. 1960. *La Calabre: Une région sous-développée de l'Europe méditerranéenne.* Paris: Armand Colin.

Miccoli, Giovanni. 1973. "La chiesa e il fascismo." In Guido Quazza, ed. *Fascismo e società italiana.* Torino: Einaudi, 183–208.

———. 1976. "Chiesa, Partito Cattolico e Società Civile (1945–1975)." In Valerio Castronovo, ed. *L'Italia contemporanea, 1945–1975.* Torino: Einaudi, 191–252.

Misra, Joya, and Alexander Hicks. 1994. "Catholicism and Unionization in Afflu-
ent Postwar Democracies: Catholicism, Culture, Party, and Unionization."
American Sociological Review 59: 304–26.

Mitchell, Maria. 1995. "Materialism and Secularism: CDU Politicians and National Socialism, 1945–1949." *Journal of Modern History* 67 (June): 278–308.

———. 1999. "Protestants, Priests, and Catholic Politics: The Early Contours of
Christian Democracy." Franklin and Marshall College. Typescript.

Mitchell, William C. 1990. "Interest Groups: Economic Perspectives and Contributions." *Journal of Theoretical Politics* 2 (1): 85–108.

Mitchell, William C., and Michael C. Munger. 1991. "Economic Models of Interest Groups: An Introductory Survey." *American Journal of Political Science* 35
(2): 512–46.

———. 1993. "Doing Well While Intending Good: Cases in Political Exploitation." *Journal of Theoretical Politics* 5 (3): 317–48.

Moe, Terry. 1980. *The Organization of Interests: Incentives and the Internal Dynamics of Political Interest Groups*. Chicago: University of Chicago Press.

Mohr, Lawrence B. 1982. *Explaining Organizational Behavior*. San Francisco: Jos-
sey-Bass.

Mojzes, Paul. 1996. "Ecumenism, Evangelism, and Religious Liberty." *Religion
in Eastern Europe* 16 (2): 1–7.

Morelli, Dario. 1985. "Il clero Bresciano nella Resistenza." In *Antifascismo Resistenza e Clero Bresciano*. Centro di Documentazione. Brescia: CEDDC, 57–78.

Moro, Renato. 1979. *La formazione della classe dirigente cattolica (1929–1937)*.
Bologna: Il Mulino.

Morsey, Rudolf. 1983. "Adenauer und Kardinal Frings 1945–1949." In Dieter
Albrecht et al. *Politik und Konfession*. Berlin: Duncker und Humblot, 483–501.

Mouvement Républicain Populaire. [1946?]. *Pourquoi et Comment créer une
Equipe ouvrière: Plan d'organisation et de Travail*. Paris: Imprimerie du Palais-
Royal.

Mulè, Cesare. 1975. *Democrazia Cristiana in Calabria (1943–1949)*. Roma:
Cinque Lune.

Munck, Gerardo L., and Carol Skalnik Leff. 1997. "Modes of Transition and Democratization: South America and Eastern Europe in Comparative Perspective." *Comparative Politics* 29 (3): 342–62.

Nettl, J. P. 1968. "The State as a Conceptual Variable." *World Politics* 20:
559–92.

North, Douglass C. 1981. *Structure and Change in Economic History*. New York:
W. W. Norton.

———. 1990. "A Transaction Cost Theory of Politics." *Journal of Theoretical
Politics* 2 (4): 355–67.

North, Douglass C., and Robert P. Thomas. 1973. *The Rise of the Western World:
A New Economic History*. Cambridge: Cambridge University Press.

Novick, Peter. 1968. *The Resistance versus Vichy: The Purge of Collaborators in Liberated France*. New York: Columbia University Press.

Oberreuter, Heinrich, and Alf Mintzel, eds. 1992. *Parteien in der Bundesrepublik
Deutschland*. München: Opladen.

O'Donnell, Guillermo, and Philippe C. Schmitter. 1986. *Tentative Conclusions about Uncertain Democracies.* Baltimore: Johns Hopkins University Press.

Olson, Mancur. 1965. *The Logic of Collective Action: Public Goods and the Theory of Groups.* Cambridge: Harvard University Press.

Ouchi, William G., and Alan L. Wilkins. 1985. "Organizational Culture." *Annual Review of Sociology* 11: 457–83.

Pallotta, Gino. 1972. *Il Qualunquismo e l'avventura de Guglielmo Giannini.* Milano: Bompiani.

Panebianco, Angelo. 1982. *Modelli di partito: Organizzazione e potere nei partiti politici.* Bologna: Il Mulino.

Pattnayak, Satya R., ed. 1995. *Organized Religion in the Political Transformation of Latin America.* Lanham, Md.: University Press of America.

Paul, Harry W. 1967. *The Second Ralliement: The Rapprochement between Church and State in France in the Twentieth Century.* Washington, D.C.: Catholic University of American Press.

Payne, Stanley G. 1995. *A History of Fascism, 1914–1945.* Madison: University of Wisconsin Press.

Pelztman, Sam. 1976. "Toward a More General Theory of Regulation." *Journal of Law and Economics* 19 (3): 211–40.

Petracca, Mark, ed. 1992. *The Politics of Interests: Interest Groups Transformed.* Boulder, Colo.: Westview.

Phillips, Charles Stanley. 1966. *The Church in France, 1789–1848: A Study in Revival.* New York: Russell and Russell.

———. 1967. *The Church in France, 1848–1907.* New York: Russell and Russell.

Pierrard, Pierre. 1986. *Histoire des Curés de Campagne de 1789 à nos jours.* Paris: Plon.

———. 1991. *L'Église et les ouvriers en France (1940–1990).* Paris: Hachette.

Pierson, Paul. 1996. "The Path to European Integration: A Historical Institutionalist Analysis." *Comparative Political Studies* 29 (2): 123–63.

———. 1997. "Path Dependence, Increasing Returns, and the Study of Politics." Paper presented to the seminar "The State and Capitalism since 1800," Harvard University, November.

Pius IX. 1864. "The Encyclical Letter of Pope Pius IX and the Syllabus of Modern Errors." Widener Library, Harvard University photocopy (C 71.188.9).

Pius XII. 1954. *Acta Apostolicae Sedis.* 46. Vatican City: Typis Polyglottis Vaticanis.

Poggi, Gianfranco. 1967. *Catholic Action in Italy.* Stanford: Stanford University Press.

Pollard, John E. 1985. *The Vatican and Italian Fascism, 1929–1932.* Cambridge: Cambridge University Press.

———. 1996. "Italy." In Tom Buchanan and Martin Conway, eds. *Political Catholicism in Europe, 1918–1965.* Oxford: Oxford University Press, 69–96.

Pombeni, Paolo. 1979. *Il gruppo dossettiano e la fondazione della democrazia italiana (1938–1948).* Bologna: Il Mulino.

Posner, Richard A. 1974. "Theories of Economic Regulation." *Bell Journal of Economics and Management Science* 5 (3): 335–58.

Poulat, Emile. 1985. "Chiesa e mondo moderno: il caso dei preti operai." In Andrea Riccardi, ed. *Pio XII*. Bari: Laterza, 295–306.

———. 1986. "Autorità ed obbedienza nell'Eglise de France." In Andrea Riccardi, ed. *Le chiese di Pio XII*. Bari: Laterza, 135–42.

Prandi, Alfonso. 1968. *Chiesa e politica: La gerarchia e l'impegno politico dei cattolici in Italia*. Bologna: Il Mulino.

Pridham, Geoffrey. 1977. *Christian Democracy in Western Germany*. London: Croom-Helm.

———. 1988. *Political Parties and Coalitional Behaviour in Italy*. London: Routledge.

Prieur, Christian. 1956. *Les Élections Législatives du 2 janvier 1956 dans l'Aveyron*. Thèse du Troisième cycle, Institut d'Études Politiques de Paris.

Pütz, Helmut. 1971. *Die Christlich Demokratische Union*. Bonn: Boldt Verlag.

Quazza, Guido, ed. 1973. *Fascismo e societa italiana*. Torino: Einaudi.

Rauch, William R., Jr. 1972. *Politics and Belief in Contemporary France*. The Hague: Martinus Nijhoff.

Ravitch, Norman. 1990. *The Catholic Church and the French Nation, 1589–1989*. London: Routledge.

Reese, Thomas J. 1996. *Inside the Vatican: The Politics and Organization of the Catholic Church*. Cambridge: Harvard University Press.

Riccardi, Andrea. 1983. *Il "partito romano," nel secondo dopoguerra (1945–1954)*. Brescia: Morcelliana.

———. 1985a. "Governo e 'profezia' nel pontificato di Pio XII." In Andrea Riccardi, ed. *Pio XII*. Bari: Laterza, 31–92.

———, ed. 1985b. *Pio XII*. Bari: Laterza.

———, ed. 1986. *Le chiese di Pio XII*. Bari: Laterza.

———. 1988. *Il potere del Papa da Pio XII a Paolo VI*. Roma: Laterza.

Richardson, Jeremy J. 1993a. "Introduction: Pressure Groups and Government." In Jeremy Richardson, ed. *Pressure Groups*. New York: Oxford University Press, 1–22.

———, ed. 1993b. *Pressure Groups*. New York: Oxford University Press.

Rioux, Jean-Pierre. 1987. *The Fourth Republic, 1944–1958*. Trans. Godfrey Rogers. Cambridge: Cambridge University Press.

Rokkan, Stein. 1977. "Towards a Generalized Concept of *Verzuiling:* A Preliminary Note." *Political Studies* 25 (4): 563–70.

Rossi, Ernesto. 1965. *Viaggio nel feudo di Bonomi*. Roma: Riuniti.

Rossi-Doria, Manlio. 1963. *Rapporto sulla Federconsorzi*. Bari: Laterza.

Rousso, Henri. 1991. *The Vichy Syndrome: History and Memory in France since 1944*. Trans. Arthur Goldhammer. Cambridge: Harvard University Press.

Rugafiori, Paride. 1974. *Il triangolo industriale tra ricostruzione e lotta di classe 1945–1948*. Milano: Feltrinelli.

Sa'adah, Anne. 1987. "Le Mouvement Republicain Populaire et la Reconstitution du Système Partisan Français, 1944–1951." *Revue française de Science Politique* 37: 33–58.

Sabel, Charles F. 1981. "The Internal Politics of Trade Unions." In Suzanne Berger, ed. *Organizing Interests in Western Europe*. Cambridge: Cambridge University Press, 209–44.

Sala, T. 1972. "Un'offerta di collaborazione dell'Azione cattolica italiana al governo Badoglio (agosto 1943)." *Rivista di storia contemporanea* 1 (4): 519–33.

Salisbury, Robert H. 1984. "Interest Representation: The Dominance of Institutions." *American Political Science Review* 78: 64–76.

Salvati, Mariuccia. 1982. *Stato e industria nella ricostruzione*. Milano: Feltrinelli.

Sartori, Giovanni. 1967. *Parties and Party Systems*. New York: Harper and Row.

Sbarberi, Franco. 1980. *I comunisti italiani e lo stato, 1929–1956*. Milano: Feltrinelli.

Scarrow, Susan E. 1996. *Parties and Their Members: Organizing for Victory in Britain and Germany*. New York: Oxford University Press.

Schelling, Thomas. 1990. *The Strategy of Conflict*. Cambridge: Harvard University Press.

Schmid, Josef. 1990. *Die CDU*. Opladen: Leske und Budrich.

Schmidt, Ute. 1983. "Die Christlich Demokratische Union Deutschlands." In Richard Stöss, ed. *Parteien-Handbuch: Die Parteien der Bundesrepublik Deutschland 1945–1980*. Vol. 1: *AUD bis EFP*. Opladen: Westdeutscher Verlag, 490–660.

———. 1987. *Zentrum oder CDU: Politscher Katholizismus zwischen Tradition und Anpassung*. Opladen: Westdeutscher Verlag.

Schmitter, Philippe C. 1974. "Still the Century of Corporatism?" *Review of Politics* 36 (1): 85–131.

Schmitter, Philippe C., and Gerhard Lembruch, eds. 1979. *Trends towards Corporatist Intermediation*. London: Sage.

Schwarz, Edward P., and Michael R. Tomz. 1997. "The Long-Run Advantages of Centralization for Collective Action: A Comment on Bendor and Mookherjee." *American Political Science Review* 91 (3): 685–94.

Schwering, Leo. [1952]. *Vorgeschichte und Entstehung der CDU*. Köln: Deutsche Glocke.

Scoppola, Pietro. 1980. *Gli anni della Costituente fra politica e storia*. Bologna: Il Mulino.

———. 1988. *La proposta politica di De Gasperi*. 3d ed. Bologna: Il Mulino.

———. 1991. *La repubblica dei partiti*. Bologna: Il Mulino.

Sedgwick, Alexander. 1965. *The Ralliement in French Politics, 1890–1898*. Cambridge: Harvard University Press.

Settembrini, D. 1964. *La Chiesa nella politica italiana*. Pisa: Nistri-Lischi.

Shefter, Martin. 1977. "Party and Patronage: Germany, England, and Italy." *Politics and Society* 7 (4): 403–51.

Siegfried, André. 1956. *De la IIIe à la IVe République*. Paris: Grasset.

Simoni, Carlo. 1988. *Oltre la Strada: Campione sul Garda: Vita quotidiana e conflitto sociale in un villagio operaio periferico*. Brescia: Graffo.

Smith, Huston. 1991. *The World's Religions*. San Francisco: Harper.

Soave, P., and P. G. Zunino. 1977. "La Chiesa e i cattolici nell'autunno del regime fascista." *Studi Storici* 18: 69–95.

Sperber, Jonathan. 1984. *Popular Catholicism in Nineteenth-Century Germany*. Princeton: Princeton University Press.

Spezzano, Francesco. 1968. *La lotta politica in Calabria (1861–1925)*. Manduria: Lacaita.

Spotts, Frederic. 1973. *The Churches and Politics in Germany.* Middletown, Conn.: Wesleyan University Press.

Stabile, Francesco Michele. 1986. "Palermo, La Chiesa Baluardo del Card. Ruffini (1946–1948)." In Andrea Riccardi. *Le Chiese di Pio XII*. Bari: Laterza, 367–92.

Stark, Rodney. 1993. "Europe's Receptivity to New Religious Movements: Round Two." *Journal for the Scientific Study of Religion* 32 (4): 389–97.

Stark, Rodney, and Laurence Iannaccone. 1994. "A Supply-Side Reinterpretation of the 'Secularization' of Europe." *Journal for the Scientific Study of Religion* 33 (3): 230–52.

Stark, Rodney, and James C. McCann. 1993. "Market Forces and Catholic Commitment: Exploring the New Paradigm." *Journal for the Scientific Study of Religion* 32: 111–23.

Steinmo, Sven, Kathleen Thelen, and Frank Longstreth, eds. 1992. *Structuring Politics: Historical Institutionalism in Comparative Analysis*. Cambridge: Cambridge University Press.

Stigler, George, and C. Friedland. 1962. "What Can Regulators Regulate? The Case of Electricity." *Journal of Law and Economics* 5 (3): 1–16.

Stille, Alexander. 1995. *Excellent Cadavers*. New York: Pantheon Books.

Streeck, Wolfgang, and Philippe C. Schmitter. 1991. "From National Corporatism to Transnational Pluralism: Organized Interests in the Single European Market." *Politics and Society* 19: 133–64.

Strøm, Kaare. 1994. "The Presthus Debacle: Intraparty Politics and Bargaining Failure in Norway." *American Political Science Review* 88 (1): 112–27.

Tackett, Timothy. 1977. *Priest and Parish in Eighteenth Century France: A Social and Political Study of the Curés in the Diocese of Dauphine*. Princeton: Princeton University Press.

———. 1986. *Religion, Revolution, and Regional Culture in Eighteenth-Century France: The Ecclesiastical Oath of 1791*. Princeton: Princeton University Press.

Tarrow, Sidney. 1990. "Maintaining Hegemony in Italy: 'The Softer They Rise, the Slower They Fall!' " In T. J. Pempel, ed. *Uncommon Democracies: The One-Party Dominant Regimes*. Ithaca: Cornell University Press.

Tassello, Graziano, and Luigi Favero, eds. 1983. *Chiesa e mobilità umana: Documenti della Santa Sede dal 1883 al 1983*. Roma: Centro Studi Emigrazione.

Tavernier, Yves. 1969. *Le Syndicalisme Paysan F.N.S.E.A./C.N.J.A.* Paris: Armand Colin.

Thomas, Clive S., ed. 1993. *First World Interest Groups: A Comparative Perspective*. Westport, Conn.: Greenwood.

Thomson, David. 1964. *Democracy in France*. 4th ed. Oxford: Oxford University Press.

Tranfaglia, Nicola. 1992. *Mafia, Politica e Affari nell'Italia Repubblicana*. Bari: Laterza.

Traniello, Francesco. 1988. "Il mondo cattolico italiano nella seconda guerra mondiale." In Francesca Ferratini Tosi, Gaetano Grassi, and Massimo Legnani, eds. *L'Italia nella seconda guerra mondiale e nella Resistenze*. Milano: Angeli, 325–69.

Truman, David B. 1951. *The Governmental Process: Political Interests and Public Opinion*. New York: Alfred A. Knopf.

Tullock, Gordon. 1967. "The Welfare Costs of Tariffs, Monopolies, and Theft." *Western Economic Journal* 5 (2): 224–32.

Vaillancourt, Jean-Guy. 1980. *Papal Power: A Study of Vatican Control over Lay Catholic Elites*. Berkeley and Los Angeles: University of California Press.

van Kersbergen, Kees. 1994. "The Distinctiveness of Christian Democracy." In David Hanley, ed. *Christian Democracy in Europe*. London: Pinter Press, 31–47.

Vassort, Brigitte Marie-Odette. 1984. *Politics and Catholic Hierarchy in France*. 2 vols. Ph.D. diss., Yale University.

Velain, Serge, and Corinne Nadin. 1990. *Les Leaders de la Démocratie Chrétienne dans le Morbihan sous la IVe République*. Unpublished manuscript, École de droit et des sciences économiques, DEUG II, Vannes.

Verhoeven, Joseph. 1979. *Démocratique chrétienne: Origines et perspectives*. Brussels: Labor.

Vezzoli, Affra. 1965. *Il Partito Popolare a Brescia visto attraverso "Il Cittadino di Brescia "1919–1926*. Brescia: Commentari dell'Ateneo di Brescia.

Vignaux, Paul. 1980. *De la CFTC à la CFDT syndicalisme et socialisme "reconstruction" (1946–1972)*. Paris: Les Éditions Ouvrières.

Vinatier, Jean. 1983. *Cardinal Suhard, 1874–1949: L'Évêque du renouveau missionnaire en France*. Paris: Le Centurion.

von Beyme, Klaus. 1985. *Political Parties in Western Democracies*. Aldershot, England: Gower.

Walker, Jack L. 1983. "The Origins and Maintenance of Interest Groups in America." *American Political Science Review* 77: 390–406.

———. 1991. *Mobilizing Interest Groups in America: Patrons, Professions, and Social Movements*. Ann Arbor: University of Michigan Press.

Walston, James. 1988. *The Mafia and Clientelism: Roads to Roma in Post-war Calabria*. London: Routledge.

Ward, James E. 1964. "The French Cardinals and Leo XIII's *Ralliement* Policy." *Church History* 33 (March): 60–73.

Warner, Carolyn M. 1994. "Priests, Patronage, and Politicians." Ph.D. diss., Harvard University.

———. 1997. "Political Parties and the Opportunity Costs of Patronage," *Party Politics* 3 (4): 533–48.

———. 1998. "Getting Out the Vote with Patronage and Threat: Constructing the French and Italian Christian Democratic Parties, 1944–1958." *Journal of Interdisciplinary History* 28 (4): 553–82.

Wattebled, Robert. 1990. *Stratégies Catholiques en monde ouvrier dans la France d'après-guerre*. Paris: Les Éditions Ouvrières.

Webb, Leicester C. 1958. *Church and State in Italy, 1947–1957*. Carlton, Australia: Melbourne University Press.

Weber, Eugen. 1962. *Action Française: Royalism and Reaction in Twentieth Century France*. Stanford: Stanford University Press.

———. 1976. *Peasants into Frenchmen: The Modernization of Rural France, 1870–1914*. Stanford: Stanford University Press.

Weber, Max. 1978. Guenther Roth and Claus Wittich, eds. *Economy and Society.* Vol. 2. Berkeley and Los Angeles: University of California Press.

Webster, Richard A. 1959. "La rinascita della Democrazia Cristiana in Italia (1929–1945)." *Il Mulino* 90 (1): 7–63.

———. 1960. *The Cross and the Fasces: Christian Democracy and Fascism in Italy.* Stanford: Stanford University Press.

Weitz, Margaret Collins. 1995. *Sisters in the Resistance.* New York: John Wiley and Sons.

White, Steven F. 1999. "The Roman Question Reopened: Pius XII, De Gasperi, and the Sturzo Operation." Paper presented to the annual meeting of the American Historical Association, Washington, D.C.

Whittam, John. 1995. *Fascist Italy.* Manchester: Manchester University Press.

Whyte, Glen. 1994. "The Role of Asset Specificity in the Vertical Integration Decision." *Journal of Economic Behavior and Organization* 23 (3): 287–302.

Whyte, John H. 1981. *Catholics in Western Democracies: A Study in Political Behaviour.* Goldenbridge, Dublin: Gill and Macmillan.

Wieck, Hans Georg. 1953. *Die Entstehung der CDU und die Wiedergründung des Zentrums im Jahre 1945.* Düsseldorf: Droste Verlag.

Williams, Philip M. 1964. *Crisis and Compromise: Politics in the Fourth Republic.* Hamden, Conn.: Archon Books.

Williamson, Oliver E. 1979. "Transaction-Cost Economics: The Governance of Contractual Relations." *Journal of Law and Economics* 22 (2): 233–61.

Wilson, Frank. 1987. *Interest Group Politics in France.* Cambridge: Cambridge University Press.

Wilson, James Q. 1989. *Bureaucracy: What Government Agencies Do and Why They Do It.* N.p.: Basic Books.

———. 1995. *Political Organizations.* Princeton: Princeton University Press.

Wimmer, Bradley S., and John E. Garen. 1997. "Moral Hazard, Asset Specificity, Impact Bonding." *Economic Inquiry* 35 (3): 544–54.

Woodward, Kenneth L. 1998. "In Defense of Pius XII." *Newsweek,* March 30, 35.

Wright, Gordon. 1964. *Rural Revolution in France.* Stanford: Stanford University Press.

———. 1970. *The Reshaping of French Democracy.* 2d ed. Boston: Beacon Press.

Zapf, Wolfgang. 1965. *Wandlungen der deutschen Elite: Ein Zirkulationsmodell deutscher Füchrungsgruppen 1919–1961.* München: Piper.

Zariski, Raphael. 1993. "Italy: The Fragmentation of Power and Its Consequences." In Clive S. Thomas, ed. *First World Interest Groups: A Comparative Perspective.* Westport, Conn.: Greenwood, 127–38.

Zeigler, Harmon. 1993. *Political Parties in Industrial Democracies.* Itasca, Ill.: F. E. Peacock.

Zwier, Robert. 1991. "The Power and Potential of Religious Interest Groups." *Journal of Church and State* 33 (2): 271–85.

Zuckerman, Alan S. 1979. *The Politics of Faction: Christian Democratic Rule in Italy.* New Haven: Yale University Press.

All foreign nouns are alphabetized under the noun (i.e., without the definite article). Names that include possessive articles are listed thereunder (e.g., de Gaulle, under D). Political parties are listed under their English translation and in the original language. **Boldface** indicates a major entry on a subject.

CPSIA information can be obtained at www.ICGtesting.com
Printed in the USA
LVOW050803250712

291302LV00001B/9/P